Capital Accumulation
and Income Distribution

Capital Accumulation and Income Distribution

DONALD J. HARRIS

Stanford University Press, Stanford, California   1978

Stanford University Press
Stanford, California
© 1978 by the Board of Trustees of the
Leland Stanford Junior University
Printed in the United States of America
ISBN 0-8047-0947-5
LC 76-54097

To Kamala and Maya

Preface

The aim of this work is twofold. It seeks to provide a systematic interpretation and critical assessment of the main, contemporary lines of
approach to a theory of accumulation and income distribution in the
capitalist economy. At the same time, an attempt is made to develop an
analytic reconstruction of some of the substantive problems and issues
that arise in such a theory.

A basic reference point for the discussion is the system of ideas developed
by the English Classical economists and by Marx. This is a necessary
point of departure, since it is in these ideas, and especially in the work of
Marx, that some of the main conceptual foundations for theoretical
analysis of accumulation and distribution in the capitalist economy were
laid. From this vantage point it is possible to gain both a critical understanding of contemporary approaches to that analysis and a conceptual
framework for developing a more adequate theory. To this end, the
integrated structure of this system of ideas is reviewed in Part One.
A sharp contrast is drawn with the later neoclassical system based on
marginal productivity and subjective preference theory. Against this
background the problematic character of modern growth theory is
identified and discussed as it has taken shape in the work of contemporary
writers beginning with Harrod and Domar.

In Part Two a scheme of analysis is rigorously developed in terms of a
linear model of production with heterogeneous commodities under
conditions of simple and expanded reproduction. In this context a number
of theoretical problems are examined, pertaining to the relation between
labor values and prices of production, the nature of the wage-profit

relation, the choice of techniques of production, the role of different saving conditions, the meaning of Harrod's antinomy between the "warranted" and "natural" rates of growth, and the significance of the "golden rule" of accumulation. These problems are considered as arising at the level of an abstract specification of the requirements for reproduction of the capitalist economy as a whole, with no necessary implication of how, if at all, those requirements could be met.

Part Three goes on to consider critically and in depth how the process of expanded reproduction in the capitalist economy, with the distributional relations it entails, is accounted for within various contemporary theoretical approaches. Specific and detailed attention is given to the neo-Keynesian and neoclassical approaches. Following from this, an analytic reconstruction of the problem is presented, drawing upon certain elements of Marxian theory.

There is no pretense of completeness with regard to the area that is covered in this work. The most glaring omissions have to do with the process of *technical change*, the role of *money*, and the *cyclical dynamics* of capitalist economies. These particular omissions are by no means accidental. It is because the treatment of these problems, which are mutually related aspects of the process of expansion of capitalist economies, constitutes the weakest link in the chain of contemporary theoretical analysis. There is, indeed, in these areas not much theory as such to be concerned with. Technical change, for instance, has been mostly treated as if it were an exogenous condition taking place outside of, but imposing itself upon, the overall economic process. Similarly, the nature and role of money in an expanding capitalist economy have not been adequately clarified within contemporary theory. The problem of cyclical fluctuations has been mostly suppressed within the framework of a concern for analysis of the properties of steady states and the "approach" to a steady state.

The task of providing a systematic and integrated treatment of these problems within a coherent conception of the economic process as a whole is long overdue. Meanwhile, there are certain necessary preliminaries to this task, which involve sorting out and assessing the main lines of analysis and elaborating a consistent conceptual framework appropriate to the task. It is to this purpose that the present work is directed.

I am indebted to Joan Robinson for helpful discussion and comments during the preparation of this work from the time of its initial conception. I am especially grateful to David Levine for reading and discussion of the work as a whole. Comments of Krishna Bharadwaj, Maurice Dobb, John Eatwell, Luigi Pasinetti, and Bob Rowthorn on an early draft of particular chapters are gratefully acknowledged. Duncan Foley and Geoff Harcourt provided useful suggestions at a later stage. Comments of Harvey Gram, Basant Kapur, and John Roemer have aided the technical exposition at various points. To all these persons, and many others with whom at one time or another I have shared discussion of the ideas that are now presented here, I express my appreciation. They are, of course, not to be implicated in the outcome, whatever be the remaining agreement or disagreement, or the remaining errors.

All along the way, my interest in setting out the material in the present form has been sustained by the keen participation of students in my graduate classes taught at the University of Wisconsin (Madison) and at Stanford University. For their interest and encouragement I am very grateful. Since the first draft was circulated among them some time ago, some of them have gone on themselves to break new ground.

Acknowledgment is made to the editors of *Australian Economic Papers*, *American Economic Review*, and *Journal of Political Economy* for permission to include revised parts of papers of mine that they have published. A special word of thanks goes to Beverly Hallak and Ann Vollmer for their patience in typing the drafts, and to the editors of Stanford University Press for their ready cooperation throughout the process of publication.

Finally, if there is any virtue in the writing of this book, it springs from the sacrifices knowingly or unknowingly made by my two daughters, Kamala and Maya. In return, it is dedicated to them.

D.J.H.

Stanford University
Stanford, California
1977

Contents

Part One. The Setting

Chapter One

Theoretical Perspectives

The Classical Economists

Interest in the analysis of economic growth is not new. It was a central feature of the work of the English Classical economists (chiefly Smith, Malthus, and Ricardo). Despite the speculations of others before them, they must be regarded as the main precursors of modern economic theory. The ideas of this school reached their highest level of development in the works of Ricardo (see Ricardo, *Works*).

The interest of these economists in problems of economic growth was rooted in the concrete conditions of their time. Specifically, they were confronted with the facts of change taking place in contemporary English society as well as in previous historical periods. Living in the eighteenth and nineteenth centuries as they were, on the eve or in the full throes of the industrial revolution, they could hardly help but be impressed by the fact of such change. They undertook their investigations against the background of the emergence of what was to be regarded as a new economic system—the system of industrial capitalism. Political economy represented a conscious effort on their part to develop a scientific explanation of the forces governing the operation of the economic system, of the actual processes involved in the observed changes that were going on, and of the long-run tendencies and outcomes to which they were leading.

The interest of the Classical economists in economic growth derived also from a philosophical concern with the possibilities of "progress," an essential condition of which was seen to be the development of the material basis of society. Accordingly, it was felt that the purpose of analysis was to identify the forces in society that promoted or hindered this development, and hence progress, and consequently to provide a basis for policy and action to influence those forces.[1] Ricardo's campaign against the corn laws must obviously be seen in this light, as also Malthus's concern with the problem of population growth and Smith's attacks against the monopoly privileges associated with mercantilism.

Of course, for these economists, Smith especially, progress was seen from the point of view of the growth of national wealth. Hence, the principle of national advantage was regarded as an essential criterion of economic policy. Progress was conceived also within the framework of a need to preserve private property and hence the interests of the property-owning class. From this perspective, they endeavored to show that the exercise of individual initiative under freely competitive conditions to promote individual ends would produce results beneficial to society as a whole. Conflicting economic interests of different groups could be reconciled by the operation of competitive market forces and by the limited activity of "responsible" government.

As a result of their work in economic analysis the Classical economists were able to provide an account of the broad forces that influence economic growth and of the mechanisms underlying the growth process. An important achievement was their recognition that the accumulation and productive investment of a part of the social product is the main driving force behind economic growth and that, under capitalism, this takes the form mainly of the reinvestment of profits. Armed with this recognition, their critique of feudal society was based on the observation, among others, that a large part of the social product was not so invested but was consumed unproductively.

The explanation of the forces underlying the accumulation process was seen as the heart of the problem of economic growth. Associated with accumulation, and indeed an essential part of it as Marx later emphasized, is technical change as expressed in the division of labor

---

[1] To the extent that economic analysis was thus concerned with the contribution to "progress" by the operation of a particular economic system—the emerging system of industrial capitalism—it would be relatively easy to go from an analysis of the operation of that system to either justification or critique of it. By the same token, the need to justify the existing economic system on the part of dominant groups in it could serve to support and reinforce one set of ideas against another. This dialectical connection between justification or critique and scientific explanation cannot be escaped. It provides also the key to an understanding of the historical development of economic analysis and the far-reaching controversies that have characterized political economy from the beginning to this day. For a relevant treatment of the general issues and of specific lines of analysis in the history of economic thought, see Dobb 1973. See also Marx, *Theories of Surplus Value*, for an exhaustive treatment of the history of political economy up to Marx's time.

and changes in methods of production.[2] To these basic forces in economic growth they added the increase in the supply of labor available for production. Their analysis of the operation of these forces led them to the common view, though they quite clearly differed about the particular causes, that the process of economic growth under the conditions they identified raises obstacles in its own path and is ultimately retarded, ending in a state of stagnation—the "stationary state."[3] There was a certain logical coherence to this view.[4] It was founded, however, upon the twin laws of diminishing returns and of population growth which proved to be inadequate as a scientific basis on which to sustain a theory of long-run development of the capitalist economy.[5]

In examining the work of the Classical economists we find also that problems of economic growth were analyzed through the application of general economic principles, viewing the economic system as a whole, rather than in terms of a separate theory of economic growth as such. These principles were such as to recognize basic patterns of interdependence in the economic system and interrelatedness of the phenomena of production, exchange, distribution, and accumulation. We may briefly go into the nature of these interrelations as they appear within the Classical analysis.

Exchange of commodities was seen as necessarily connected with specialization of the labor of individuals in society to the production of different *use values*. More precisely, specialization of labor in production, or the social division of labor, was seen as the determining condition underlying the exchange of commodities. The activity of labor itself,

---

[2] There is no systematic treatment of the relation between capital accumulation and technical change in the work of the Classical economists. It is, however, a central theme in the work of Marx and is subjected there to detailed analysis. See, for instance, *Capital* I, part 4.

[3] The conception of the stationary state as the ultimate end of the process of economic growth is often interpreted as a "prediction" of the actual course of economic development in nineteenth-century England. There is no doubt that it was for a time so regarded by some, if not all, of the economists and their contemporaries, though the weight that was assigned to this particular aspect of the conception by Ricardo himself is a matter of some dispute. What is more significant, however, is that this conception served to point the finger at a particular social group, the landlord class, who benefited from the social product without contributing either to its formation or to "progress" and who, by their support of the corn laws and associated restrictions on foreign trade, acted as an obstacle to the only effective escape from the path to a stationary state, that is, through foreign trade.

[4] For an exposition of the argument see Blaug 1968, chs. 2–4.

[5] Detailed criticisms of Malthus's views were made by Marx and Engels. On this see Meek 1954.

specialized to the production of different commodities and utilizing means of production that were themselves the product of past labor as well as natural objects (e.g. "land"), was regarded as the central feature of production. Consequently, in seeking a principle that would explain the *exchange values* of commodities,[6] the Classical economists came naturally to find such a principle in the quantity of labor expended in production: commodities exchange at ratios that are determined by the quantity of labor directly and indirectly employed in their production. In this way was founded the Classical Labor Theory of Value.

In arriving at this conception it was explicitly recognized that, in order to be an object of exchange, commodities had to have use value. This was identified as an objective character in commodities that made them capable of satisfying human wants. It was taken as a condition for the existence of exchange value but could not itself be the determinant of exchange value. In this regard, there is a basic difference between the Classical analysis and that of the later Marginal Utility School. The latter locates "utility" as a subjective (or psychological) satisfaction derived from the consumption of commodities and gives it a role in determining the magnitude of exchange value.

Furthermore, the Classical economists did not rule out the existence of "scarce" commodities (e.g. art objects), which are not the product of current labor but which remain nevertheless the "object of desire of the wealthy classes" and therefore continue to command a market price. In such cases, price would significantly depart from value without altering the magnitude of value itself. But these commodities were regarded as being on the margins of a system of production dominated by industrial capitalism and could therefore be safely neglected in constructing an analysis of the system as a whole. As Ricardo pointed out (*Works* I:12): "By far the greatest part of those goods which are the objects of desire are procured by labour; and they may be multiplied, not in one country alone, but in many, almost without any assignable limit, if we are disposed to bestow the labour necessary to obtain them."

Distribution of the social product was seen to be connected in a definite way with the performance of labor in production and with the pattern of ownership of the means of production. In this regard, Labor, Land, and

---

[6] The exchange values that were relevant for this analysis were the natural prices of the commodities, or prices of production, around which the observable market prices would fluctuate from day to day owing to the vagaries of demand and supply.

Capital were distinguished as *social categories* corresponding to the prevailing class relationships among individuals in contemporary society: the class of laborers consisted of those who performed labor services, landlords were those who owned titles or property in land, and capitalists were those who owned property in capital consisting of the sum of exchangeable value tied up in means of production and in the "advances" which go to maintain the laborers during the production period. Each class received income or a share in the product according to specified rules: for the owners, the rule was based on the total amount of property which they owned—so much rent per unit of land, so much profit per unit of capital (and, for the class of finance capitalists or "rentiers" who lent money at interest, so much interest per unit of money lent). For laborers it was based on the quantity of labor services performed: so much wages per manhour.

Accumulation and distribution were seen to be interconnected through the use that was made by different social classes of their share in the product. Basic to this view was a conception, taken over from the Physiocrats, of the social surplus as that part of the social product which remained after deducting the "necessary costs" of production consisting of the means of production used up and the wage goods required to sustain the laborers employed in producing the social product. This surplus was distributed as profits, interest, and rent to the corresponding classes of property owners. For the Classical economists, the possibility of accumulation was governed by the size and mode of utilization of this surplus. Accordingly, their analysis placed emphasis upon those aspects of distribution and of the associated class behavior which had a direct connection with the disposal of the surplus and therefore with growth. In particular, it was assumed that, typically, workers consumed their wages for subsistence, capitalists reinvested their profits and landlords spent their rents on "riotous living." On the other side, accumulation would also influence the distribution of income as the economy expanded over time.

It was this absolutely strategic role of the size and use of the surplus, viewed from the perspective of the economy as a whole and of its process of expansion, which dictated the significance of the distribution of income for Classical economic analysis. Thus, for Ricardo especially, investigation of the laws governing distribution became the central focus of analysis. In a letter to Malthus, Ricardo wrote (*Works* VIII: 278–79): "Political

Economy you think is an inquiry into the nature and causes of wealth; I think it should rather be called an inquiry into the laws which determine the division of the produce of industry among the classes which concur in its formation." What was of crucial significance in this connection was the rate of profits because of its connection with accumulation, both as the source of investment funds and as the stimulus to further investment.

The distribution of income also acquired significance for another reason. In particular, it was recognized that, under normal conditions of commodity exchange, exchange values of commodities were subject to a definite rule: they must equal costs of production consisting of wages of labor, profits on capital, and rental on land. Thus, exchange values depended on the respective incomes of the different classes. In order to determine exchange values, these incomes would therefore have to be known. It required, in other words, a prior theoretical solution of the problem of distribution.

At the same time, in order for the analysis to yield unambiguous statements about the size and variation of the surplus, it was necessary to have an independent theoretical measure of its magnitude. For this purpose, the heterogeneous commodities composing the surplus product had to be reduced to a common standard—a standard of value. This was clearly so, for instance, when the surplus was analyzed in terms of the overall rate of profits and outside of the most simplified conditions of a corn-wage economy.[7] One possible measure might be the relative

---

[7] Having "got rid of rent" as the difference between the product on marginal land and that on intra-marginal units, the Ricardian analysis focused on profits as the residual component of the surplus. Under the simplifying conditions on which the analysis was constructed, there emerged a very clear and simple relationship between the wage rate and the overall rate of profits, determined within a single sector of the economy—the corn-producing sector. The special feature of corn as a commodity was that it could serve both as capital good (seed corn) in its own production and as wage good to be advanced to the workers. With the wage rate fixed in terms of corn, the rate of profit in corn production is uniquely determined as the ratio of net output of corn per man minus the wage to the sum of capital per man consisting of seedcorn and the fund of corn as wage good. Competition ensures that the same rate of profit enters into the price of all other commodities that are produced with indirect labor. The overall rate of profits, determined in this way, varies inversely with the corn wage. But as soon as it is recognized that the wage and/or the capital goods employed in corn production consist of other commodities besides corn the rate of profits can no longer be determined in this way. For the magnitude of the wage and of the total capital then depends on the prices of those commodities, and these prices incorporate the rate of profit. Attention then has to be directed to explaining the rate of profit in terms of the production system as a whole.

prices (in terms of some *numéraire*) at which the commodities exchange. But those prices, being themselves dependent on distribution, would vary with the distribution of the product. This meant that the measure of value could not itself be an exchange value, that is, dependent on distribution. The problem of exchange values of commodities and that of distribution were thus inseparable. It was the role of a theory of value to provide a solution for both.

The solution of this problem, the problem of an "invariable standard of value," remained a crucial obstacle which the Ricardian analysis was unable to overcome. Ricardo struggled with it until the end of his life.[8] A formal solution of the Ricardian problem has been provided in recent times by the analysis of Sraffa (1960).

In sum, what we find in Classical economic analysis is a necessary interconnection between the analysis of value, distribution, and growth. Because of these interconnections it was by no means possible to draw a sharp dividing line between the inquiry into economic growth and that into other areas of political economy.[9] The difference must be seen rather as a matter of emphasis. The particular form of these interconnections and the substantive propositions that were made in this framework constitute the defining characteristics of the Classical analysis.

It cannot be said that the Classical economists had succeeded in working out a fully integrated theoretical system, or that they had satisfactorily, even to themselves, resolved the conceptual problems inherent in their analysis, or that they had provided adequate answers to all the relevant questions. In general, they failed to consummate a theory appropriate to the conditions of industrial capitalism.[10] Their ideas were essentially limited to the conditions of a simple agrarian system, without significant

[8] For a discussion of Ricardo's problem, see the editor's Introduction in Ricardo, *Works* I: xl–xlix, which makes it clear that "the problem of value which interested Ricardo was how to find a measure of value which would be invariant to changes in the division of the product; for, if a rise or fall of wages by itself brought about a change in the magnitude of the social product, it would be hard to determine accurately the effects on profits." The significance of this problem in the context of the Classical theory of distribution is examined by Garegnani (1960).

[9] As Meek (1967: 187) notes: "To Smith and Ricardo, the macroeconomic problem of the 'laws of motion' of capitalism appeared as the primary problem on the agenda, and it seemed necessary that the *whole* of economic analysis—including the basic theories of value and distribution—should be deliberately oriented towards its solution."

[10] For a penetrating analysis of the causes of this failure within the internal logic of their own reasoning, see Levine 1977.

change in methods of production, in which, because of the limited quantity and diminishing fertility of the soil, growth is arrested by increasing costs of production of agricultural commodities.

It remained for Marx to pinpoint some of the major limitations and deficiencies of the Classical analysis and to develop an analysis of the capitalist economy that went beyond that of the Classical economists in many respects.

Marx: Surplus Value and Accumulation

For Marx, a necessary basis for the discussion of accumulation under capitalism was an analysis of the nature of capitalism itself—its essential and distinguishing features as *a mode of production*. The objective of the analysis was to discover the immanent laws of capitalist development or the "economic laws of motion" of this form of society. The overall perspective of the analysis was one of viewing the production system as a whole in perpetual historical motion and in accordance with the principles of dialectics and historical materialism.

From this perspective Marx saw capitalism as a historically specific form of commodity production within the general form of commodity-producing societies. Its characteristic feature is that labor power itself becomes a commodity, and ownership of the means of production becomes concentrated in the hands of a class that, by its monopoly of ownership as a class and control over the use of labor in production, is able to appropriate a part of the product of labor in the form of surplus value. All of this presupposes a historical process through which the means of production come to constitute property in the various forms of Land, Capital, etc., and through which a class of laborers owning nothing but their labor power is formed. Marx called this the process of "primitive accumulation" (see Marx, *Capital* I, chs. 26–28; and Dobb 1963, ch. 5).

A central problem for Marx is to explain the existence of surplus value consistent with the rules of competition and equal exchange that are assumed to characterize the sphere of exchange under capitalism. In working out his analysis, Marx started from the Classical Labor Theory of Value and proceeded to broaden and deepen it in a number of directions. The basis of his reformulation was the perception that the complex of exchange relations existing in the market is but a reflection of the link between the productive labor of individuals, a link that arises from the social or collective nature of productive activity: "A relation of commodities as exchange-values is nothing but a mutual relation between persons in their productive activity." Like the Classical economists, he was thus concerned to explain exchange values in terms of production viewed as consisting of the "labor process." To this extent, the labor theory of value was seen as correctly incorporating the determining role of the "real relations of production." But in addition, Marx sought to bring the social relations of production to the forefront of the analysis, emphasizing that these relations have a definite class character—the capital-labor relation—which is by nature antagonistic. The role of value theory therefore becomes not only a matter of explaining quantitative exchange ratios but, more fundamentally, a matter of exhibiting the qualitative nature of the social relations within which exchange phenomena are located.

One may note here that, even though Marx started from a common ground with the Classical economists in the labor theory of value, his concerns in the theory of value were quite different from those of Ricardo, as was also the place that the labor theory of value occupied in his theoretical system.[11] For instance, as indicated in the previous section, Ricardo's chief concern in the theory of value was with the problem of an "invariable standard of value" as an adjunct to the analysis of income distribution. The difference between Ricardo and Marx is evident also in their treatment of the quantitative relation between relative prices of commodities and labor values. Ricardo regarded this relation as one of strict proportionality between values and prices. For Marx it was a matter of values being transformed into prices, the conditions of this transformation being theoretically determinate but not necessarily yielding proportionality, except under the condition (assumed throughout Volume I of *Capital*) of an equal organic composition of capital in all branches of production. Smith was unable to go beyond the conception of a society of simple commodity producers (hunters of deer and beaver) where, profits being nonexistent, it could be presumed that relative prices are necessarily proportional to relative values.

The problem of surplus value is solved in Marx's theory by applying the labor theory of value to the determination of the value of labor power. The distinction between labor and labor power as analytical

---

[11] For a comprehensive discussion of the different treatments of the labor theory of value by Smith, Ricardo, and Marx, see Meek 1973 and Rubin 1972.

categories is crucial here. Labor power is the capacity to labor, embodied in the worker and consisting of the ability to exercise muscle, nerve, and brain at an appropriate level of skill. Labor is the setting into motion of this capacity, or the actual use of labor power in the performance of a specific task. The introduction of this distinction was of fundamental significance in the advance that Marx made upon the analysis of the Classical economists. With it he was able to clear up the confusions that surrounded the use of the labor theory of value, especially by Smith.

Specifically, it is assumed that labor power, like other commodoties, has a value. This value is equal to the amount of labor embodied in the commodities required to sustain and reproduce the labor power of the worker.[12] But labor employed in production is capable of creating more value than is used up in the maintenance and reproduction of labor power. It is this difference between the value of the product of labor and the value of labor power which constitutes surplus value. The origin of surplus value lies, then, in an excess of the value produced, say, in a day's labor, over the value paid to the worker for a day's use of his labor power. Surplus value thus originates from the exploitation of labor in production. It is "unpaid labor." This pool of surplus value is, in turn, the source from which is derived all categories of property income in the form of profits, interest, rent, etc.[13] Marx distinguished between production of absolute surplus value and relative surplus value.[14] The former is due to quantitative extension of the working day or intensification of labor with a given quantity and quality of means of production, and with workers' consumption remaining the same. The latter is due to changes in the technical quality of means of production and organization of the labor process such as to reduce the labor embodied in producing wage goods.

---

[12] "The value of labour-power is determined, as in the case of every other commodity, by the labour-time necessary for the production, and consequently also the reproduction, of this special article. . . . Given the individual, the production of labour-power consists in his reproduction of himself or his maintenance. For his maintenance he requires a given quantity of the means of subsistence. Therefore the labour-time requisite for the production of labour-power reduces itself to that necessary for the production of those means of subsistence; in other words, the value of labour-power is the value of the means of subsistence necessary for the maintenance of the labourer." (*Capital* I: 171–72.)

[13] In a letter to Engels, Marx noted that "the best points in my book are . . . the treatment of surplus value independently of its particular forms as profit, interest, ground rent, etc. . . . The treatment of the particular forms by classical political economy, which always mixes them up with the general form, is a regular hash." See Marx and Engels n.d.: 232.

[14] See *Capital* I, chs. 12, 16.

There is, of course, as Marx noted, a fundamental difference between labor power and all other commodities, which arises from the fact that labor power is not produced within the same process as that of other commodities. This difference would require, however, that the value of labor power be established on the basis of some principle other than that which applies to the value of other commodities. For other commodities this principle was based on the expansion and contraction of production occurring in response to short-term deviations of price from value. But an equilibrating mechanism of this sort would clearly not apply to labor power. For the Classical economists the principle was provided by the Malthusian Law of Population, according to which population changes in response to variations in the wage were held to account for the maintenance of the "natural price of labor" at a level equal to the customary subsistence of workers. Marx rejected this principle as theoretically and historically unfounded.[15] Instead, in his analysis the resolution of the problem is found to lie in the process of accumulation and technical change through the continued creation of a "reserve army" of unemployed labor (or a "relative surplus-population") and within the framework of an ongoing struggle between workers as a class and capitalists as a class.[16] But the precise analytical meaning and implications of this idea have not been fully worked out.

In Marx's theory, surplus value is a category that is logically prior to and determining of the various categories of income distribution. It therefore requires analytical treatment prior to the problem of income distribution. Marx's treatment is such as to give a theoretical account for the nature and origin of profits as a specific form of surplus, namely surplus value. The magnitude of surplus value sets the limit on the average rate of profits. It also fixes thereby the boundary within which capitalists' accumulation and consumption can take place.

The analysis of value and surplus value lays the foundation for Marx's analysis of accumulation. In this connection, it is recognized that the production and expansion of surplus value are the basic motivating force

[15] See for instance *Capital* I: 637–39.
[16] "Relative surplus-population is therefore the pivot upon which the law of demand and supply of labour works. It confines the field of action of this law within the limits absolutely convenient to the activity of exploitation and to the domination of capital." (*Capital* I: 639.) For a discussion of the place of this principle in Marx's theory, see Sweezy 1956: 87–91.

that underlies the behavior of capitalists as a class. The drive to accumulate comes out of this quest for surplus value and, as such, is inherent in the system of capitalist production. Accumulation is the process of converting surplus value into capital for the purpose of producing more surplus value, which in turn is converted into additional capital, and so on. In this sense, the essential feature of capital is that it is "self-expanding value." Correspondingly, the rate of profits, representing the money form of surplus value as it accrues to capitalists, is seen as "the rate of self-expansion of the total capital."

Like the Classical economists, Marx saw accumulation of capital as the main driving force of capitalist development. But, in addition, in Marx's analysis it is identified as a process that is rooted in the class position of the capitalists and hence in a historically specific mode of production. It is also explained as the outcome of objective factors operating upon each and every individual capital. In particular, Marx noted, with regard to "the tendency to accumulate, the drive to expand capital and produce surplus value on an extended scale":

This is law for capitalist production, imposed by incessant revolutions in the methods of production themselves, by the depreciation of existing capital always bound up with them, by the general competitive struggle, and the need to improve production and expand its scale merely as a means of self-preservation and under penalty of ruin. (*Capital* III: 244–45.)

Marx's analysis of the process of capital accumulation indicates a number of essential elements involved in that process. It involves, first, a continuing revolution in the technical methods of production accompanied by quantitative and qualitative changes in economic and social organization. These changes are such as to raise over time the organic composition of capital and continuously reproduce a reserve army of unemployed labor. There is an associated tendency for the average rate of profits to fall. There occurs also an increasing concentration of capital into larger and fewer units, which come to exercise greater control in the economy and over the state. Accumulation has the effect, moreover, of increasing the size of the proletariat through the global expansion of the capitalist mode of production and by breaking up noncapitalist modes. It also gives rise to "increasing immiserization" of the proletariat. Finally, it is associated with continually recurring crises. At the heart of the whole process is an inherent contradiction due to the increasing socialization of production which runs into conflict with the continued private appropriation of the product by individual capitals. This contradiction is resolved only by the ultimate break-up of the capitalist system.

Marx was the theorist of economic growth par excellence. He conceived of the capitalist economy as an inherently expansionary system having an inner logic of its own. It was his purpose to discover the abstract and general principles underlying the operation of this form of society and the contradictions it entailed, so as to account for its process of change and supersession. Out of this scientific endeavor, Marx developed an integrated system of analysis with a distinctive method and quite specific formulation of the laws of motion of the capitalist economy. Others, after Marx, have attempted to elaborate upon and develop further this system of analysis, recognizing the changing conditions of capitalism as it develops.[17] Specific elements of Marx's own formulation as concerns, for instance, the law of the falling tendency of the rate of profit and a tendency of the organic composition of capital to rise, are subject to an ongoing debate within the Marxian tradition. The system of analysis is also incomplete in some of its essentials. Nevertheless, the Marxian system remains today as a powerful basis upon which to construct a theory of growth of the capitalist economy appropriate to modern conditions. Accordingly, an attempt is made below (see Chapters 3 and 10) to develop some elements of the Marxian theoretical system that are relevant to this purpose.

The Neoclassical Tradition

The problem of accumulation and growth of the capitalist economy is not a major focus of neoclassical economics.[18] The typical feature of this tradition has been its focus on the properties of the static equilibrium that is imposed upon an economic system by the existence of "fixed factors of production" or "scarce resources." The basic analytical problem that is raised in this context concerns the efficient allocation of available resources in relation to consumers' preferences. The theorems that have been

---

[17] See, for instance, Luxemburg 1951, Hilferding 1923, Sweezy 1956, and other references cited in Chapter 10 below.

[18] In accordance with general usage, the term "neoclassical" is taken here to refer to the body of ideas developed by Jevons, Menger, Walras, Wicksell, Marshall, J. B. Clark, and Fisher, among others, and more recently by Arrow and Debreu. Of course, in speaking of this body of ideas as one system or tradition, one has to have in mind a certain stylized conception of it since its exponents did not agree on all matters. A comprehensive statement of the modern version of neoclassical theory is to be found in Arrow and Hahn 1971 and Hirshleifer 1970.

developed from this analysis, concerning the optimality of a competitive market solution of the allocation problem, represent an elaboration of Adam Smith's notion of the beneficial results to society as a whole of the operation of the "invisible hand."

The neoclassical conception of society is one of a class-*less* society or property-owning democracy consisting of atomistic individuals or "households" with particular preferences and ownership of given "endowments" of physical resources and specialized skills. Schumpeter (1954: 889) views this conception as a matter of "methodological individualism" suitable "for the special purposes of a particular set of investigations." This view is evidently concerned more with the formal character of the theory than with its substantive content. By contrast, Bukharin (1972: 35–36) correctly points out:

> Political economy is a social science and its presupposition—whether the theorists of political economy are conscious of this fact or not—is some conception or other as to the essence of society and its laws of evolution. In other words, any economic theory depends on certain presuppositions having a sociological character and serving as the basis of an investigation of the economic phase of social life. Such presuppositions may be clearly expressed or may remain unformulated; they may be enuciated as an orderly system, or they may remain an "indefinite general view"—but they cannot be absent.

In this setting, the central economic problem for neoclassical theory is one of exchange of goods and factor services among the individuals and the existence of a set of prices at which the plans of the individuals can become consistent. Some versions of the theory are set out in terms of pure exchange without production. For Marx and the Classical economists this would have been an inconceivable situation, since exchange was necessarily connected with the social division of labor in production.

In neoclassical theory, prices and the allocation of factors in production are determined, in equilibrium, so as to be appropriate to the given preferences of individuals, the technology of production and the supply of factors. The distribution of income among the individuals emerges from the distribution of endowments, which is unexplained by the theory, and the rental price of their services. The rental price of each factor service can be shown to correspond to the marginal physical product of the factor times the price of output in each line of production. This is a consequence of cost minimization in production and competition in the market for factors. If the total supply of factors or the preferences of individuals change, prices change. The rental price of each factor is higher or lower according as the factor is relatively more or less "scarce." A different pattern of distribution corresponds to the endowments and the prices ruling in the new situation. In this sense, it is said that the distribution of income—payments to factors and to individuals—is determined by supply and demand consistent with marginal productivity pricing of factor services.

If any factor is in excess supply in a given situation, its price is supposed to fall to zero. This means that the problem every society faces, that of consistency of the pattern of prices and income distribution with the social requirement of reproduction of the material conditions of production (means of production and labor), is not explicitly recognized. When it is assumed that all "resources" are fixed and nondepreciating, this problem drops out altogether. Otherwise, the problem is admitted only indirectly through ad hoc assumption of conditions on the components of the vector of individual endowments, on the technical substitutability of factors in production, and on the degree of substitutability of goods in consumption.[19]

In order to have a determinate set of prices, including rental prices of the factors, the total supply of factors has to be taken as given for each equilibrium situation. It is therefore necessary to have a measure of their quantity independent of those prices. This poses no problem so long as each factor is conceived of in physical terms with its own technical unit of measurement.[20] The problem comes with trying to conceive of capital as a factor in the same terms, that is, as a homogeneous entity the quantity of which is independently given and the marginal product of which can be made to correspond to the rate of profit. In general, no such entity exists. Capital, as a property relation, can be quantitatively represented as a sum of exchange values corresponding to a given set of prices of the means of production. On the other hand, the stock of capital goods which enter into production is a collection of heterogeneous commodities. It can be regarded as a homogeneous entity only when it consists of a single commodity. When, in addition, output consists of the same commodity, the marginal product of this commodity can be thought of as a technical datum which corresponds to the rate of profit. This is a very special case which would be of little interest outside the restrictive assumptions on which it is constructed were it not for the fact that it has come to occupy a

[19] See Koopmans 1957.
[20] That this was Wicksell's conception is clear from his *Lectures* (1934: 149).

prominent place in the modern theory. We shall subsequently return to it (see Chapter 9).[21]

It is in the specific form of the marginal productivity theory that is embodied the neoclassical conception of different categories of income as returns to different factors, reflecting relative factor scarcities and technical conditions of production. It was thought that this conception would carry over to an interpretation of "capital" as a factor of production, on the same footing as labor, and of profits as a return to such a factor. Indeed, it was felt that this transition could be made logically and without hitch from one situation to the other and back again, because the interpretation of "capital" as a factor of production was presumed to be merely a special and convenient case of a more general case involving production with many different capital goods, or many factors of production, as many as one wished to assume.[22] It turns out, however, that there is no analytical basis for these presumptions. The confusion involved in this transition was pointed out by Bohm-Bawerk (1959) as early as 1884. At a much later date, Schumpeter (1954: 655–56) again called attention to it when he wrote:

For the votaries of the triad schema and of the theory that incomes are essentially prices (times quantities) of productive services, the natural thing to do was to interpret the yield of capital goods . . . as a price for the productive services of those capital goods. This again may be done in several ways, though, unfortunately, all of them meet with this fatal objection: nothing is easier than to show that capital goods or their services, being both requisite and scarce, will have value and fetch prices; nor is it difficult to show that their ownership will often yield temporary net returns; but, all the more difficult is it to show that—and, if so, why—these values and prices are *normally* higher than is necessary in order to enable their owners to replace them, in other words, why there should be a permanent net return attached to their ownership. This point was not fully brought home to the profession at large until the publication of Bohm-Bawerk's history

---

[21] Ricardo dealt with a similar case in constructing his analysis of distributive shares. With an eye to the importance of agriculture in the conditions of his time, he chose corn as the relevant commodity, arguing that the rate of profit is uniquely determined within the corn-producing sector by technical conditions and a wage rate fixed in terms of corn. On this, see above, note 7, p. 8.

[22] Walras himself was well aware of the need to modify his scheme to take account of produced inputs such as capital goods. See Walras 1954. But with different kinds of capital goods being used in production and their relative supplies allowed to vary, the Walrasian system runs up against a problem. Competitive equilibrium requires that the price of capital goods equal their cost of production and that the ratio of the net rental to the price of the capital goods (that is, their net rate of return) be equal in all lines of production. The system must then provide a solution for both the level of the uniform rate of return and the quantities of the capital goods produced. But, as Piero Garegnani (1960, chs. 2, 3) has shown, the Walrasian system is incapable of providing such a solution.

of interest theories . . . Until that time (perhaps in some cases even now) people thought (or think) that the easy proof of the proposition that capital goods must yield a return establishes *ipso facto* that they must yield an income to their owners. This confusion of two different things vitiates all the pure productivity theories of interest . . . both the primitive ones . . . and the more elaborate ones.

In another version, which is subject to the same objection, the neo-classical concept of capital is tied to the use of "roundabout methods of production" and the associated passage of time between application of physically specified inputs (capital goods and labor) and the subsequent flow of output.[23] Since such methods of production enhance the productivity of a given quantity of labor (otherwise those methods would never be adopted), it is possible to seek to attribute the extra output to the quantity of the extra inputs which may be only the extra time spent in using the roundabout method. This difference in output, in this view, constitutes the return to "capital" as a factor of production. By contrast, the Classical and Marxian theories take as given the fact that there are roundabout methods which enhance the productivity of labor. The existence of such methods is regarded as part of the description of the technical conditions of production in any society. Beyond this, and as an essential condition of capitalist society, capital is conceived to be a property relation that enables the capitalists to employ propertyless laborers in production and reap the difference between the net product and the amount paid out as wages.

In general, the central feature of neoclassical analysis is that the problem of distribution, conceived in terms of a society of atomistic individuals, is solved entirely within the sphere of exchange as related both to exchange of factor services and to exchange of products. Underlying this analysis is the conception of a society *without* classes, defined either in terms of appropriation of the product according to divisions in property ownership, as in Classical economic analysis, or in terms of a social-production relation (the capital-labor relation) based on control of labor in production, as in Marxian theory. In this respect, there is a fundamental division between the substance of neoclassical theory on the one hand and that of Classical and Marxian theory on the other.[24]

---

[23] This is the distinctively Austrian version of the neoclassical argument.

[24] The existence of this division, as well as other notable differences between Classical and neoclassical theory, begs the question as to exactly what sense is to be assigned to the term "*neo*classical." This is a far-reaching question in the history of economic thought. We simply leave this here as an open question and stick to what is commonly accepted terminology.

Without classes in the above sense there can be no meaningful distinction between income from property and income from work. There is accordingly no special significance to be attached to the value sum of capital upon which profit is to be paid and on the basis of which a share of the product accrues to a particular class. Capital as a value sum constitutes merely an "aggregation problem." What really matters is the individual capital goods and their "own rates of return" associated with exchange of those goods through time.[25] There is then some question of what reality this conception is supposed to correspond to and what bearing, if any, it may have on the actual historical conditions of capitalism. In this connection, it has been suggested that this conception can be given meaning only in the context of an artisan economy (Robinson 1962a: 1–6).

When it comes to the problem of accumulation, this is treated in neoclassical theory essentially as a matter of the exchange of commodities through time, or the exchange of "time-dated" commodities. As such, the problem of accumulation has no special significance in this theory apart from the problem of exchange per se. The only difference is in the time dimension; and time is simply another physical dimension in terms of which commodities as objects may be distinguished from each other, as height, length, weight, smell and taste.

In so far as the problem of accumulation is dealt with at all in the neoclassical tradition, the process of accumulation is constituted as a process of "deepening the structure of capital" (Wicksell 1934; Hirshleifer 1970). It is a process in which the saving decisions of atomistic individuals drive the economy to a stationary state where the ratio of the quantity of capital to labor is optimal and where there is no further inducement to save because the rate of profit has fallen to the level of the rate of intertemporal preference or the "cost of waiting." What drives the economy, in this conception, are the intertemporal preferences of individuals engaged in exchanging consumption "today" for consumption "tomorrow." The basic objective of the economy is consumption;[26] accumulation is an incidental feature of individuals' consumption decisions and comes to an end in the stationary state. In this way the theory effectively denies the continuing and self-sustaining process of expansion of capital as an essential feature of the capitalist mode of production.

[25] On this see Bliss 1975.
[26] For an early critique of this aspect of neoclassical theory, see Bukharin 1972.

Understandably, therefore, the chief locus of economic analysis in this tradition is in the fiction of a stationary state taken over from the Classical economists and reconstituted for the purposes of neoclassical theory. Problems of economic growth and evolution of the capitalist economy are evidently alien to such a system of analysis.[27] For a long time there existed no systematic treatment of them within the neoclassical tradition. It is not surprising, then, that, when these problems sharply asserted themselves during the period of world economic crisis in the 1930's and after, this tradition should prove incapable of dealing with them. Arising as they did from considerations that were *external* to the neoclassical theory, they had to be, so to speak, thrust upon the theory from outside.

The task of reconstructing the neoclassical theory fell to Keynes and his followers, who came thereby to develop what might be called a neo-Keynesian analysis. The neoclassicals, for a time, sought to rebut one of the central arguments of the neo-Keynesians, namely, that the capitalist economy is inherently incapable of following a stable path of sustained expansion. But the discussion of this issue was short-lived. Neoclassical economics soon turned once again to the problem of efficient allocation of resources in accordance with consumers' preferences, now defined to embrace the problem of "optimal growth."

Summary and Preview

The model of production based on generalized scarcity of resources was developed by Walras. We may therefore call it the Walrasian model. In the Walrasian model, production is viewed as a one-way avenue from "primary" factors of production, the services of which are used in production, to commodities that are used for final consumption. In the work of the Classical economists and of Marx, on the other hand, production as well as consumption (i.e. "necessary consumption") is viewed as a circular process by which commodities are transformed into each other through the application of labor in production. This view of production, which we might call the classical model, is formalized in the works of Neumann 1945, Leontief 1951, and Sraffa 1960.

This view does not deny the role of a fixed supply of particular "re-

---

[27] It would, in any case, be self-contradictory to conceive of a process of sustained economic growth in an economy in which all factors of production were truly "fixed." In this context, the analysis would have to both start and end with the fiction of a "stationary state."

sources" in limiting the production of particular commodities. In Classical theory this was the role of "land." For Malthus, it was a central consideration. Land being, in his view, fixed in total quantity and subject to diminishing returns as more and more labor is applied to production, it determined a maximum attainable level of output and a corresponding "optimum" level of population. For Ricardo, it was rather a matter of the existence of land of varying quality determining a rising share for its owners in the net product as more and more of such land is brought into cultivation. However, for theoretical purposes, we may legitimately abstract from the problem of "land," this being regarded as arising at a different level of the analysis from that with which we are primarily concerned. The existence of land and land rent raises complications which need to be discussed in their own right.[28] From the point of view of the problem of accumulation, the role of land has to be considered along with the possibilities of technical change. If we abstract from technical change, then it is just as well that we abstract also from the existence of land.

Associated with the Walrasian model is a conception of capitalist society as a property-owning democracy based on exchange of products and factors in accordance with independently given preferences of atomistic individuals. Classical economic analysis recognizes basic class divisions in society as related to ownership of property and appropriation of the product. In addition, for Marx, production includes not only the technical conditions of the labor process but also the specific social relations within which these conditions are put into effect. Under capitalism, these social relations embody a definite class character—the capital-labor relation—related to capitalists' control over the labor process. The technical conditions themselves are regarded as dependent upon, as well as determining, the prevailing social relations in a dialectical manner.

Starting from the classical model of production and with their conception of social classes, the Classical economists arrived at what was thought to be a striking conclusion. Production is attributable to labor, that is, to current labor services and to means of production that are themselves reducible to the labor services embodied in them.[29] Income is attributable to the ownership of property and to labor. Laborers get an

---

[28] For a modern discussion of the implications for the analysis of prices and distribution, see Sraffa 1960, ch. 11.

[29] This statement, as it stands, is entirely without ethical or normative content. Neither does it deny the simple fact that both labor and means of production are required in order to carry out production.

amount of the total product as payment for their labor services; the owners of property get an amount to cover replacement of the means of production used up and, in addition, they get the surplus that remains. Smith referred to this latter quantity as a "deduction." The point, as Marx saw, acquires an analytic content when expressed in terms of labor values and the theory of surplus value. Specifically, a part of the value which labor produces returns to it in the form of the value paid for labor power; the rest, which goes to the owners, constitutes surplus value or "unpaid labor." It was then possible to go on to ask: what is there in capitalist society which enables the owners to get that surplus as a permanent source of income? And, how does the capitalist economy, including both the technical conditions of production and the social relations of production, evolve over time consistent with the continued production and appropriation of that surplus?

Starting from the Walrasian model of production and the conception of atomistic individuals with given endowments of factors, it appears that income is attributable to the productivity of the factors and to the pattern of individual endowments and tastes. The size and composition of the individual endowments is left completely unexplained. Productivity, in this scheme, is a matter of an exogenously given technology or an exchange with Nature. Accumulation is an aspect of the consumption decisions of individuals.

It is this issue of whether profits, and other forms of property income—i.e. rent and interest—constitute a surplus which the rules of property and capitalists' control of the labor process allow the owners to appropriate, or whether they are to be considered a return to a factor of production, which remains as the source of basic theoretical divisions and controversies in economics. Tied in with this are different conceptions of the nature and meaning of capital as a category in the analysis of capitalist production. These, in turn, are rooted in different theoretical perspectives on the problem of value, and hence in the theory of value. These different conceptions, located at the level of basic theoretical principles, necessarily condition the approach adopted to an analysis of accumulation and distribution.

It is the Classical and Marxian view of production that is adopted in the analysis to be presented here,[30] in addition to which it is assumed that

---

[30] There is no intention here to equate the Classical (or Ricardian) system of thought with the Marxian theoretical system. As should be evident from the preceding discussion, there are basic distinctions and differences between them.

production takes place at constant costs in terms of labor when technology is given. The assumption that technology is given means specifically that we are here considering the economy at a given "moment" or "epoch" in its development, taking the technical conditions of the labor process then prevailing as given, without inquiring either into the process of their evolution in the past or into the process of their subsequent development. It is then only natural and consistent with this assumption to assume that costs are constant.

To emphasize, the assumption of constant costs is an entirely appropriate assumption to make at this level of analysis. It implies only that the technical methods of production are independent of the scale of operation of the economy, whatever may be the range of alternative methods that are available at the given "moment". The question of the pattern of variation of costs in relation to scale, or the degree of "returns to scale", is tied up with that of the process of technical change and development of the economy as a whole. Therefore, it can be systematically dealt with only in the framework of a systematic analysis of that process.

We shall be concerned to develop, in the above-described context, a critical view and understanding of how various approaches in contemporary theory formulate and solve the interrelated problems of accumulation and distribution in the capitalist economy.

Chapter Two

Modern Growth Theory

Introduction

The general considerations which we have said motivated the concerns of the Classical economists and of Marx might be thought to underlie current interest in the study of economic growth. However, one would be hard put to verify this from a cursory look at recent contributions to the field. They often seem to have more to do with the properties of convex polyhedral cones in finite dimensional vectorspaces than with human "progress" or the historical development of capitalism.

The fact is, as we shall see, that growth theory as currently constituted is concerned with a more limited set of questions. Such classical questions as that of the long-run outcome of the process of growth under capitalism cannot even be posed; for the analysis is set out in terms of a scheme which allows only for indefinite expansion. The term "growth" itself is often used to mean simply quantitative expansion in terms of an index of national output. In the field of the theory of optimal growth the question of "efficiency" of allocation in a growing economy is raised to a level of importance it never had for the Classical economists. Although they were aware of the existence of a problem of the efficient organization of production, this was less important for them than the question of development of the material forces of production. For Marx, both of these were subsidiary to the question of the social relations of production, that is, the social relations between people in production activity. In much of the recent theory, on the other hand, the social context of the analysis is often left unspecified or regarded as a matter of indifference whether it applies, for instance, to a socialist or a capitalist economy (cf. Solow 1963: 9–16). In its most aggregative form, a world in which only one commodity is produced, the theory completely ignores the problem of exchange values of commodities.[1] When it comes to consider a world of many commodities, it virtually abandons not only the classical search for a measure of value but also all concern for the role of a theory of value.

It will be found also that much of recent growth theory focuses on quantitative aspects of the relations involved in production and accumulation and, perhaps for that reason, has thrown up a plethora of formal mathematical models. But not all the relations that are relevant for a theory of growth are quantitative, and the qualitative ones are not all representable mathematically. Mathematics is a convenient device for ensuring precision and logical rigor, once an adequate basis for the theory has been laid out. By itself, it cannot provide either a theory of growth or a complete representation of one.

The Beginnings: Harrod's Problem

Can a capitalist economy expand continuously at a steady rate? This was the question that set modern growth theory going in the 1940's after a long hiatus during which the problem of economic growth had been all but ignored in academic discussion. In the capitalist economies a period of sustained expansion had only recently been broken by a deep depression. The problems of the depression had dominated discussion, and the analysis by Keynes of these problems was a major focus of attention. Soon, the attention of economists was increasingly turned to the problem of long-run expansion. The immediate context of their concern was the advanced capitalist economies. The specific problems of the colonial or underdeveloped economies had not yet come to the fore, and economic growth in the socialist economies was not considered of much interest.

To this question Harrod offered a two-pronged answer: there is one and only one rate at which the system can conceivably expand, and there is nothing to guarantee that it will in fact expand at that rate. (See Harrod 1939, 1948, 1960).

The argument can be set out in simple terms, starting from the familiar

---

[1] The problem does not, by this means, disappear. For, if the services of labor are viewed as a commodity, i.e. labor power, there is still a question of the rate at which this commodity exchanges against the commodity that labor produces. This is usually regarded as a question of income distribution. The point is that, in a "one-commodity" world, the problem of exchange value and that of distribution are not only inseparable but become one and the same thing.

equilibrium condition of equality between investment and saving. Harrod assumed that a uniform proportion of net income is saved by the recipients of income. For the economy to be in equilibrium, this saving must match the investment which firms are undertaking. In symbols, this condition can be written as

(2.1) $$I = sY$$

where I is net investment, Y is net income and s is the given proportion of net income saved. Viewed in the Keynesian framework of analysis, this condition has a straightforward meaning: investment generates income and demand through a "multiplier effect" and the equilibrium level of income equals the amount of investment times the multiplier $1/s$. Now let K, the total value of capital in the economy, grow at the rate g. Assume further that the ratio of the value of capital to net income (the capital-income ratio) is a given constant. Let this be v. It follows from equation (2.1) that

(2.2) $$g = \frac{I}{K} = s\frac{Y}{K} = \frac{s}{v}$$

which is Harrod's basic "dynamic equation."[2] Harrod interpreted this to mean that, if the firms, taken together, were willing to grow at the rate g given by (2.2), saving would exactly match the investment that is going on.[3] Their expectation of demand would prove to be exactly right and they could continue to grow at the same rate. The rate g is the warranted rate of growth. Under the assumed conditions, g is a unique number given by the constants s and v. Since the capital-income ratio is constant, the growth rate of capital is equal to the growth rate of income.

The question which naturally arises next is whether the firms, in the aggregate, would be willing to grow at this rate, or, in other words, whether the firms' plans for investment, given the basis upon which they are

---

[2] A similar equation was independently derived by Domar (1946), using a somewhat different approach. For a comparison of the two approaches see Harrod 1959. The interpretation given here follows that of Harrod, which had a greater bearing on subsequent development of the ideas. Strictly, Harrod's analysis was set out in terms of the *incremental* capital-income ratio, or $\Delta K/\Delta Y$.

[3] In his interpretation Domar emphasized "the dual character of the investment process": investment generates demand through the multiplier and at the same time creates additional productive capacity. On this view, g is the rate of growth of income that equates demand with productive capacity.

formed, can be brought into line with the requirements for smooth expansion along the warranted path. Harrod argued that there is no guarantee of this in a capitalist economy in which investment decisions are largely taken by individual firms holding particular expectations about the profitable rate of expansion of their productive capacity. There is therefore no reason to expect, in general, that the warranted rate would in fact be realized. And, what if firms plan to grow at a different rate from that which is "warranted"? If the planned rate is below the warranted one, it is argued, intended saving exceeds planned investment, a situation of excess capacity exists, and actual growth falls. With a planned growth rate higher than the warranted rate, investment exceeds planned saving and this generates cumulative inflation. The path of warranted growth thus constitutes a sort of knife-edge: only one such path exists, defined by a unique growth rate; if the actual growth path happens to be different from it, the actual path is unlikely ever to converge to it.[4]

One aspect of the matter, that is, the situation of excess capacity and slowed growth, can be seen as a generalization to the long run of the conditions which Keynes had earlier dealt with in the context of a slump. The root cause of both situations is regarded as the same: the failure of investment to generate sufficient demand to keep capacity fully utilized and growing. In the short run this takes the form of a slump, in the long run chronic stagnation. An alternative possibility to which the analysis points is a situation of continued boom and inflation associated with high levels of investment and growth.

All of this, it should be noted, is independent of the question of employment and availability of labor in the process of expansion. Given the rate of utilization of productive capacity, the growth rate of employment equals the overall rate at which firms expand capacity less the rate at which labor productivity grows on average, owing to the introduction of new methods of production. Suppose now we introduce a condition that expansion along the warranted path should be capable of providing just enough employment for all the additional labor that is becoming available, once all the existing labor has been fully absorbed. From the point of view of the firms themselves, this condition is meaningless except to

[4] Harrod (1948: 86) expressed the point as follows: "Around the line of advance which, if adhered to, would alone give satisfaction, centrifugal forces are at work causing the system to depart farther and farther from the required line of advance."

the extent that a shortage of labor constitutes a limit on their possible rate of expansion. This limit itself could be viewed as something which they could push out or contract by investing in methods of production that employ less or more labor per unit of investment. Nevertheless, take this "full employment" condition as given. For full employment to be maintained over time, assuming that it exists initially, employment must grow at the rate of increase of the labor force. Assume that the rates at which productivity grows, τ and the labor force increases, n, are independently given and call their sum, following Harrod, the *natural rate of growth*. Steady growth with full employment then requires that

$$(2.3) \qquad\qquad g = n + \tau,$$

where $n + \tau$ is the natural growth rate. When growth takes place at this rate the economy is said to be in a golden age.[5] The condition that $g = n + \tau$ is the golden-age condition; it requires that all parts of the system expand at a constant and uniform rate equal to the "natural rate." We could of course have a steady state, in the sense of growth at a constant and uniform rate, without the stringent requirement of continuous full employment.[6] But, with the natural rate being fixed, the growth rate of the economy could not remain permanently above this rate.

If we look again at the argument, it now appears that we have a contradiction. If the warranted rate g is a single number, given by s/v, it cannot at the same time equal the natural rate $n + \tau$ except by accident. However, it must be recognized immediately that the appearance of this contradiction does not arise from a logical flaw in the argument. On its own terms the argument is perfectly logical. First, the analysis tells us what the requirement is for equilibrium of saving and investment. Because of the particular conditions assumed to hold in the economy, there can be only one such equilibrium, one "warranted rate of growth." It is another matter whether growth at this rate could coincide with growth at the natural rate so as to provide continuous full employment. Since these two rates are independent, it turns out that they could be equal only as the result of an accident.

But the argument does not end here. It is being said furthermore that, *even if golden-age equilibrium can be shown to exist, the economy is*

---

[5] This felicitous expression is due to Robinson (1956: 99).
[6] One example is a steady state with a constant fraction of the labor force unemployed. This has been called a "bastard golden age." See Kahn 1959.

unlikely ever to achieve it. In effect, what the argument points to is the existence of some mechanism, inherent in the operation of the capitalist economy, such as to make it incapable of bringing about equilibrium growth, whether at the natural rate or at any other rate.

The preceding is a schematic presentation of the main lines of the argument. As an analysis of the process of expansion of the capitalist economy, it identifies, as an essential requirement of that expansion, a steady accumulation of capital by firms such as to absorb the saving that is available. It points to technical invention or innovation and increase of the labor supply as independent limits on the rate of expansion. Because there is no mechanism to bring these elements into appropriate relation with each other, it sees the process of expansion as being inherently unstable. In particular, Harrod goes on to show that, owing to the interaction of these different elements, the economy does not actually maintain an equilibrium of steady growth but might proceed by a series of investment booms interrupted by slumps or relapse into a state of complete stagnation.[7] To this extent, it is held that the "dynamic equation" and the relations it identifies provide the key to the existence of the business cycle and periods of chronic stagnation in capitalism.

If we view the argument in broad terms, it may be said here that what Harrod, and Keynes before him, had rediscovered was the problem of periodical crises which Marx had long before shown to be an inherent feature of the process of expansion and development of the capitalist economy.[8] Harrod's analysis of this problem is set out within the framework of a distinctively Keynesian analysis, while constituting also an extension of Keynes's own analysis to the "long run." There are certain similarities with the Marxian analysis, but the two are in fact substantially different, as is indicated in Chapter 10.[9]

In examining the analytical basis of Harrod's argument there are several questions to be considered. At the heart of the matter is a question of what governs the investment decisions of firms in a capitalist economy

---

[7] Harrod regarded the situation in which the warranted rate is the greater of the two rates as the most likely to be found in reality. Kaldor (1960: 230–31, 253–55) takes a similar view, but holds that "the more the warranted rate tends to exceed the natural rate, the more it will bend the natural rate in its own direction."

[8] Robinson (1965: 96) points out that "Keynes could never make head or tail of Marx. . . . But starting out from Marx would have saved him a lot of trouble."

[9] For relevant discussions of the relation between Marxian and Keynesian analysis, see also Mattick 1969; Meek 1967: 179–95; Robinson 1947; Robinson 1951b: 133–45; Robinson 1960: 1–17; Sweezy 1953: 253–62; Sweezy 1972: 79–91.

and whether the firms, taken together, can be relied upon to carry out accumulation at the rate appropriate to steady growth. In formal terms, this is a question of the investment function which describes their behavior. Harrod adopted an investment function based on the *acceleration principle*, according to which investment depends on the rate of increase of income.[10]

Another question concerns the role of saving. The argument assumes that a uniform proportion of income is saved regardless of its source. Given the rate at which firms plan to grow and the capital-income ratio, this proportion may be too high or too low. If it is too high, actual growth falls. Far from promoting growth at a high rate, a high rate of saving thus tends to slow it down. If, on the other hand, the saving rate is too low, a high rate of accumulation cannot be sustained. Thus, the argument suggests that, from the side of saving behavior, there is nothing to ensure that growth will proceed at a steady rate. Under alternative assumptions about saving behavior, the case would turn out rather differently. Specifically this is so, as we shall see, if it is assumed that saving is related to the share of income going to profits.

The argument assumes also that the capital-income ratio is fixed. Underlying this ratio are various conditions related to the composition of the stock of capital goods and the flow of output which is being produced, the technology of the economy which governs the pattern of physical inputs required to produce the flow of output, and the prices at which that output and the stock of capital goods are valued. For the capital-income ratio to be fixed it must be assumed that these conditions are such as to make it so. It needs to be shown what the specific conditions are and alternatives to these might be considered.

Finally, we are directed to a concept of the "natural growth rate," which sets a ceiling on the possible rate of expansion. The rate of accumulation must be equal to it for there to be steady growth with full employment. If the rate of accumulation is less, there is growing unemployment. If the rate of accumulation is greater, it cannot be indefinitely maintained. Underlying the natural rate are technical change and population growth, which are seen as constant factors determined independently by exogenous forces. These together govern the growth rate of the "effective" supply of labor. Whether these factors are to be considered exogenous ("natural")

[10] For a discussion of this aspect of Harrod's model, see Baumol 1959, ch. 4.

or not is a matter that needs further investigation. We also need to ask why it is that unemployment should be ruled out and what role it actually plays in a capitalist economy.

These questions suggest the routes along which it is possible to go in order to examine further Harrod's formulation of the problem. All of them have been pursued in subsequent work, some more vigorously than others. One must of course have some reason for wanting to choose one route or another. That reason, in turn, must derive from some systematic conception of the way in which the capitalist economy works and the forces which govern its expansion. It must derive, in other words, from a theory that is applicable to the situation being examined.

Harrod's argument provided a lead which set off an extended discussion and controversy. The specific problems he posed and the analysis he offered provided a focus for much of the ensuing discussion. In the course of it other problems were raised. Some of these problems arose in a different context. This was so, for instance, in the case of problems concerning the meaning and measurement of "capital," the nature of technology, the choice among methods of production, and the determination of the rate of profits in the capitalist economy.[11] These problems were all nevertheless related to each other at the level of basic theoretical principles. Their solution accordingly required drawing upon such principles wherever they were to be found or fashioning new ones to suit the task. From the attempts to do this, various theoretical "models" have emerged which incorporate different approaches to these problems. It is our purpose in this book to investigate the logical basis and substantive content of these approaches.

A significant line of development of analysis not dealt with here is the large literature on formal models of the business cycle (see, for instance, the collection of papers presented in Gordon and Klein 1965). This literature was concerned with explaining the mechanism of endogenous generation of cyclical fluctuations in the capitalist economy. But it did not get very far as a whole. Among other things, it left the explanation of forces causing recurrence of the cycle to exogenous "random shocks." It also failed to integrate a theory of growth and the business cycle as aspects of the same phenomenon. In later work the problem of the business cycle was altogether displaced by a preoccupation with the properties of

---

[11] For a review of some of the controversies on these issues see Harcourt 1972.

steady-state growth. For instance, there is no mention of that problem at all in Kaldor's [1965] definitive list of the "stylized facts" appropriate to the construction of a theory of economic growth.

On Equilibrium and Golden Ages

The concept of a steady state or a golden age, as an equilibrium of balanced expansion at a given uniform rate, underlies most of the analysis with which we shall be dealing in this book. It would seem, on the face of it, that this concept is far removed from the actual historical process of *cyclical* expansion under capitalism. In that connection, one may want to question the relevance of a concept such as this. On the other hand one finds an idea similar to the concept of a steady state in Marx's schemes of "simple reproduction" and "expanded reproduction" as well as in Schumpeter's "circular flow of economic life."[12] The steady state has a close resemblance also to the concept of a stationary state found in the work of the Classical economists. In view of the central role of this conception in the analysis presented here, it is essential that we should have a clear idea both of its meaning as a theoretical construct and of its possible relevance to an analysis of concrete historical conditions. The first of these two considerations is taken up in this section. The second is postponed until the next section.

There are two strands of recent theory which make use of this conception. One follows in a line of development directly from the formulation given by Harrod and Domar. Its characteristic feature is that it focuses on the aggregate conditions of equilibrium. It therefore deals with the relations between such aggregates as the value of capital, income, employment, investment, and saving, broadly defined for the economy as a whole. The other is associated with the work of Neumann (1945), Leontief (1951), and Sraffa (1960).[13] It views the economy in disaggregated terms, explicitly recognizing the fact of a multiplicity of production sectors and interdependence in production between different sectors. The focus is upon the pattern of prices, the commodity composition of output, and the technical conditions of production in the various sectors.

[12] See Marx, *Capital* I, ch. 23; II, chs. 20, 21; and Schumpeter (1934, ch. 1). The concept of a "uniformly progressing state," which is the same in all essentials as a steady state, was employed by Cassel (1932, ch. 1).
[13] Sraffa's analysis, unlike that of the others, is based on a system in which there are no changes in the scale of production.

These two strands at first evolved quite separately from each other, but over time have tended to be brought together.[14] This was only natural since the two are merely different ways of looking at the same problem. Bringing them together makes it possible to have an integrated picture of the structural relations that characterize a growing economy, albeit one which is growing only by a steady expansion of all its units. It is in the framework of this integrated picture that some of the central problems of the modern theory will be examined in subsequent chapters. We shall of course simplify where necessary in order to make the analysis manageable. For this purpose the analysis is presented, in part, in terms of a simple model of an economy with only two sectors of production. This model is a direct descendant of Marx's two-department scheme and effectively combines an aggregative analysis with some degree of disaggregation.

The formal features of an economy in a steady state can be easily set out. *The central feature is that accumulation is going on at a steady rate through time.* We need not suppose that net accumulation is positive, that is, that there is net expansion of the stock of means of production. It could be that the stocks accumulated in the past are only being replaced as they depreciate. In this case the system is said to be in a *stationary state.*

It must be supposed that the technical conditions are such as to allow growth to continue at a steady overall rate. Under the assumption that all commodities are produced except labor and with an unchanging technology, the upper limit on the expansion of the system would be either the rate of growth of labor supply or the smallest of the rates at which the technology makes it possible to expand net output of each commodity. As long as the limiting rate is positive, the system can expand at any positive rate within that limit. The actual rate need not be constant, but, with constant returns to scale, a constant rate would be technically feasible even in the absence of technical change.

The context of the analysis is taken to be a capitalist economy in which production is organized by capitalist firms which own capital in means of production, hire labor, and sell the product on a market in the expectation of profit for the owners. Units of labor are assumed to be homogeneous and a uniform wage is paid per unit. Competitive conditions are assumed to exist. This means, in particular, that capital is free to move

[14] See, for instance, Morishima 1964, 1969.

into any line of production, going from one line to another according to which yields the higher profits. These conditions ensure that a uniform rate of profit is established throughout the system. Prices are then such as just to cover costs of production, consisting of wages at a uniform rate per unit of labor and gross profits sufficient to pay for replacement of commodities used up plus net profit at the ruling rate on the value of the stock of capital evaluated at those prices. These are "prices of production" or "normal prices."

The various types of capital goods in existence embody the technique that has been selected from the available alternatives in accordance with the ruling rate of profit on the principle of minimizing costs (or maximizing prospective profits on the amount of finance committed). The composition of the stock of capital goods is adjusted to the technique in use and to the composition of output. The composition of output is such that consumers are able to buy the output of consumption goods at the associated distribution of purchasing power and firms obtain the capital goods appropriate to the rate of accumulation that is going on. In all sectors, a "normal" rate of capacity utilization is being realized on average and is being maintained over time as demand grows along with the expansion of capacity.

The overall equilibrium of the system requires that saving equals the value of investment. When replacement is being met out of gross profits, this means that saving out of the incomes derived from net profits and from wages must match net investment. It follows that the volume of expenditure for consumption is equal to the value of output of consumption goods.

Technical change can be introduced into this scheme. For it to be consistent with steady growth it must go on at a steady pace in all lines of production. It must also be *neutral* in the sense that the value of the capital goods employed per unit of output remains constant as output per unit of labor rises. With a constant rate of profit, this means that the real wage per unit of labor rises with the productivity of labor. Hence the overall shares of labor and of capital in net income remain constant. It is evident that this is merely an ad hoc treatment of the problem of technical change, a treatment that is solely geared to preserving the conditions assumed to characterize a steady state. Therefore, it could just as well be omitted.

"Money" can also be introduced into this scheme. Assume that the wage bargain is struck in terms of money and commodities are sold at money prices using money as the medium of exchange. For owners of wealth, money is a store of wealth. Firms borrow finance for the purpose of carrying out investment. Equilibrium requires that the rate of interest on money, allowing for a risk premium, be equal to the rate of profit on capital, and the supply of money must expand to meet requirements so as to keep the rate of interest at that level. The level of money prices follows its own course consistent with the underlying conditions and with the trend in the money wage rate. For the prices of commodities in general to remain constant, the money wage rate must rise at the rate of increase of labor productivity so as to keep the real wage growing at the same rate.

Now, there are several things to note about this scheme. First, it is a moving equilibrium to the extent that production, employment, and income are growing over time. However, the type of motion taking place here is somewhat deceptive. Since all the relevant variables are changing at the same rate, if the growth rate itself is constant it is easy to convert the system to ratios that are constant. Even in the presence of positive net accumulation and technical change, the system would then *appear* no different from what it would be in a stationary state. In recognition of this feature the name *quasi-stationary equilibria* has been given to equilibria of this type. The difference is of course that in a stationary state there is no net accumulation or technical change; but in some respects, as we shall see, the results turn out to be hardly different.

Another element in the scheme is that decisions are being taken in the light of expectations about "the future." Most clearly is this so in regard to investment decisions. Given the fact that production takes time, the decision to invest is a decision to commit an amount of finance to the future through the purchase of capital goods and the hiring of labor in the expectation of profits (i.e. net profits plus amortization) on the capital advanced.[15] Equilibrium, in this situation, must therefore mean that those expectations are being fulfilled: the current rate of profit is equal to the expected one.[16] For this purpose, it could be imagined that the rate of

---

[15] Each individual firm, seeing the problem in this way, has to decide how much to invest even though there may be no other choice but to invest. There is then a problem of ensuring that, for the system as a whole, the individual plans for investment add up to just the right amount, that is, the amount which enables the firms to realize the profits expected on the investments already made.

[16] This has a further implication. The stock of capital goods in existence at any moment, fully specified in all its diversity, has been brought into existence by decisions taken "in the

profit has been constant for some time, so that everyone comes to know what it is on the basis of experience and confidently expects it to continue at that level. There exists what has been called a state of *tranquillity*.[17] It may then be supposed that the economy follows the equilibrium path because the experience, expectations, and behavior of the actors in it are allowing it to do so. It must be admitted, however, that this is simply a way of fitting expectations to the assumed condition of equilibrium and not a satisfactory treatment of the problem of expectations as such.[18]

A particular steady state is based on a given set of conditions and interrelations among them: a given rate of accumulation of capital, given rates of saving from the stream of net income, a given state of technical knowledge (or rate of technical innovation), a given rate of increase of the labor force, and given set of expectations. To ask whether such a situation exists is to ask whether the conditions which define it are mutually compatible or self-consistent. There may be one or many such equilibria, each corresponding to a different set of conditions, or none at all. This is usually referred to as the problem of *existence of equilibrium*.

Given the nature of steady-state or golden-age equilibria, a question of movement from one equilibrium to another cannot arise. Every equilibrium involves a specific stock of means of production appropriate to the technique in use and an appropriate set of expectations about the future which will be fulfilled. The description given so far provides no information on how such movement or process of change could occur. The situation is rather like that of a train moving along a fixed track, the path of which is known beforehand and the path from which it comes is also known. Once the track is laid out and the train is put on it, there is

---

past" in the light of particular expectations held by firms about what the present was likely to be. For the stock of capital goods to be different from what it is, expectations would have had to be different and a different pattern of accumulation would have had to take place in order to have brought it into existence. Thus, equilibrium in this sense is not a state that is to be reached "in the future" or "in the long run."

[17] The concept of *tranquillity* was introduced in this context by Joan Robinson who attributes it to M. Kalecki. See Robinson (1956: 59, 66–67; 1952: 159). She points out that this way of handling expectations is "a simple device which enables us to conceive of beliefs about the future which are going to be proved correct (in stable conditions) without being obliged to deprive those who hold them of Free Will." It yields results similar to the assumption of perfect foresight. Compare also the concept of "normalcy"; see Baumol 1959: 54–55.

[18] For a relevant methodological critique of the traditional treatment of expectations in theoretical models, see Sweezy 1937–38.

nowhere else it can go but forward.[19] To consider a process of change from one position to another, that is to say, from one track to another, would be wholly incongruous under the stated conditions of the problem.

It is possible to examine different equilibrium positions (regarding them as if they were different tracks) and compare the conditions and interrelations prevailing in them. This is what is called *comparative equilibrium analysis*. It corresponds to a comparison of different economies, each moving through time along its own equilibrium path without any relation existing between them. In this context, several questions arise, for instance, about the determination of the equilibrium levels of the rate of profit and the rate of growth, the distribution of the net product between the owners of means of production and workers supplying labor services, the valuation of the stock of means of production and the choice of technical methods of production. One can begin to tell a "story" in answer to such questions. It cannot, of course, be presumed or pretended that in doing this one has as yet begun to discuss actual history.

The equilibrium relations are necessarily "true," that is, they follow from the assumed conditions regarding saving, investment, pricing, distribution, technology, etc. The main interest is in the "story" that is told about those relations and in the answers that are given to the relevant questions. Different stories are based on different assumptions; they ask different questions and provide different answers to the same questions. One problem is, of course, to determine which is the "better" story in some sense. It must be insisted, however, that a minimum condition to be met by any story is that it should be internally consistent. As we shall see, this can be a problem for some types of stories.

A sharp distinction has to be made between comparisons of equilibrium positions in the sense defined above and a process of change and adjustment. For instance, suppose we find from equilibrium comparisons that a higher rate of saving by the recipients of net income is associated with a higher growth rate. This would be a consequence of what had been shown to be the conditions prevailing in each of two separate equilibria. It would be quite illegitimate to conclude from this finding that a rise in the rate of saving above that which has existed in the past would bring about a higher rate of accumulation. It could well bring about a recession or a slump. The point is that one cannot say what would happen in such

---

[19] The analogy breaks down insofar as the train, but not the golden-age economy, can move backward on its track.

circumstances until one has specified the process of change that would take place when such an event occurs. Under the assumption that tranquillity prevails, it can be taken for granted that an equilibrium is stable in the sense that a chance change in any direction will soon reverse itself. This is because of the assumption that all actors in it have acquired a clear view of what the equilibrium is and confidently expect it to continue. This is evidently the simplest case that could be imagined and can be viewed merely as an analytical convenience. In a world in which frequent disturbances occur and expectations are continually being falsified, expectations of what is "normal" cannot be held with confidence. Moreover, incompatible relations or "internal contradictions" are liable to upset the situation from within. Reactions may then be such as to make the situation highly unstable. Whatever the case, it is necessary to explain the behavior of the actors, the interactions between them, and what forces keep the situation within bounds, if at all.

Now, the fact is that, if the "story" that was told in the previous step were sufficiently elaborated, it would of course be possible to say what the process of change would be. Thus, what we can now see is that a theory, if it is to be adequate, must provide an explanation not only of the structure of equilibrium relations and the differences among equilibria but also of the process of change through which an economy moves. Only then does a theory begin to acquire a "historical" character.[20] As it turns out, it is the former set of problems, those of existence and comparative analysis of growth equilibria, which have been mostly dealt with in recent work.

Equilibrium and History

The conditions of a steady state only have to be stated in order to appear "unrealistic." But the question of their realism or unrealism is not at issue. The important question is whether, as an abstraction, the concept of a steady state *distorts* reality in a significant way, or whether it helps in some sense to *illuminate* reality.

It has sometimes been claimed on behalf of this conception that, in some respects, it approximates certain "stylized facts" of history in some

---

[20] For a relevant discussion of the distinction between historical and equilibrium models, see Robinson 1962a: 22–34. The concept of "historical" being used here is used in a very limited sense as referring to "disequilibrium" situations, not in the broader sense of qualitative change in structural conditions.

of the advanced capitalist economies (see Kaldor 1957, 1965). In particular it is said that, in these economies aggregate output and output per worker tend to grow at a steady rate over time, whereas the real capital stock, however measured, grows at about the same rate as aggregate output. Together these imply that capital per man rises over time and the capital-output ratio remains constant. The overall *ex post* rate of profit on capital has also been found to be constant. It follows that the share of profits in income, which is the rate of profit multiplied by the capital-output ratio, has been constant.

All of these "facts" are seemingly consistent with the picture of a steady state and, for this reason, the conception has been thought to have validity as a factual description, at least in regard to this range of facts. These are, furthermore, the facts that, it is suggested, a theory of growth should explain. Additionally, it is suggested that a theory of growth should explain also the observations, across different economies, of (a) significant differences in the rate of growth of output and output per worker, (b) differences in the share of wages in net product, and (c) a high positive correlation between the share of profits in income and the share of investment in output. The comparative analysis of steady-state equilibria is supposed to throw light on such observations.

There has been considerable discussion about the empirical basis of some of these "stylized facts" that calls into question their status as facts.[21] Quite apart from the empirical validity of this range of "facts," we know also that the historical pattern of growth has not been one of uniform sectoral expansion but, characteristically, one of uneven or nonproportional growth.[22] This is inconsistent with the steady-state assumption of a uniform rate of expansion.

The question of what the facts show and what is therefore to be explained is of considerable importance. Much work also remains to be done in gathering the facts. Nevertheless, discussion of these problems need not delay us here. One could be agnostic or skeptical about the validity of the "stylized facts" and still find the concept of a golden age analytically useful. Joan Robinson, who gave the concept this name, regards it as "a mythical state of affairs not likely to obtain in any actual economy" (Robinson 1956: 99). Its usefulness is seen rather as "a means of distin-

---

[21] See, for instance, Domar 1961, Anderson 1961, Solow 1958, Urquhart 1959.
[22] For some evidence on this, see Chenery 1960.

guishing various types of disharmony that are liable to arise in an uncontrolled economy" (Robinson 1962a: 99). On the other hand, Kaldor, who introduced the "stylized facts," seems to regard the concept as broadly consistent with those facts. It is therefore seen as an appropriate basis for constructing explanatory hypotheses directly applicable to actual historical experience. Solow (1970a) takes a similar view as well as considering it a suitable framework with which to examine policies for "managing" the economy and to undertake empirical estimation of "production functions" and the "sources of growth." Pasinetti (1962: 279) views it as "a logical framework to answer interesting questions about what *ought* to happen if full employment is to be kept over time, more than as a behavioural theory expressing what actually happens." Others see it, if not as a description of the normal state of affairs in advanced capitalist economies, perhaps as a situation that could be brought about by state intervention and planning (cf. Meade 1961: 3–4; Swan 1956).

From the various uses that have been made of the concept of a steady state, it seems possible to distinguish three different approaches to its use as an analytical scheme. One is to regard it as an abstract formulation of the conditions required for the economy to continue to reproduce itself from one period to another at, say, a given level of the rate of profit or at a given rate of growth. These are the necessary conditions, so to say, for *balance* with either growth or stagnation. The scheme enables identification of the relevant economic relations, examination of the requirements for their consistency, and comparison of the structure of different possible sets of conditions. It also provides, at this level of abstraction, a vehicle for an initial statement of what is perceived within the framework of a particular theory to be the direction of causation or the "determining conditions" among the economic relations.

Starting from this conception and without any commitment to the view that balance (or equilibrium) as defined is ever, or tends to be, actually established, it is possible to go on to analyze possible sources of *imbalance*. The steady state serves as a reference point against which various patterns of imbalance can be studied and their causes investigated. The theory of growth is contained in the hypotheses that the analysis offers about the causal factors determining the imbalance. In this way, the theory provides a basis for understanding and interpreting history after it (that is, the theory, *not* history) has been appropriately modified to take account of time and place.

Marx's scheme of reproduction was constructed on this basis and was so used by Rosa Luxemburg (1951) and others for examining the causes of crises and imperialism. There is no need however, in the Marxian usage, to anchor the conception of a state of reproduction (whether it is "simple" or "expanded") in a subjective principle such as the "expectations" of individual capitalists. It is rather a condition that derives from the *social* requirement of reproduction of capital as a whole.[23]

In some respects, Harrod's use of the steady-state concept has a formal resemblance to this approach. The approach taken by Robinson (1962a) is also consistent with it. The different "ages" of growth which she constructs can be seen as a taxonomy of possible historical patterns of growth, each drawn with reference to the "mythical" pattern of a golden age but lacking any continuing evolution from one age to another.

There is a second approach according to which there is held to be some correspondence between the steady-state path and the actual historical experience of capitalist economies (if only in broad outline and allowing for the controls provided by the state). On this view, it becomes a crucial problem to show that a golden-age equilibrium is *stable* in the sense that a departure from the equilibrium values would set in motion forces such as to produce a return to those values. This is the role of *stability analysis* in this context. A theory of growth thus seeks to account for how the conditions and relations characterizing the equilibrium path, including the given level of the rate of profit and rate of growth, are maintained and reinforced. This general viewpoint appears to be broadly characteristic of Kaldor's approach. It seems to represent also the position of Solow. Additionally, Solow holds that the relationships obtained from steady-state models, whether of the more complex and "quasi-realistic" type or in the form of simple "parables," can be used to "predict" actual behavior and statistical trends.[24]

The distinctions between these two approaches should be clearly recognized. The second approach is basically pragmatic and tends to follow an empiricist method. Its emphasis on a direct correspondence between the steady-state path and the actual history of capitalist economies presumes the existence of some sort of self-regulating mechanism in such economies. The first approach does not presume any such corres-

[23] On this see Marx, *Capital* I, ch. 23; II, part 3. For a relevant discussion of Marx's concept of reproduction, see Althusser and Balibar 1970, part 3, ch. 3.

[24] See Solow 1957. For a complementary statement of this position, see Samuelson 1962.

pondence or self-adjusting mechanism. In particular, Marx viewed the historical process of capitalist expansion and development as inherently prone to recurring economic crises of various forms. Such crises are due to internal contradictions, which themselves produce qualitative changes in the social system and which it was the purpose of his analysis to identify. In this sense, Marx's approach is *dialectical-historical*. Outside of the Marxian tradition, this concept of inherent contradictions in the operation of the capitalist economy has not received much attention in the recent work. It was noticed "in passing" by Schumpeter (1954: 971) as a matter of "far-reaching importance."

A third approach to use of the steady-state concept is in the context of attempts to rank different growth paths in terms of some independently established criterion of "social welfare" as related exclusively to consumption. This line of inquiry began with the work of Ramsey (1928). It was revived by Dorfman, et. al (1958) and flourished for a time, becoming known as the *theory of optimal growth*.[25] The analytical problem posed is to determine which is the best or optimal path in the sense of maximizing an index of welfare. It has been shown that, under certain conditions, a steady-state path is itself the optimal path or serves as a "turnpike" for reaching some defined objective. To solve this problem, one must have some criterion for evaluating the welfare of society as a whole, and there must be more than one path from which to choose. It must also be presumed that there is some social context in which such an analysis makes sense.

To distinguish this approach from the previous ones, we may call it the *technocratic approach*. It is concerned less, if at all, with explaining the actual historical pattern of production and accumulation in capitalist economies than with the derivation of rules for the ideal organization of production.

A rationale of the technocratic approach seems to lie in the presumption of neoclassical theory, going back to Bohm-Bawerk and Fisher, that intertemporal preferences regarding consumption enter into the accumulation process through the savings decisions of the rentier class. Koopmans (1976b: 97) notes in this connection that "the main aim is to obtain insight into the effect of, and the scope for, time preference." In defense of this approach, Solow (1963: 15) claims that it is "the easiest

---

[25] For a review of this literature, see Koopmans 1967a,b.

and safest route to a simple but rigorous view of the subject" and that "By asking planning questions, allocation questions, we can ... dodge many embarrassing questions of definition and their ideological over-tones." Against that claim it could be argued, as Solow recognizes (*ibid.*, p. 16) that "a capital theory erected on planning grounds has no relevance to the actual behavior of any real capitalist economy." This argument has never been effectively rebutted.[26]

It is the first, or Marxian, approach to interpretation and use of the steady-state concept that is adopted in the present work. The technocratic approach and the analysis following from it will be ignored. We shall also be entirely concerned with theoretical analysis and not at all with problems of empirical application.

A process of nonproportional growth is what is most directly relevant to the uneven development of the world economy and to the situation of the underdeveloped economies or underdeveloped regions within national units. To the extent that it ignores this dimension of the growth problem, it is perhaps in this respect that the concept of steady-state growth does most violence to our sense of historical reality. What is needed in this connection is a *theory of uneven development*.

Profits and Interest

For the purpose of the subsequent discussion, a sharp distinction is to be made between the rate of profit and the rate of interest. We examine here the meaning and significance of these two concepts.

The concept of (net) profit refers to the excess of total income above wage costs and depreciation that is earned from the employment of wage labor in production. It bears a more or less regular proportion to the sum of money values (or capital sum) used directly or indirectly in the employment of labor in whatever sphere such capital is employed. That proportion is the *rate* of profit. Several different uses of the concept of rate of profit may be distinguished.

First, this concept is commonly used with reference to the total amount of profits generated in the economy as a whole. In this context, it is customary to speak of the rate of profits (that is, profits in the plural). As a quantity, it is a quotient consisting, in the numerator, of the total

[26] For a use of the golden age scheme to answer planning questions in the context of a planned economy, see Mathur 1965.

profits (or the share of profits in the total product) and, in the denominator, of the total value of invested capital in the economy (or the capital-output ratio). It is thus a combination of two other quantities, one of which refers to the overall distribution of the product between profits and wages, the other to the value of total capital.

A rate of profits in this sense always exists as a problem to be explained in the context of a capitalist economy. It is a *macroeconomic* quantity, itself a combination of other macroeconomic quantities, all of which relate to the economy as a whole regardless of the level of disaggregation of the economy. Its level must therefore be explained with reference to the economy as a whole.[27] As a concept, it must be located in a theory that is explicitly stated in macroeconomic terms. In a similar vein, Pasinetti (1962: 278) notes, in regard to his own analysis of this problem, that "the foregoing investigation is not 'macroeconomic' in the sense of representing a first simplified rough step towards a more detailed and disaggregated analysis. *It is macro-economic because it could not be otherwise.* Only problems have been discussed which are of a macro-economic nature; an accurate investigation of them has nothing to do with disaggregation" (emphasis added).

A different concept is that of the rate of profit generated within a single industry or firm. As a quantity, this may be higher or lower than the overall rate of profits. As a concept, it relates to the individual firm or industry. For the economy as a whole, there may be a hierarchy of different rates of profit in this sense, ranging from the highest to the lowest. The pattern of individual rates of profit is a problem to be explained on its own terms quite apart from the explanation of the overall rate of profits. Explanation of the former must also be imbedded within a theory that focuses upon individual sectors and firms in the economy and the differences that exist between them. The theoretical models considered here have very little to say on this problem.[28]

On the assumption that competition exists in the sense that capital

[27] Although the need for explaining a macroeconomic quantity in terms of macroeconomic relations can be readily granted, it needs to be shown also how these relations are consistent with individual and group behavior affecting formation of prices, wages, and decisions concerning production, saving, and investment. But such problems arise at a different level of the argument.

[28] A major effort in the direction of a systematic treatment of this question is that of Kalecki (1954). Another is that of Steindl (1952). The question is also taken up by Leon (1967).

is free to move from one industry to another in order to capture differences in the rate of profit, it is reasonable to assume a tendency towards a uniform rate of profit in the economy. The condition of a uniform rate of profit is then a consequence of the assumption of competition in this sense and of the tendencies associated with competition. On this assumption, it becomes possible to speak of the individual rate of profit as if there were just one such rate. There is then no distinction to be made between the overall average rate of profits and the individual rate.[29] This is a matter of great analytical convenience and, in this respect, could be regarded as a useful first approximation. It is this assumption which is made in the analysis presented in subsequent chapters. It is, moreover, the theoretically appropriate assumption to make if it is believed that strong competitive forces exist in a particular historical situation so as to create a tendency toward a uniform rate of profit.

All of this relates to the realized rate of profit as viewed either from the level of the overall rate for the economy as a whole or from that of the individual rates for particular industries and firms. We may distinguish, next, the expected rate of profit which is a matter of the income that is *expected* to be generated in the future by investments that are being planned. This concept is used in the context of decisions by firms concerning the rate of investment and the technical form in which such investments are to be embodied (or the "choice of technique"). Other terms like "rate of discount," "marginal efficiency of capital" and "rate of return on investment," which are often used in this context, have a similar meaning. Determination of the expected rate of profit has to be made in the light of what a theory says about the formation of expectations. It is common to assume that expectations are formed on the basis of past experience. This assumption then provides a link between the expected and the realized rate of profit. The two need not be the same. In a state of steady growth when expectations are consistently fulfilled so that long-period equilibrium prevails, the expected rate of profit then turns out to be equal to the realized rate, which is constant.

Interest is the payment for financial wealth. That is to say, it is the payment received by the owners of the existing *stock* of financial assets of various sorts (securities, bonds, bank deposits, etc.), representing loans

[29] Strict equality of the rate of profit in all sectors is not a necessary feature of this assumption. Profit rates may be higher or lower than the average, reflecting elements of risk and uncertainty that are specific to each sector.

made in the past and accumulated cash reserves. Each type of financial asset has its corresponding rate of interest which is the rate at which interest is paid on the value of the asset. Assuming, for simplicity, that there is one such asset, say, "money," then there is only one such rate, and we can speak unambiguously of *the* rate of interest on money. A theory of interest is directed to explaining how the market for financial assets works to determine the pattern of rates of interest appropriate to each type of financial asset. It can be assumed that on a steady-state path (with constant prices) the rate of profit is equal to the rate of interest, allowing for a risk premium on capital invested in production. However, to say that the rate of profit and the rate of interest are equal is not to say that they are one and the same thing.

The analysis which follows has nothing to say about the determination of the rate(s) of interest. It is focused exclusively on the rate of profit. This bias reflects the relative emphasis placed upon these matters in the theoretical approaches discussed here. This procedure is also consistent with the Classical and Marxian view of profits as a generic type of *class* income, interest being a derivative form which is paid out of (gross) profit and ultimately regulated by it. Analysis of the rate of interest is, nevertheless, within the purview of a theory of economic growth. It requires a conception of the role of money and finance in the capitalist economy. Precisely what this role is and how it is to be incorporated in a theory of growth are questions that have so far been relatively neglected.[30]

Finally, there is the Marxian concept of *rate of exploitation*, which differs from all the foregoing. It refers to the excess of the value, measured in units of labor time, of the current product of labor above the value, similarly measured, which the workers get in the form of wages for their labor time. The ratio of that excess or surplus to the value of wages constitutes the rate of exploitation or rate of surplus value. Like the rate of profits, it is a macroeconomic concept. Similarly, it has a counterpart at the level of individual firms and industries. But it is a broader category than those discussed above for the reason that it includes them all, that is to say, it includes all nonwage income consisting of profits, interest, and rent as component parts of total surplus value. In Marx's analysis, as

---

[30] For various attempts to deal with this problem, see Tobin 1955, 1965; Davidson 1968, 1969; Robinson 1971a, chs. 5, 6; Foley and Sidrauski 1970.

we shall see, it plays a central role, to which all the other categories are subsidiary.

Conclusion

The concerns of modern growth theory are more narrowly focused than those of Classical or Marxian theory and derive from the historically specific situation of contemporary capitalism. Nevertheless, these concerns must be seen to relate fundamentally to the same level and scope of theoretical reasoning. Accordingly, their resolution requires a similarly integrated theoretical conception of the capitalist economy as a whole and its process of expansion, explicitly recognizing interrelatedness of the phenomena of production, exchange, distribution, and accumulation.

It is our task in what follows to develop a critical understanding of contemporary theoretical approaches to the analysis of growth of the capitalist economy, while drawing upon the conceptual foundations that were laid by Classical and Marxian theory. This is a necessary first step in seeking to advance the development of a theory appropriate to modern conditions.

Part Two. A Scheme of Analysis

Chapter Three

Value, Distribution, and Accumulation

Introduction

To try to take account of all the features of reality that might be considered relevant for economic analysis would be a futile, if not impossible, task.[1] An appropriate scientific procedure is to start with simple cases, focusing on those features that are considered to be essential and leaving out the inessential complications. This process of theoretical abstraction is, moreover, an essential and indispensable requirement for the purpose of scientific analysis of economic and social relations.[2] In this process, we should of course choose our assumptions carefully with an eye to the problem at hand and the historical reality to which it relates. If the choice is well made, we should be able to get useful analytical results that are not drastically altered when the complications are introduced.

With these general considerations in mind, we proceed in this chapter to present the elements of an abstract economic model or scheme as a basis for the analysis of accumulation and distribution in the capitalist economy.[3] We start off from a specification of the "technical" conditions of production and build upon these other economic and social relations,

---

[1] Joan Robinson (1962a: 33) aptly notes, in this connection, "A model which took account of all the variegation of reality would be of no more use than a map at the scale of one to one."

[2] As Marx put it: "In the analysis of economic forms . . . neither microscopes nor chemical reagents are of use. The force of abstraction must replace both." (*Capital* I: 8.)

[3] This scheme follows, in part, that of Sraffa (1960), but differs from his in regard to the assumptions made here that the economy is expanding and that production coefficients are invariant to changes in the scale of output. A relevant mathematical treatment of Sraffa's model is given by Newman (1962). The schema presented here also draws upon certain formal properties of the dynamic model of Leontief (1951) and Neumann's (1945) model without joint production. The mathematical aspects of the analysis, which are essentially

leading thereby to a sharp characterization, in schematic form, of some abstract and general conditions of the capitalist economy. Certain analytic properties are shown to hold in such a system with regard to the inter-relations between labor values, prices, profits, and accumulation. Within this framework some links with the concepts and method of Classical and Marxian economic analysis can be clearly drawn.[4] The precise theoretical limitations of this scheme are also indicated.

A Model of Production

Within the broad framework of a production system in which com-modities are produced by commodities and labor (the "Classical model of production"), there are various "technical" conditions of production that need to be taken into account.[5] These have to do with the number and types of commodities, whether they are capital goods, consumption goods, or intermediate goods, the number of methods available for producing each commodity, the possibility of joint production, the time pattern of production, the durability of capital goods, and so on. For full generality in describing technology, attention should be paid to all of these dimensions. But, as a first approximation, we can afford to sim-plify.

Assume, therefore, a system in which there are n produced commodities. For full generality, n may be large or small ($1 \leqq n < \infty$). Any commodity may serve either as consumption good or as capital good or as both. Intermediate goods are ignored. Each commodity is produced in a single industry using homogeneous labor and stocks of some or all of the same n commodities as inputs. Joint production of two or more commodities in one industry is excluded. Production takes one period, the same for all commodities. The production process thus has a time dimension,

---

connected with the properties of nonnegative square matrices, have been widely studied and the key theorems are reported in both the mathematical and economic literature. See Dorfman et al. 1958: 253–60; Gale 1960, chs. 8, 9; Morishima 1964; and Takayama 1974, ch. 4.

[4] For a relevant discussion of the connection between Sraffa's scheme and Classical economic analysis, see Meek 1967: 161–69. Some of the distinctions to be drawn in this context between Classical economic analysis and that of Marx are discussed by Rowthorn (1974).

[5] There is no implication of these conditions being purely physical or "natural." They are governed by social and historical factors that are being taken as given for purposes of the present analysis. Compare Marx's description of "the elementary factors of the labour-process," *Capital* I, ch. 7, sec. 1.

which means that stocks of commodities (capital goods) must be available at the start of production before the outputs are available. Assume that the stock of each type of capital good depreciates over time at a given rate per period, δ_i, which is independent both of the industry in which it is used and of the age of the capital good.[6]

A method for producing the jth commodity is characterized by the quantities $a_{ij}(i = 1, 2, \ldots, n)$ of the stock of the ith commodity employed per unit of output of the jth commodity and the quantity a_{0j} of labor per unit of output.[7] The quantities a_{ij} and a_{0j} are fixed constants independent of the scale of output.[8] A technique of production consists of a set of n methods for producing the different commodities, one method for each commodity.[9] It is assumed, for the sake of simplicity, that there is a single unchanging technique of production. The central economic question involved in the existence of more than one technique is that of the choice among them. In the context of our steady-state assumptions, when technology is taken as given, the technique chosen in accordance with the ruling conditions remains the same on a particular steady-state path. Therefore, nothing is lost in assuming one technique. However, in comparing different paths, we must take account of the possibility that the technique used in each may be different. As a matter of convenience this issue may be usefully postponed for the moment. (The existence of

---

[6] The assumption of a fixed rate of depreciation independent of the age of the capital good is a convenient device. This makes it possible to regard each type of capital good as homogeneous regardless of its age and, by a simple specialization, to deal with the case of pure circulating capital. It must be granted, however, that this is not a satisfactory method of dealing with fixed capital. In ruling out joint production we are giving up one possible way of dealing with this problem, which is to recognize that a capital good, on becoming one period older, is a type of joint product of the industry in which it is used. On this, see Sraffa 1960, ch. 10. It turns out that the introduction of this type of joint production leaves unaltered the main conclusions derived from the present scheme of analysis. See Schefold 1971.

[7] Stocks are measured in physical units of each type of commodity. Labor is measured in homogeneous units of its duration over a given uniform period (the same as the production period) and at a constant intensity of application. We may refer to this unit as a "man-hour (day/week/year)" or, for short, a "man."

[8] We are here neglecting complications due to variations in the duration of the work period and in the intensity of application of labor during a given period. These omissions are a cause for serious concern with regard to the actual historical conditions of capitalist production. Neglect of variations in the work period would, however, be legitimate where a fixed length of the working day has become incorporated into law and custom. The classic treatment of these dimensions of the capitalist labor process is that of Marx. Their theoretical and practical significance is discussed throughout *Capital* I (see esp. chs. 10 and 17).

[9] Heterogeneity of commodities is here defined in terms of a difference in their method of production within a given technique.

many alternative techniques of production will be introduced in Chapter 5.) For present purposes, there is no harm in assuming also that technology is unchanging.[10]

We may represent the technique of production in the form of a matrix

$$\left[\frac{a_0}{A}\right] = \begin{bmatrix} a_{01} & a_{02} & \cdots & a_{0j} & \cdots & a_{0n} \\ \hline a_{11} & a_{12} & \cdots & \cdot & \cdots & a_{1n} \\ a_{21} & a_{22} & \cdots & \cdot & \cdots & a_{2n} \\ \cdot & \cdot & \cdots & \cdot & \cdots & \cdot \\ \cdot & \cdot & \cdots & \cdot & \cdots & \cdot \\ a_{i1} & a_{i2} & \cdots & a_{ij} & \cdots & a_{in} \\ \cdot & \cdot & \cdots & \cdot & \cdots & \cdot \\ \cdot & \cdot & \cdots & \cdot & \cdots & \cdot \\ a_{n1} & a_{n2} & \cdots & \cdot & \cdots & a_{nn} \end{bmatrix}$$

where the jth column defines the method of production of the jth commodity; the ith row gives the pattern of utilization of the ith commodity in different industries, and the 0th row gives the pattern of utilization of labor. The rates of depreciation form a ($n \times n$) diagonal matrix

$$\delta = \begin{bmatrix} \delta_1 & & & & & \\ & \delta_2 & & & 0 & \\ & & \delta_3 & & & \\ & & & \delta_4 & & \\ & 0 & & & \cdot & \\ & & & & & \delta_n \end{bmatrix}$$

where $0 < \delta_i \leqq 1$. In the special case where $\delta_i = 1$ for all i, we have a model of pure circulating capital goods.

We need not assume that every commodity enters directly into the production of every other commodity; only that production does not require negative amounts of any commodity (the matrix A is nonnegative) and that some labor is directly required to produce every commodity (a_0 is strictly positive). It is assumed also that each commodity is required

---

[10] Recall that, by saying technology is taken as given, we mean specifically that we are holding constant the social and historical conditions which govern the available methods of production. (On this, see pp. 21–24.) It needs to be added here that the quantities entering into the matrix of production coefficients represent only what is "socially necessary" under the given conditions. Cf. *Capital* I: 195–96.

directly or indirectly in the production of every commodity (A is indecomposable).

The exercise of labor in production involves the using up of commodities for the maintenance of the laborer. In this respect, we could say that consumption (here, individual consumption) itself has a purely productive aspect. The specific character of labor, however, is that it is *not* produced within the same process as the commodities that are indexed $i = 1, ..., n$.[11] Accordingly, suppose that a fixed quantity, say b_i, of each commodity is required for consumption in order that a unit of labor may be maintained in production. Call this necessary consumption. Let the column vector of necessary consumption be $b = [b_i]$. It is the same for all units of labor. As a formal matter, we could represent the conditions of production defined so far, including necessary consumption, as an $(n + 1)^2$ augmented matrix, say,

$$B = \left[\begin{array}{c|c} & a_0 \\ \hline b & A \end{array} \right]$$

where the first column, b, is necessary consumption and (a_0, A) is the technique of production as previously defined. We forgo this formal treatment, however, in order to keep in full view the distinction between labor and produced commodities. This is to emphasize that the social process of production and reproduction of labor requires further study and analysis on its own terms.

Of course, the assumption that the vector of necessary consumption is the same for all units of labor follows naturally from the prior assumption that all units of labor are the same. But what accounts for the condition that all units of labor are the same? This is an important question and we shall return to it in the subsequent discussion. In contrast, we do not have a problem associated with all means of production (stocks of capital goods) being the same. They are strictly defined not to be the same; and there are as many different types as is considered to be appro-

---

[11] Marx expressed another aspect of the difference in the following terms: "Labour uses up its material factors, its subject and its instruments, consumes them, and is therefore a process of consumption. Such productive consumption is distinguished from individual consumption by this, that the latter uses up products, as means of subsistence for the living individual; the former, as means whereby alone, labour, the labour-power of the living individual, is enabled to act. The product, therefore, of individual consumption, is the consumer himself, the result of productive consumption, is a product distinct from the consumer." *Capital* I: 183.

priate. This is a perfectly general and reasonable assumption which is consistent with the diversity of means of production associated with an advanced division of labor.

To produce the vector of outputs $X = [x_i]$ requires capital stocks AX and total labor $a_0 X$. For production to be technically feasible it must be assumed that available capital stocks and labor are sufficient to meet these requirements. Since capital stocks are produced commodities, we need only assume in their case that the required stocks have been built up from production in the past—a condition which holds on the steady-state path. In the case of labor, however, since labor is not produced within the same process as that of means of production, we cannot resort to the same condition. Special attention therefore needs to be given to the conditions governing the availability of labor. We leave this here as an open question. Even so, there is of course no necessary reason why the available stocks of capital goods and supply of labor should be fully utilized. Whether they are or not is an additional condition of the problem which requires to be explained. An answer could perhaps be found by appealing to Say's Law of Markets, which denies the possibility of unemployment or overproduction. This appeal may be granted under the highly restrictive conditions of a barter economy. But the applicability of Say's Law to societies based on generalized exchange of products by individual producers through the medium of money is doubtful. In the case of capitalist economies, it is necessary to recognize the existence of unemployment or overproduction as a continually recurring phenomenon which requires theoretical explanation.

Given the preceding conditions, we can go on to conceive of a number of additional conditions regarding production, exchange, and distribution. Accordingly, in the following sections several such sets of conditions are distinguished. We seek to determine the consistency among those conditions, the prices that would prevail under those conditions, and the interrelations between prices, production, and distribution. In this way it is possible to construct the concepts and relations which enter into the theoretical analysis of the capitalist economy and to identify the specific form of the analytical problem which arises in that context.

A Pure Subsistence Economy

Suppose that an economy is just capable of producing as much output as is required to provide for replacement of commodities used up in production including necessary consumption. This feature defines the character of this economy as a subsistence economy.[12] It implies the following conditions for total output of each commodity:

(3.1) $$x_i = \delta_i \sum_j a_{ij} x_j + b_i \sum_j a_{0j} x_j \qquad i = 1, \ldots, n$$

This is, furthermore, a condition of reproduction of the production system as a whole in the sense that the quantities of commodities that are used up in production must be replaced from current production if production is to continue at the same level in the next period. From this statement of its specific character we can go on to derive particular features of the economy and the requirements for its self-consistency.

The system of output equations (3.1) is a simple linear equation system consisting of n equations in the n unknowns x_i. We may rewrite this in matrix notation as

(3.2) $$X = \delta A X + b a_0 X$$

By rearranging terms we get

(3.2a) $$[I - b a_0 - \delta A] X = 0$$

where I is the $(n \times n)$ identity matrix. Mathematically we have to solve this system for the unknowns X. It is also required for economic reasons that X is nonnegative, since production cannot be negative. Being homogeneous, the system (3.2a) can have a nontrivial solution[13] if and only if the matrix $[I - b a_0 - \delta A]$ has a vanishing determinant, that is

(3.3) $$|I - b a_0 - \delta A| = 0$$

This can be seen as a restriction on the conditions of production, including necessary consumption, which characterize the economy. Since it is assumed further that each commodity is used directly or indirectly in the production of every commodity (the matrix A is indecomposable), then it is a theorem that there exists a positive output vector X that is unique up to multiplication by a positive constant. (See Gale 1960: 266.) The solution of (3.2a) is uniquely determined by the conditions of

[12] This concept of a subsistence economy is not to be confused with the notion of subsistence production as a process taking place on the part of an isolated individual or self-subsistent household (e.g. Robinson Crusoe) outside of society. The concept of subsistence as used here refers, rather, to a characteristic of the production system as a whole within organized society.

[13] We ignore the trivial solution $X = 0$.

production. These equations yield a solution for the *ratio* of outputs and not the absolute *levels*. This means that the system has one possible solution of relative outputs x_i/x_j, but the scale of output is undetermined. To determine the scale, additional conditions have to be introduced. One such condition might be, for instance, that the total quantity of available labor is fully employed. But this begs the question of how such a situation of "full employment" could arise. Without seeking to impose or justify any such condition, we prefer simply to leave the matter open in the present case.

As a further condition of the problem, assume that the output of commodities is exchanged on a market by the producers. The condition that goods are thus regularly acquired through private exchange by individual producers may be taken to define the status of such goods as commodities. The condition that social production is permeated and spontaneously organized by such exchange defines the character of the economy as a *commodity-producing economy*. It follows that, if the system is to be able to reproduce itself, there is a further condition of reproduction that must be satisfied within the sphere of exchange. Specifically, exchange must enable the producers, each in his own line of production, to obtain the means to provide for necessary consumption and replacement of that part of the stock of commodities which depreciates during the production period. These are the "necessary" costs of production in the strict sense that these commodities are used up in production. The coverage of these costs is also required for continued production. For these costs to be exactly covered, the set of equilibrium prices or exchange ratios for each commodity is[14]

$$(3.4) \qquad p_i = \sum_j a_{ji}\delta_j p_j + a_{0i}\sum_j b_j p_j \qquad i = 1, \ldots, n$$

In matrix notation we have

$$(3.5) \qquad P = A'\delta P + a_0' b' P$$

or

$$(3.5a) \qquad [I - a_0' b' - A'\delta]P = 0$$

[14] It is assumed here and throughout the subsequent discussion, without loss of generality, that the prices which prevail at the end of the period are the same as at the beginning. The word "equilibrium" is used simply as an expression for the condition that, at those prices, the accounts of the producers are fully balanced.

where, for economic reasons, it is assumed that P is nonnegative. Solution of the price system requires

(3.6) $$|I - a_0'b' - A'\delta| = 0$$

which is mathematically the same condition as that for the output system (only the columns and rows of the matrix are interchanged) and has the same economic meaning. These equations, being homogeneous, also yield a solution only for the ratio of prices and not the levels. That is to say, for any choice of numeraire, equilibrium *relative* prices p_i/p_j are fully determined.[15] Furthermore, relative prices are determined independently of both the level and composition of output—they depend only on the conditions of production. This can be seen from the fact that the system of outputs and prices dichotomizes—the output equations are solved independently of the price equations and vice versa. The reason for this follows from the assumptions concerning production. Because the coefficients of production are fixed, production can be expanded to any level at constant costs per unit. Thus, if there is one set of prices that cover costs at one level of output, the same will do at any other level.

In summary, we note several characteristics of this system. Existence of a subsistence economy in the sense defined strictly requires a very special set of production conditions. These conditions are such that, in every period, the output from production just suffices to meet the replacement of depreciated stocks and consumption requirements for production. The structure of the economy, viewed in terms of both relative outputs and relative prices, is independent of the scale of output. Prices are exchange ratios: they express a quantitative relation between commodities in the sphere of exchange. But this particular set of prices has a more definite character. Specifically, they enable the exchange of commodities so that in any period each producer is provided with the means for continuing production in the next period. These prices are uniquely determined by the conditions of production and are independent of the composition of output.

We could conceive of this as a society of independent producers,

---

[15] Assume, for the sake of simplicity, that gold is the money commodity and is produced in the nth industry. Then p_i/p_n is the price of commodity i in terms of gold, or the "money price" of commodity i. In reality, the choice of a numeraire, whether it be gold, cigarettes, or cows, is not arbitrary. It is the outcome of a social and historical process that requires analysis on its own terms.

"peasants" and/or "artisans," each engaged in production with his own stock of means of production and own labor—a type of "simple commodity production" (Marx). The individual producer or unit of production may be taken in this case to be "the family." If each producer were capable of producing, as a unit in isolation, all that is required and in the right proportions for continued reproduction, then there would be no basis for exchange. Exchange of products is attributable to specialization of producers in different lines of production, that is, to a social division of labor. The basis of such specialization or division of labor may be assumed to lie in historical and social factors, for instance, in rights to particular types of means of production. How such rights could come about is of course another matter. There is no need to presuppose independent "preferences" of individual producers as between different lines of production. And with the composition of output and relative prices uniquely determined by the given conditions of production and reproduction, there is then no room for explaining any feature of this system by presumed preferences of producers as individuals.

There remains, however, an important question of how it comes about in such an economy, where labor is strictly specialized to different lines of production, that there exists a homogeneous unit of labor. There seems to be no way of resolving this problem within the framework of assumptions of this case.

Production with a Surplus

Suppose, now, that an economy is capable of producing gross outputs of commodities in excess of the amounts required to provide for replacement of commodities used up in production including necessary consumption. This means that the condition of reproduction in terms of replacement of used-up commodities can be satisfied by this economy, as a sort of "minimum" condition.

Call the excess of gross output over replacement the *surplus product*. It is defined in physical terms for each commodity. Let $Z = [z_i]$ = column vector of surplus product. Thus, gross output of each commodity is

$$(3.7) \qquad x_i = \delta_i \sum_j a_{ij} x_j + b_i \sum_j a_{0j} x_j + z_i \qquad i = 1, \ldots, n$$

or, in matrix form,

$$(3.8) \qquad X = \delta AX + b a_0 X + Z$$

We now have a system of n equations in $2n$ unknowns: x_i and z_i. Given, say, the (nonnegative) vector of surplus product, $Z = \overline{Z}$, the problem is to find a corresponding nonnegative solution for the outputs. Rewriting (3.8) we have

(3.8a) $$X = [I - ba_0 - \delta A]^{-1}\overline{Z}$$

Provided that the inverse matrix $[I - ba_0 - \delta A]^{-1}$ exists, a solution may be found for the X_i and it is nonnegative. This requires that the production system is productive, implying

(3.9) $$|I - ba_0 - \delta A| > 0$$

which is a restriction on the conditions of production including necessary consumption.[16]

The solution for the outputs corresponds to a convergent geometric series which takes the form

$$X = [I + B + B^2 + B^3 + \ldots]\overline{Z}$$

where $B = ba_0 + \delta A$. Consider the terms in this series. The first, $I\overline{Z}$, is the surplus product itself. The second, $B\overline{Z}$, consists of the commodities required as direct inputs in the form of necessary consumption for the labor directly employed in producing the surplus product and replacement of worn-out means of production. Call this the first round of production. The third term, $B^2\overline{Z}$, consists of the commodities required to produce the inputs of the first round. These are the second-round input requirements. The fourth term, $B^3\overline{Z}$, consists of the commodities required to produce the inputs of the second round, and so on ad infinitum. In general, $B^t\overline{Z}$ are the tth-round input requirements. As t increases, the terms of the series become negligible and the series converges. Thus, the gross output of commodities, item by item, is seen to be made up of the surplus product itself, plus the quantities of commodities directly and indirectly required to produce the surplus product. The rounds of production described here occur not in historical time but as a logical implication of interdependence and circularity in the production process.

Similarly, viewed from the side of the absorption of labor, production of gross outputs X requires total labor of

[16] Strictly, the necessary and sufficient condition for a nonnegative solution is that all the principal minors of the matrix $[I - ba_0 - \delta A]$ are positive. This is commonly referred to as the Hawkins-Simon condition.

$$a_0 X = a_0 [I + B + B^2 + B^3 + \dots]\overline{Z}$$

which consists of the labor directly and indirectly employed in producing the surplus product.

The solution of (3.8a) gives a unique level of the outputs. What fixes the level of output in this case is the assumed condition that the vector of surplus product is given. For a different vector of surplus product the vector of outputs would be different. The scale and composition of output thus depend on the level and composition of the surplus product as well as on the conditions of production including necessary consumption. It is interesting to note, furthermore, that if there exists a solution for one vector of surplus product, involving all the produced commodities, then there exists a solution for any other vector, provided only that the required level of capital stocks and supply of labor are available. This is a corollary of the condition that the system is productive.

Thus, a productive system is one that is capable of producing a vector of surplus product. Productivity in this sense is indifferent to the scale and composition of output, or to the particular vector of surplus product. It is a characteristic of the production system as a whole. In particular, it is a characteristic of the production conditions as represented by the whole matrix of production coefficients and the vector of necessary consumption. It gives to the economy a specific character which clearly differentiates this economy from the previous case of a subsistence economy. Insofar as this character is neither purely accidental nor a purely natural or technical feature of the given production system, and whereas it may simply be taken as given for the purposes of a particular exposition, it is a condition that remains to be accounted for within an analysis of the economy as a whole. Considered on a historical plane, it would also be the product of a specific historical development.

Consider now the matter of prices under these conditions. In the case of a subsistence economy, as we saw above, equilibrium prices enable the producers to cover exactly the "necessary" costs of production, no more and no less. Suppose that such were the prices in this case. Then we should have

(3.10) $$\hat{P} = A'\delta\hat{P} + a_0'b'\hat{P}$$

the solution of which requires that the production conditions satisfy

(3.11) $$|I - a_0'b' - A'\delta| = 0$$

But we know from the output system (3.8a) that, if a solution exists, the production conditions satisfy inequality (3.9), and this is inconsistent with the equality (3.11). Therefore, in a system that is productive, there exists no consistent set of prices having just this particular property. We can see why this is so. Premultiplying (3.8) by $\hat{P}$ and (3.10) by X gives

(3.12) $$\hat{P}'X = \hat{P}'\delta AX + \hat{P}'ba_0X + \hat{P}'Z$$

(3.13) $$X'\hat{P} = X'A'\delta\hat{P} + X'a_0'b'\hat{P}$$

Thus, when calculated in terms of such prices, total value of output in equation (3.12) exceeds total value of output in equation (3.13) by an amount exactly equal to the total value of the surplus product measured at those same prices. It is evident, then, that such prices fail to provide for distribution of the surplus product. What is missing, therefore, is a rule for distribution in this sense. Without such a rule, specification of the economy is incomplete.

It may be noted here that the surplus product, whatever its actual size and composition, originates in production. It exists by virtue of the fact that the system is productive in the sense defined above. Given the existence of a surplus product and the existence of markets for exchange of commodities, prices in such markets must provide for distribution of this surplus. By contrast, in a subsistence economy, since there exists no surplus product, then there is no such problem of distribution. Thus, this problem of distribution arises only when there exists a surplus product. In this sense, not only what exists to be distributed, but also distribution itself, is determined by production. What remains to be determined is the particular form of that distribution. The general form of distribution with which we are concerned is one that takes place through the market on the basis of exchange of products. This condition clearly rules out forms of distribution determined by factors that are outside the market, such as the "force theory" of Eugen Duhring. (See Engels 1939, part 2.) As we have seen in the previous case of a subsistence economy, the market is also the mechanism through which the economy as a whole reproduces itself. It follows that distribution must be determined jointly with relationships of reproduction and within the same process as that which enables reproduction.

One possible rule for distribution is that a uniform payment is made to each producer in accordance with the quantity of labor directly performed. This payment is included in the price of the commodity along with the necessary costs of production. We then have the equilibrium prices

$$P = A'\delta P + a_0'b'P + a_0'v$$

or, by rearranging terms,

$$P = [I - a_0'b' - A'\delta]^{-1}a_0'v$$

where v is the payment per unit of labor. This system determines the $(n - 1)$ relative prices p_i/p_n and the payment to labor in terms of numeraire v/p_n. Prices per unit of payment to labor p_i/v are uniquely determined by the conditions of production. With a higher (lower) payment to labor, the level of all prices is proportionally higher (lower) and relative prices are the same.

In this case, the whole of the surplus product is absorbed in payments to labor. Distribution is based on the principle: to each according to the quantity of labor performed. As in the previous case of a subsistence economy, we could conceive of this as a society of independent producers, each with his own stock of means of production and own labor. Now, however, an additional problem arises, namely, what accounts for the payment to labor?[17] It might seem that we could solve this problem by assuming that some producers hire themselves out for work with other producers, so that the quantity v is the hire price of labor. But this merely leads to another problem, namely, why would any producer who is an independent producer, and is therefore capable of carrying out production with his own means of production and own labor, hire himself out to another producer? Or, viewing the matter the other way round, why would any producer who has his own labor available for production, seek to hire "outside" labor?[18] Besides all this, we still have a problem

[17] It is being assumed that the total labor available is at least sufficient to meet the aggregate requirement of labor at the given level of production. In this respect there is no "scarcity" of labor. Moreover, the conditions of production and reproduction are such as to yield the appropriate quantities of necessary consumption for all labor that is employed in production. In this sense, the requirement of necessary consumption is being met. The requirement of a payment to labor is a quite separate and distinct condition that is now being added to the system.

[18] To retain a hired worker the employer must pay at least as much per unit of hired labor (and he could not pay more if his accounts are to balance) as the worker could obtain by working with his own means of production. The total payment to hired labor would exactly equal the difference between the price of the product and the necessary costs of production. Hence, there would be no margin left over for the employer after meeting these costs. Viewing the matter from his side, and since all labor is the same, the employer could obtain the same payment per unit of labor as hired labor by working for himself. It follows that there would be no reason, on either side, for hiring labor.

of explaining how, with each producer specialized to a particular line of production, all units of labor come to be the same. There seems to be no way of resolving these problems within the framework of assumptions of this case.[19]

What if it were assumed instead that there is hiring of means of production? As a formal matter, this condition provides a rule for distribution of the surplus product in accordance with the payment for hiring means of production. The payment is calculated at the hire price of each type of means of production times the quantity of each utilized in production and is included in the price of the product along with the necessary costs.

In a society of independent producers this case is formally no different from that of hired labor and raises some, though not all, of the same problems. The problem in this case, as in the case of hired labor, is one of explaining why any producer would hire means of production from/to another producer. In addition, we have a problem of explaining what determines the level of the hire price of each type of means of production. Evidently, we cannot rely for this explanation on a condition of "limited supply" of such means of production. For the stock of each type can be expanded through production to any level appropriate to the requirements of the vector of gross output.[20] What we do not have, unlike the case of labor, is a problem associated with all means of production being the same.

Consider another possible rule for distribution. In this case there is a uniform payment that is proportional to the prices of both the stock of means of production and the commodities required for necessary consumption. The equilibrium prices are, then,

$$(3.14) \quad p_i = \sum_j \delta_j a_{ji} p_j + a_{0i} \sum_j b_j p_j + r\left(\sum_j a_{ji} p_j + a_{0i} \sum_j b_j p_j\right) \quad i = 1, \ldots, n$$

---

[19] In seeking to resolve these problems it would be of no help to introduce any presumed preference of the producers as individuals between employment in the different lines of production or between "inside" and "outside" labor. For, once the choice of occupation has been made in accordance with such preferences, each producer thereby becomes "specialized." And the hiring of an individual's labor when all individuals already own the means to be independent producers cannot be considered simply a matter of choice or preference.

[20] Since the available stock of capital goods, item by item, is sufficient to meet aggregate requirements, there can be no "scarcity" of means of production. Furthermore, the conditions of production and reproduction are such as to enable replacement of stocks that are used up in production.

where r is the factor of proportionality, a pure number per unit of time. In matrix form, equation (3.14) is

(3.15) $P = A'(\delta + rI)P + a_0'b'P(1 + r)$

Rearranging terms we get

(3.15a) $[I - (1 + r)a_0'b' - A'(\delta + rI)]P = 0$

the solution of which requires

(3.16) $|I - (1 + r)a_0'b' - A'(\delta + rI)| = 0$

This condition determines the magnitude of r as a function of the particular set of production conditions a_0, b, A, δ.[21] Substituting this value of r in (3.15a) determines $n - 1$ relative prices in terms of any one commodity as numeraire.

This situation could be taken to represent an economy in which the laborers are slaves. The labor of slaves is wholly owned by slave owners, who provide necessaries for their maintenance as well as means of production. For the purchase of means of production and necessaries the slave owners receive "advances" or loans from a class of merchants.[22] Call them merchant capitalists, and their loans merchant capital. The merchant capitalists receive, in turn, a payment from the slave owners in the form of profits on their capital. Competition among merchant capitalists, involving free mobility of their capital between different in-

---

[21] For convenience define the matrices: $B = ba_0 + \delta A$ and $D = ba_0 + A$. Algebraically we have:

$$[I - (1 + r)a_0'b' - A'(\delta + rI)] = [I - a_0'b' - A'\delta - r(a_0'b' + A')]$$
$$= [I - rD'(I - B')^{-1}](I - B')$$
$$= r\left[\frac{1}{r}I - D'(I - B')^{-1}\right](I - B')$$

Condition (3.16) requires the determinant of this last expression to vanish. Owing to condition (3.9), the determinant of $(I - B')$ cannot vanish. Therefore the determinant of

$$\left[\frac{1}{r}I - D'(I - B')^{-1}\right]$$

is required to vanish. This occurs if $1/r$ is chosen so as to be a characteristic root of the matrix $D'(I - B')^{-1}$. If the solution is to have economic meaning, the prices must be nonnegative. For this additional requirement to be satisfied, a necessary and sufficient condition is that $1/r = \alpha$, where α is the dominant characteristic root of the matrix $D'(I - B')^{-1}$. Thus the equilibrium value of r is equal to $1/\alpha$.

[22] It could be that slave owners receive advances only for purchase of means of production and provide necessaries out of current production. In this case, the price system is $P = a_0'b'P + A'(\delta + rI)P$.

dustries, dictates that the rate of profit is uniform in all lines of production.

We have a solution, in this case, for the problem of distribution of the surplus product in terms of the rate of profit under the assumed conditions of a "slave economy" with merchant capitalists. The concept of a rate of profit thus refers to an economy in which capital exists as a sum of exchange value the ownership of which is vested in a specific class. Distribution is based on the principle: to each according to the sum of exchange value that he owns. Under the present assumptions, the rate of profit is that number which, when it is applied to this sum of exchange value in each and every industry and the resulting amount is added to the necessary costs of production, gives a set of prices which enable the whole surplus product to be distributed. The equilibrium level of the rate of profit emerges as part of the solution: it is uniquely determined by the conditions of production. Relative prices of commodities are also fully determined. They depend only on the conditions of production and are independent of the level and composition of output. These prices enable the exchange of commodities so as to satisfy the condition of reproduction, including, in this case, the distribution of the surplus product among the merchant capitalists.

It may be noted also that distribution of the surplus product among the capitalists (that is, the amount each gets) cannot be determined before the prices are determined. This follows from the condition that distribu-- tion is based on capital as exchange value, since the amount of such exchange value depends on the prices of the commodities which make up the means of production and necessaries. At the same time, the prices themselves depend on the rate of profit in terms of which distribution is to be determined. Thus, the prices cannot be determined before distribution is determined. We conclude, therefore, that the prices of commodities and the distribution of the surplus product are simultaneously determined.

The actual physical amount of the surplus product (the vector Z) is taken as given and is therefore not explained by this analysis. It might be said that Z represents "demand" in some sense. But this leaves open the question of how such demand is determined.

Under the assumed conditions of this case, labor is slave labor, which means that laborers as such are freely bought and sold or hired on the market—the laborer himself is a commodity exchanged for other commodities. If there is, in addition, an actual production of slaves through breeding—as, for example, with cattle—then this condition would provide a full determination of the availability of labor for production. The price of a slave is then determined, like that of every other commodity, by the conditions of production. The hire price of a slave is also determined. With competition in the market for slaves, it is equal to the cost of necessaries plus profit at the going rate on the advances that go to purchase necessaries. Similarly, the hire price of means of production is determined. It is equal to the cost of depreciation plus profit at the going rate on the advances that go to purchase those means of production. Hiring of labor and of means of production takes place because of the opportunity this affords of making profit. All profits accrue ultimately to merchant capitalists and on the basis of their ownership of capital.[23] These profits stem from the employment of labor and means of production in production, and the generation thereby of a surplus product. That the system is productive, in the sense that it is capable of yielding a surplus product, can be seen in this case to be an expression of the specific social conditions of slavery within which production is carried out, entailing a definite structure of interrelated productive activities, a definite effectiveness of labor in those activities, and definite requirements of maintenance for the laborer. The institutions of slavery and of the market are the social mechanisms through which this whole process is effected.

Nevertheless, despite all these determinations, we are still left with one further problem. What accounts for the condition that all labor is the same? In a system of slavery the continued exercise of ownership rights in slaves necessitates restrictions on the ability of the laborer to pass from one occupation to another. Therefore, the existence of an objective standard, uniform throughout the system, by which one unit of labor may be determined to be equal to another unit is inconsistent with such a system.

A Capitalist Economy

Suppose that, instead of the condition of slave labor, we have a condition of "free" laborers, which means that the laborer owns his own

---

[23] In this system, as constructed, the slave owners have no basis for claiming a share in the total pool of profits. They exist solely on the strength of their ownership rights in slaves, which must in turn have a social and historical base. It would be otherwise if slave owners were themselves merchant capitalists. Introduction of land ownership on the part of slave owners would also bring them back into the picture so far as distribution of the surplus product is concerned.

capacity to labor and is free to sell it for a period of time to the highest bidder. The laborer is also "free" in another sense, which is that he has no means of obtaining a living except through the sale of his capacity to labor. For the purpose of carrying out production, labor has to be united with means of production and these are wholly owned by a class who themselves control the activity of production. Call this class the pure capitalists.[24] This is the case of a pure capitalist economy.

It is to be noted that we now have a real basis for the assumption that all units of labor are the same. This basis lies in the freedom of the laborer as defined in the above twofold sense. With laborers being free to take employment in one line or another and compelled by the necessity of finding a living to seek for such employment, an objective standard could come about, uniform throughout the system, by which one unit of labor might be determined as equal to another.[25] In the final analysis, it is the social process of mobility of labor in this sense and its adaptability through learning to different uses that accounts for the homogeneous quality of labor and, therefore, for its reduction to a homogeneous quantitative measure. The same cannot be said of material means of production, which, once designed and constructed as physical objects, have a relatively fixed technical quality and are not capable, except within very narrow limits, of the same adaptability as human labor.

The conditions of the problem now differ qualitatively from what we had before. A new commodity has now entered the market in the form of the labor capacity of the laborer, which is owned by the laborer himself and freely bought and sold in exchange for other commodities. It would be useful to have a name for this new commodity to identify and distinguish it from all others. In recognition of this, Marx called it "labor power." We call it simply labor time, recognizing that it is measured by

---

[24] Capitalists may continue to make loans, in this case to one another. We abstract from such considerations in order to focus on the position of the class as a whole.

[25] Call this socially determined homogeneous unit of labor a unit of "simple" labor. Once the analysis has been worked out on this basis, it is a straightforward matter to go on to introduce "complex" labor, defined to be as heterogeneous as is appropriate, provided only that such heterogeneity (or "skills") can be assumed to be produced within the system. Skills that are somehow "innate" in the laborer, or "natural," are a special case that can be treated in a way analogous with "land." For the sake of simplicity these complications are being left out of the present analysis, which is concerned solely with "simple" labor. This procedure is, furthermore, the appropriate one for an analysis that focuses on the class position of workers, that is, their homogeneity as a class, rather than on the differences within the working class.

the duration of time over which it is expended in production.[26] There is also a relation of economic dependence of laborers upon the capitalists and a corresponding control of the production process by the capitalists. In this sense, there is a specific social relation of capital to labor that we may call the *capital-labor relation*. The laborer is paid a price, the wage rate, per unit of his labor time. The level of this price now has to be introduced as part of the problem. Exchange of products, or the circulation of commodities, is now attributable to the capitalists' quest for profits and the organization of labor within firms (units of capital) for producing commodities for sale on the market. Competition among firms, or competition of capitals, means that firms are free to move from one line of production to another according to which yields the higher profits, thereby bringing about a uniformity in the rate of profit. Specialization of firms to any one line of production is not a necessary condition of the problem.

If it could be assumed that the conditions of production, including necessary consumption, and the vector of physical surpluses remain the same as in the previous case, the production equations would not be altered by introduction of the capital-labor relation. But, in general, this would not be the case. For instance, the size and composition of the bundle of commodities constituting necessary consumption would be different in the new situation because of the altered position of laborers, from that of slaves to "free" laborers. That is to say, the quantity of necessary consumption would be different and would have a qualitatively different determination corresponding to the qualitative change in the position of the laborer. This would hold also for the vector of surplus product and for the whole matrix of production coefficients.

It must be assumed that the wage is at least sufficient to provide for necessary consumption. If the wage were to consist entirely of necessary consumption—and this would be a special case—the problem would become formally the same as that of the previous case of a "slave econ-

---

[26] Recall that the length of the working day is assumed here to be fixed, which ignores an important dimension of the problem. Specifically, this means that we are ignoring one aspect of what Marx called the production of absolute surplus value. On this, see above, Chapter 1, pp. 11–12. Marx also draws a distinction between the categories "labor" and "labor power" which is of basic theoretical significance. This distinction is sometimes glossed over in the present work, but the meaning should be clear from the context of the discussion.

omy."[27] We simply set the wage equal to the value, at ruling prices, of the commodities constituting necessary consumption, and the price system can be solved accordingly. But if the wage exceeds this amount, the problem becomes quite different, since the amount of the wage above necessary consumption—call this a "bonus"—now has to be determined. This is not to be taken to reflect an actual division of the wage into two separate parts. It indicates rather that there are two distinct sets of forces acting to determine the wage. One set is that dictating the quantity of necessary consumption. The other, which remains to be specified, is that determining the amount of the wage in excess of necessary consumption. At the same time, however, the rate of profit on capital continues to be part of the problem. For it has to be assumed that the owners of capital continue to receive profits on the capital they own. The problem is then to determine both the wage rate and the profit rate. For the solution of this problem, the rule of a uniform rate of profit on capital is clearly not enough.

In formal terms, the price equations in this case become

(3.17) $$P = a'_0 w(1 + r) + A'(\delta + rI)P$$

where the wage rate in unit of account is

$$w = b'P + w_0 \qquad w_0 \geq 0$$

and w_0 is the amount of the bonus. It is assumed that the wage is "advanced" by the capitalists at the start of production; that is to say, wages are paid out of capital. If $w_0 = 0$, this system becomes formally the equivalent of equation (3.15) and is solved in the same way. But if $w_0 > 0$, we have a system of n equations in $n + 2$ unknowns: the prices p_i, the profit rate r, and w_0. Choosing any one price or w_0 as numeraire leaves us with $n + 1$ unknowns. The system therefore remains open with respect to one of the variables. Given the level of any one variable, say w_0 or r, the rest can be determined. The important question is: what determines the level of the variable that is taken as given?

Alternatively, assume that wages are paid at the end of the production

---

[27] The identity of the formal problem in the two cases should of course not be mistaken as an identity of the underlying conditions of the problem: the difference is that, for instance, in the one case the laborer owns his own labor power whereas in the other he does not.

period out of current revenue of the capitalists.[28] The price equations then become

$$(3.18) \qquad\qquad P = a_0'w + A'(\delta + rI)P$$

It is evident that, though the conditions of the problem differ, the formal problem remains the same: the system remains open with respect to one of the variables.

What is missing here is a rule for determining the quantitative relation between wages and profits. What that rule is and how it accounts for the quantities involved are matters for further analysis. This is the purview of a theory of distribution for the capitalist economy. The concept of distribution as used in this context refers specifically to the relation between wages and profits or between workers and capitalists.

Several points may be noted in this connection. First, when the wage is set equal to the necessary consumption of workers, all relative prices and the rate of profit are fully determined. What closes the system in this case is the condition that the wage is tied to necessary consumption. The wage rate is the variable which is here taken as given, and it is given in terms of a specified bundle of commodities. This is a particular rule which could come out of a particular theory of distribution. What that theory is would remain to be spelled out, and the question would remain whether it is a correct theory for the capitalist economy.

A striking implication, following from this point, is that the possibility arises of determining one or another of the variables, the wage rate or the profit rate, before the prices are determined. Thus, determination of distribution in this sense is logically prior to the determination of prices. This is in sharp contrast to the previous case of a "slave economy," where distribution of the surplus product has to be determined simultaneously with the prices.

As a formal matter, any variable could be taken as the independent variable and so provide for closing the system. It is not, however, only a formal matter. Special significance is attached to one or another way of closing the system, depending upon the particular theory which goes

---

[28] Whether the wage is to be considered as paid out of capital or out of revenue is not merely a formal matter. It is a real, substantive matter which requires a correct understanding of the institutional conditions of the capitalist economy. Without going into this matter, in the analysis which follows we assume for simplicity the form of the price system specified in (3.18). In the Appendix we examine the implications of the price system (3.17) appropriate to the assumption that wages are paid out of capital.

with it. To say, for instance, that the wage is given in terms of a specified bundle of commodities is consistent with a view of the wage as being determined by conditions which are themselves independent of prices and the rate of profit. On this view, the investigation of these conditions is a matter that falls largely outside the domain of the analysis of prices. This was the particular conception upon which the Classical theory of distribution was based, and this procedure therefore has special significance from the viewpoint of that theory. Its significance remains even if it is granted that the specific bundle of commodities constituting the wage depends on the magnitude of the relation between wages and profits, as long as variations in this magnitude are considered to be independently determined.

Concerning the rate of profit, the argument has been made that "the rate of profits, as a ratio, has a significance which is independent of any prices, and can well be 'given' before the prices are fixed. It is accordingly susceptible of being determined from outside the system of production" (Sraffa 1960: 33). This argument does not, however, provide an answer about the particular theory in which such significance is to be located and by which, therefore, the level of the rate of profit may be explained.

From the standpoint of Marxian theory, this question of distribution can be put rather differently. The distinctive feature of the situation for a capitalist economy is that there exists a unique commodity, labor power, that is specific to the capitalist economy. The problem is, then, essentially one of determining the exchange value of this commodity as against all other commodities. In other words, it is an aspect of the problem of determining the value of commodities, in this case the value of labor power. Since the existence of this particular commodity is a condition specific to the capitalist economy, it is a necessary starting point for the analysis of that system. Moreover, the existence of labor power as a commodity is associated with a distinctive social relation, the capital-labor relation. The analysis must therefore be situated in an adequate conception of the capital-labor relation as a whole. From this point of view, Marxian theory seeks to solve the problem of distribution within the framework of the theory of surplus value or theory of exploitation. Some elements of this conception are developed in the following sections and in Chapter 10.

We note here that in the model of a capitalist economy, once the problem of distribution or the exchange value of labor power is solved, providing thereby a quantitative determination of the wage-profit relation, then relative prices follow logically from the condition of competitive equilibrium in the sphere of exchange. Under competition, relative prices are determined by the conditions of production and the given magnitude of the wage-profit relation. These prices are independent of the level and composition of gross output and the surplus product. They also incorporate the specific quantitative relation between wages and profits. We may call these "prices of production" or "normal prices."

Prices and Labor Values

Let us consider further the nature of the relations between prices, production, and distribution in the model of a capitalist economy. We are simply concerned here with the logically necessary properties of these relations under the assumed conditions of the problem. Moreover, since the system dichotomizes, we can also ignore the output relations.

For convenience, take the case of the price system represented by equation (3.18). Rewriting (3.18) we get

$$(3.18a) \qquad P = [I - A'\rho]^{-1} a_0' w$$

where $\rho = (\delta + rI)$. The solution of this system corresponds to a convergent geometric series such as we have seen before in the analysis of the output system.[29] It takes the form, in this case, of

$$(3.19) \qquad P = [I + A'\rho + (A'\rho)^2 + (A'\rho)^3 + \ldots] a_0' w$$

The right-hand side of this equation can be interpreted as follows. The first term, $I a_0' w$, is the cost, evaluated at the wage rate w, of labor directly employed in producing each commodity. The second term

$$A'\rho a_0' w = (A'\delta + A'r) a_0' w$$

is the cost of "indirect" labor employed in producing the commodities that are used up in production ($A'\delta a_0' w$), plus the labor associated with

---

[29] For the solution to have economic meaning, it is required that the prices be nonnegative. This requirement is satisfied if the rate of profit r is less than the maximum value r^*, where $r^* = 1/\gamma$ and γ is the dominant characteristic root of the matrix $A'[I - A'\delta]^{-1}$. When it is recognized that the vector of necessary consumption is a requirement for labor to be available for production, then the effective maximum value of r would be lower than this. It would be the reciprocal of the dominant characteristic root of the matrix

$$A'[I - a_0' b - A'\delta]^{-1}.$$

the stock of capital goods, weighted by the profit rate $(A'ra_0'w)$. The third term

$$(A'\rho)^2 a_0'w = [(A'\delta + A'r)(A'\delta + A'r)]a_0'w$$

is the cost of labor employed to produce the commodities that are used up in producing the commodities counted in the previous round (including in the latter both the commodities that are used up and the weighted stock of capital goods), plus the labor associated with the stock of capital goods, weighted by the profit rate. The same holds for the fourth term, the fifth, and so on through the various rounds of indirect production. In general, for the tth round the relevant term is

$$(A'\rho)^t a_0'w = [(A'\delta + A'r)^{t-1}(A'\delta + A'r)]a_0'w$$

As t increases, the terms of this series become negligible and the series converges.

The rate of profit plays here the role of a weighting factor applied to the stock of capital goods. In each round, starting with the first, this weighted stock of capital goods is added, item by item, to the commodities that are used up in production.[30] The resulting total of commodities is carried over to the next round; the commodities that are used up in producing it are calculated and to the latter are added a corresponding stock of capital goods similarly weighted. The same holds for the next round, and the next, and so on ad infinitum. The weighted stock of capital goods, having once been included, is compounded through further additions to the commodities that are used up in each successive round of production. To arrive at the price of each commodity, the labor associated with the weighted stock of capital goods is similarly added to the cost of direct labor plus indirect labor employed to produce the commodities that are used up. It is as if a mark-up that is proportional to the labor associated with the stock of capital goods were added, beginning with the first round, and subsequently compounded.

The price of each commodity thus consists of amounts of labor summed over the successive rounds of direct and indirect production involved in producing that commodity. Define the resulting sum of labor terms (in units of labor) for the ith commodity as the amount $A_{0i}(r) = a_{0i} +$

[30] This means that the stock of capital goods is, so to speak, counted twice: once in terms of that part of it which is used up and again in terms of the quantities obtained by applying the profit rate as a weighting factor.

$A_{0i}(r)$, where a_{0i} is direct labor, and $A_{0i}(r)$ is indirect labor inclusive of the mark-up and is an increasing function of r. Let $A_0(r) = [A_{0i}(r)]$ be the corresponding column vector. Then we can write

(3.20) $P = A_0(r)w$

We know that

$$\frac{d(p_i/w)}{dr} = \frac{dA_{0i}(r)}{dr} > 0$$

Thus, prices in terms of wage units are an increasing function of the profit rate (except for the prices of those commodities which employ only direct labor). The wage rate in terms of any one commodity as numeraire is the inverse of that commodity's price in terms of wage units.

(3.21) $w/p_i = 1/A_{0i}(r)$

It follows that $d(w/p_i)/dr < 0$. Thus the "real" wage rate, defined in this way, is a decreasing function of the profit rate.

Consider now a situation in which the rate of profit is equal to zero. This implies that $P = A_0(0)w$. Prices in terms of a chosen numeraire are now simply the sum of direct and indirect labor costs evaluated at the wage rate in terms of that numeraire, without the addition of a markup. The labor included here consists entirely of direct labor plus indirect labor employed in producing the commodities that are used up in production. The labor associated with the stock of capital goods is assigned a zero weight and is therefore excluded. Taking the wage rate itself as numeraire, we find that prices in terms of wage units are simply the sum of direct and indirect labor expended in the production of each commodity, that is, $P/w = A_0(0)$.

Call the amounts of labor $A_{0i}(0)$ the labor value of each commodity. At $r = 0$, prices are equal to labor value in this sense. This is a special case which conforms to the Classical Labor Theory of Value in its simplest form: the "law of value" holds with strict equality of prices and labor values. The rate of profit being equal to zero, it could be assumed that the whole surplus product is distributed to the laborer who owns both his labor and the means of production.[31] We have then the equivalent of

---

[31] At $r = 0$ the real wage rate in terms of the ith commodity is $w/p_i = 1/A_{0i}(0)$. The ratio $1/A_{0i}(0)$ is the inverse of the labor value of the ith commodity and can be interpreted as net output of the ith commodity per unit of direct and indirect labor. Thus, at a zero rate of profit, real wages in terms of the numeraire commodity exhaust the whole net product measured in terms of that commodity.

what Adam Smith called "the original state of society" in which "the laborer had neither landlord nor master to share with him" or what Marx called "simple commodity production."

Consider next a situation in which the profit rate is positive (but less than the maximum) and compare it with the previous situation. If we measure all prices in terms of the wage rate as numeraire, it will be found that all prices are higher in the new situation (except for the prices of those commodities, if there are such which employ only direct labor). In this sense, prices depart from labor values. The difference reflects the role of the markup: the markup adds to labor costs in every round and hence to total costs and price. The extent of the difference is itself determinate: it depends on the level of the profit rate and on the particular conditions of production of each commodity viewed in terms of the exact pattern of application of direct and indirect labor in successive rounds of production. In general, some prices will rise more than others. Thus prices in relation to each other, or relative prices, may be higher or lower. The reason for this ambiguity is straightforward. There are two elements in the price of a commodity which vary in opposite directions. One is the wage rate. The other is the profit rate applied to indirect labor. An increase in price due to a rise in one element may be greater or less than the corresponding decrease due to the fall in the other. To see this, note that

$$(3.22) \qquad p_{ij} = \frac{p_i}{p_j} = A_{0i}(r)\frac{w}{p_j}$$

It follows that

$$\frac{dp_{ij}}{dr} = \frac{dA_{0i}(r)}{dr}\cdot\frac{w}{p_j} + \frac{d(w/p_j)}{dr}\cdot A_{0i}(r) \gtreqless 0$$

The outcome depends on the conditions of production. Specifically, what matters is the ratio of indirect to direct labor in production of the different commodities.[32] This is apparent from rewriting

$$p_{ij} = \frac{a_{0i}}{a_{0j}}\left[\frac{1 + \tilde{A}_{0i}(r)/a_{0i}}{1 + \tilde{A}_{0j}(r)/a_{0j}}\right]$$

which expresses the relative price in terms of the ratios of indirect to direct labor.

[32] Cf. Sraffa (1960: 12): "The key to the movement of relative prices consequent upon a change in the wage lies in the inequality of the proportions in which labor and means of production are employed in the various industries."

There is one special case in which relative prices are the same whatever the level of the profit rate may be. This would be so, in particular, if the ratio of indirect to direct labor were the same for all commodities. For if these ratios are the same at one level of the rate of profit, they must be the same at all levels of r. In this case the conditions of production are such that, for every commodity, when the wage rate (or profit rate) is different, the difference in wage costs is exactly offset by the difference in profits so that relative prices are invariant. Prices in terms of wage units vary with the profit rate and therefore do not equal labor values except at $r = 0$. But prices do not vary in relation to each other.[33] Relative prices are therefore strictly proportional to labor value at all levels of the profit rate, not only at $r = 0$. We have here another case that demonstrates a simplified Labor Theory of Value. This case is the equivalent of that considered by Marx in which the "organic composition of capital" is equal in all industries.

We conclude from our analysis in this section that, in general, the system of prices depends on production conditions and on the rate of profit. More specifically, prices are related to labor values in a determinate way and under special conditions turn out to be proportional to labor values. These are characteristics of "prices of production" or "normal prices."

The result that prices are independent of the level and composition of output (and, hence, of demand) is a striking one.[34] It provides a logical justification for the Classical presumption that analysis of the formation of prices under given conditions of production could be carried out independently of the analysis of output as a whole. At the same time, it contrasts sharply with a traditional neoclassical conception of "rising

[33] For an example of this, see Burmeister 1968: 85.

[34] This result follows from the assumptions concerning production and the existence of competition. A simple sketch of the argument is as follows. Given the rate of profit that can be obtained in production, firms hire labor for production, and competition ensures that they pay the maximum wage rate consistent with the available technique at that rate of profit. The same reasoning applies when there is a given wage rate. (As we shall see, when more than one technique is available, they would adopt the technique that affords the maximum wage rate or the maximum profit rate, as the case may be.) By assumption, the output of any commodity produced with that technique can be increased to any level at constant cost in terms of labor—the only nonproduced input. Therefore, if there is one price that covers cost at any level of output, the same will do at any other level. The conditions strictly required for this result to hold are constant returns to scale, a single nonproduced input, and absence of joint production. A rigorous proof of the argument is provided by the "nonsubstitution theorem." On this, see for example Dorfman et al. 1958 and Morishima 1964.

supply prices" which vary with the level and composition of output owing to the assumed existence of scarce or fixed factors of production and operation of the law of diminishing returns.

What is at issue in this connection is the conception of production itself. When production is conceived as a process of production of commodities including means of production, then the presumption of "scarcity" of factors has no logical basis, even if it is assumed that production conditions are given and unchanging, and regardless of whether or not there exists a choice of techniques of production. The analysis of prices thereby becomes liberated from supposed conditions of scarcity. What then becomes crucial for analysis is precisely the way in which conditions of production change over time owing to the process of technical change and development of the economy as a whole. In that context, there may be attendant changes in the pattern of prices. But that result would then be a consequence of the process of technical change and development as posited, and not of any arbitrary specification of the degree of "returns" to factors of production associated with changes in the scale of production. Similarly, the question of the role of inaugmentable resources has to be treated in the context of analysis of technical change. In abstracting from technical change, we abstract from these complications. It is then appropriate to make the assumption that production costs are invariant to changes in scale.

On the side of demand for output, it is not denied that demand may have an influence on the price system. What is at issue is exactly how that influence may operate and how demand itself is conceived to be determined. This issue requires further consideration. For present purposes, this analysis simply takes as given the demand for output as represented by the vector of surplus product Z. There is no necessary presumption that such demand reflects independently given preferences of atomistic individuals as in a well-known neoclassical construction. Demand may be seen rather as determined by social conditions, including the class position of individuals and the requirements of production itself.

There remains also a problem of the mechanism of price formation in the context of changes in demand and supply associated with "day-to day" fluctuations in the market for commodities. This problem is not dealt with here. It arises at a more concrete level of analysis, that is, at the level of what the Classical economists called "market prices," as distinct from that of prices of production.

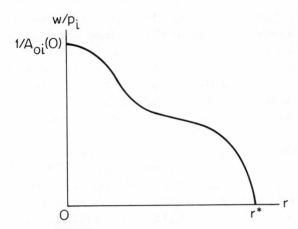

Figure 3.1. The wage-profit curve

The Wage-Profit Relation

Now consider further the nature of the wage-profit relation. In the previous section we saw that, at a zero rate of profit, all prices in terms of wage units are at their lowest. The real wage rate, measured in terms of any one commodity as numeraire, is therefore at its highest and wages absorb the whole net product. As the rate of profit is varied from zero through successively higher levels, the associated level of prices in terms of wage units is higher and the real wage lower. When the real wage equals zero, the rate of profit is at its maximum, $r = r^*$, and the whole net product is absorbed in profits. We can express this relation between the real wage rate as defined and the profit rate in the form of a wage-profit curve for the given technique of production. This is depicted in Figure 3.1.

The concept of the "real wage" used here is one that is measured in terms of a single commodity arbitrarily chosen. But choice of the standard in which the wage is measured is not a matter of indifference. It depends on the theory in which the problem of wages, and hence of distribution, is located. From the viewpoint of a theory of distribution such as that of the Classical economists, it is a matter of considerable significance. This is because of the way in which the wage is conceived to be determined in that theory.

For the Classical economists, as for the Physiocrats before them, the wage is assumed to be given at a customary subsistence level determined by demographic factors (the Malthusian Law of Population). The amount of subsistence is specified in terms of a "basket" of given quantities of the commodities the workers consume. Therefore, the relevant concept of the wage is that measured in terms of such a basket. We may take, for this purpose, the column vector of commodities $b = [b_i]$, which we have been calling necessary consumption. Accordingly, let

(3.23)
$$\hat{w} = \frac{w}{b'P}$$

The real wage rate $\hat{w}$ is here defined as the number of baskets of commodities that can be obtained with a given nominal wage rate w at prevailing prices, P. Then $\hat{w} = 1$ would represent the floor of subsistence. Substituting the price equations (3.18a) into (3.23), we get

(3.23a)
$$\hat{w} = \frac{1}{b'[I - A'(\delta + rI)]^{-1}a'_0} = \frac{1}{b'A_0(r)}$$

which is the relevant wage-profit curve for this concept of the wage.[35] There is an inverse relation between the wage as thus defined and the rate of profit. This confirms the view that the Classical economists had of this relation.[36]

For Marx, the concept of the wage that is crucial is one measured in terms of labor value, as a definite quantity of labor time. Marx states the rationale for this as follows (*Theories*, part 2 [1968], p. 419):

The value of wages has to be reckoned not according to the quantity of the means of subsistence received by the worker, but according to the quantity of labour which these means of subsistence cost (in fact the proportion of the working-day which he appropriates for himself), that is according to the *relative share* of the total product, or rather of the total value of this product, which the worker receives. It is possible that, reckoned in terms of use-values (quantity of commodities or money), his wage rise as productivity increases and yet the value of the wages may fall and vice versa. It is one of Ricardo's great merits that he examined relative or proportionate wages, and established them as a definite category. Up to this time, wages had always been regarded as something simple and consequently the worker was considered an animal. But here he is considered in his social relationships. The position of the classes to one another depends more on relative wages than on the absolute amount of wages.

[35] At $r = 0$, $\hat{w} = 1/b'A_0(0)$. Here, $b'A_0(0)$ is the labor value of the subsistence basket or composite commodity. The inverse, $1/b'A_0(0)$, is output of the composite commodity per unit of direct and indirect labor, and this is the maximum wage rate in this case. At $\hat{w} = 0$, then $r = r^*$, where r^* is the maximum profit rate. Recognition of a subsistence minimum means, of course, that any value of $\hat{w} < 1$ must be viewed as purely notional.
[36] As exemplified by the following: "... however abundant capital may become, there is no other adequate reason for a fall of profit but a rise of wages" (Ricardo, *Works* I: 296).

Thus this concept of the wage is crucial because it reflects "the position of the classes to one another." In the next section, we construct the quantitative relations involved in the Marxian conception.

It is evident from the foregoing that the wage-profit curve, specified in terms of an appropriate measure of the real wage, has an analytic interest as a representation of the technically feasible range of the quantitative relation of wages and profits. Specifically, it shows the various wage and profit rate combinations that are consistent with a given technique of production. Furthermore, this relation has the remarkable implication that a higher wage rate is necessarily associated with a lower profit rate and vice versa. This is a basic property of the production system. Given the wage rate, we can obtain from this curve the associated profit rate. Alternatively, given the profit rate, we can obtain the wage rate. A determinate solution of the problem of distribution is associated with a definite point on the wage-profit curve.

There still remains a question of what accounts for the rate of profit (or the wage rate) and its quantitative determination. Without such an account, analysis of the system of exchange and distribution for the capitalist economy is necessarily incomplete.

Value, Surplus Value, and Profits

Viewing the system of commodity production from the side of production, it is seen that the production of commodities involves a definite application of labor and using up of means of production where those means of production are themselves the product of labor. This is the basic preconception upon which, at an abstract level, the Marxian theory of value and surplus value is constituted. A formal representation of the quantitative relations involved in this conception can be set out as follows.

Define the labor value of a commodity, λ_i, as the quantity of labor directly and indirectly required in its production. This quantity is derivable from the conditions of production. Specifically, for a given technique of production we have

(3.24) $$\lambda_i = a_{0i} + \sum_j a_{ji}\delta_j\lambda_j \qquad i = 1, \ldots, n$$

In matrix notation this can be written

(3.25) $$\Lambda = a_0' + A'\delta\Lambda$$

where $\Lambda = [\lambda_i]$ is the vector of labor values of the different commodities. It follows that

$$(3.25a) \qquad \Lambda = [I - A'\delta]^{-1}a_0' = \sum_{t=0}^{\infty}(A'\delta)^t a_0'$$

The products of labor are thus reducible to a definite quantity of labor, the quantity of labor which those products embody. It is evident from previous discussion (p. 76) that $\Lambda = A_0(0)$.

As a commodity, labor power also has a value. In Marx's theory, that value is equal to the quantity of direct and indirect labor required to produce the means of consumption "necessary for the maintenance of the laborer" (*Capital* I, 170–73). Let b be the vector of necessaries in Marx's sense.[37] Then the value of labor power is

$$(3.26) \qquad \omega = b'\Lambda$$

Since the unit of abstract labor is homogeneous, ω is the same for all units.

Now, from the standpoint of the production system as a whole and its reproduction, a part of the total value of commodities produced goes to maintain and reproduce the labor power employed. This is equal to ωa_{0i}. Another part goes to replace commodities that are used up in production. This is equal to $\Sigma_j a_{ji}\delta_j\lambda_j$, The rest constitutes surplus value. Surplus value in this sense consists of a definite amount of labor embodied in the product in excess of what is contained in the articles of necessary consumption of workers and in the materials that are used up in production. The amount of surplus value per unit of each commodity is

$$(3.27) \qquad s_i = \lambda_i - \omega a_{0i} - \sum_j a_{ji}\delta_j\lambda_j \qquad i = 1, \ldots, n$$

It follows from (3.24) and (3.27) that

$$(3.28) \qquad s_i = a_{0i}(1 - \omega)$$

---

[37] Concerning the determination of the magnitude of necessaries, Marx rejected the Malthusian Law of Population with which the Classical economists had sought to account for a level of workers' subsistence. Instead, Marx took the magnitude of necessaries simply as given in the first instance, indicating some of the broad and general conditions which enter into its formation. (See, for instance, *Capital* I, ch. 6, and Marx and Engels 1968: 186–299.) However, the precise theoretical determination of the value of labor power and its relation to the wage in Marxian theory remain problematical.

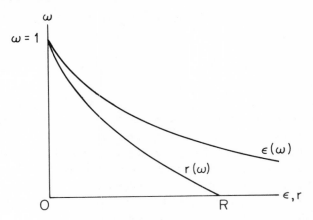

Figure 3.2. The exploitation curve

which says that the amount of surplus value is obtained by applying a weighting factor or discount to the labor currently employed, the size of that discount depending on the magnitude of the value of labor power. Define $\epsilon = s_i/a_{0i}\omega$ as the rate of surplus value or rate of exploitation. It is apparent that

$$(3.29) \qquad\qquad \epsilon = \frac{1 - \omega}{\omega}$$

Various features of this relation may be noted. In particular:

1. $\epsilon > 0$ if and only if $\omega < 1$. For the rate of exploitation to be positive, ω must be less than unity.

2. ϵ depends only on the level of ω, which is uniform. It follows that the rate of exploitation is the same regardless of the industry in which labor is employed.

3. $\omega + \epsilon\omega = 1$. Whatever the unit in which labor time or the product of labor is measured, the value of labor power ω and the amount of surplus value $\epsilon\omega$ add up to unity. Thus ω represents the relative share that the worker receives, "the proportion of the working-day [or month, or year] which he appropriates for himself."

4. $d\epsilon/d\omega < 0$. The rate of exploitation and value of labor power are inversely related to each other.

The relation between ω and ϵ is depicted as the curve $\epsilon(\omega)$ in Figure 3.2. We may call this the exploitation curve.[38] Given the value of labor

[38] For a similar construction see Morishima 1973.

power, we obtain from this curve the rate of exploitation. Alternatively, given the rate of exploitation we obtain the value of labor power. The striking feature of this relation is that every point on it gives a direct measure of the relative share of the labor expended in production which goes to the workers as against that which goes to the owners of property. It expresses the relation between workers and capitalists from the point of view of production. This measure is independent of the units in which the product is measured and independent of the associated prices. It is independent also of the specific form in which surplus value is paid out, whether as profits, interest, or rent. As between one point and another, we can therefore speak unambiguously of a difference in the relative position of workers and capitalists independent of the associated prices and level of output. In this respect the exploitation curve provides a unique, independent, and unambiguous representation of "the position of the classes to one another." It also reveals the relative position of the classes to be an antagonistic one and not one of partnership.

This construction follows from a consistent application of the Marxian concepts of value and surplus value within the framework of the production system assumed here. At the base of the construction is a concept of surplus, namely *surplus value*. It is different from the concept of *surplus product* introduced previously (see pp. 60–63) and provides an alternative theoretical grounding of the problem of distribution. Surplus value in this sense is the difference between the amount of labor time expended in the process of production and the amount of labor time the workers get back as wages. It is "unpaid labor." In Marx's theory, this pool of surplus value is the source from which is derived the profits that go to the capitalists (and other forms of nonlabor income).

It is possible to show analytically a correspondence between these relations in the production sphere, that is, in the sphere of the using-up of labor, and the relations that are established in the sphere of exchange. In particular, there exists a definite connection between the rate of surplus value and the rate of profit. For this purpose, consider the price equations (3.17),

$$P = a'_0 w(1 + r) + A'(\delta + rI)P$$

where it is assumed that wages are paid out of capital. (See Appendix for the case of wages paid out of revenue.) Now, assume that

(3.30) $w = b'P$

which says that the wage is just sufficient to purchase the bundle of necessaries at existing prices. In this sense it is assumed that the price of labor power is equal to its value, thus ignoring conditions that would bring about a systematic deviation between price and value of labor power. It follows that

(3.31) $$P = a_0'b'P(1 + r) + A'(\delta + rI)P$$

which implies

$$[I - a_0'b'(1 + r) - A'(\delta + rI)]P = 0$$

Under the usual assumptions about the production coefficients, this system yields a solution for the rate of profit r^* and the relative prices. The quantity r^* is the reciprocal of the dominant characteristic root of the matrix

$$(a_0'b' + A')[I - a_0'b' - A'\delta]^{-1}$$

and it is positive and real. Associated with r^* is a characteristic vector that is strictly positive and unique except for scale. Let this be the row vector h^*, which may be normalized by any appropriate standard; h^* may be interpreted as a composite commodity representing a specific ratio of outputs of the different commodities produced in the economy. Call this the *standard commodity*.[39] It satisfies the equation

(3.32) $$h^* = h^*[a_0'b'(1 + r) + A'(\delta + rI)]$$

Post-multiplying this equation by the vector of labor values gives

(3.33) $$h^*\Lambda = h^*a_0'b'\Lambda(1 + r) + h^*A'\delta\Lambda + rh^*A'\Lambda$$

from which, by substituting (3.25) and (3.26), we get

(3.34) $$r = \frac{h^*a_0'(1 - \omega)}{h^*a_0'\omega + h^*A'\Lambda}$$

$$= \frac{\epsilon}{1 + \kappa}$$

where $\epsilon = (1 - \omega)/\omega$, and $\kappa = h^*A'\Lambda/h^*a_0'\omega$. This result expresses a direct connection between the rate of profit and the rate of surplus value,

[39] The concept of a standard commodity was introduced by Sraffa (1960). For further discussion of the analytical meaning and significance of this concept, see Eatwell 1975.

and hence between profits and the exploitation of labor in production.[40] The corresponding relation between the rate of profit and value of labor power is shown as the curve $r(\omega)$ in Figure 3.2. It is related to the exploitation curve by a factor of proportionality equal to $1/(1 + \kappa)$ and has a maximum at $R = h^*a_0'/h^*A'\Lambda$.

The result (3.34) conforms to Marx's formula for the rate of profit. To see this, note that in accordance with (3.27) and (3.28) the value system can be written as

$$\Lambda = A'\delta\Lambda + \omega a_0' + (1 - \omega)a_0'$$

The three terms on the right-hand side correspond respectively to vectors of constant capital $C = A'\delta\Lambda$, variable capital $V = \omega a_0'$, and surplus value $S = (1 - \omega)a_0'$. In addition, define $K = A'\Lambda$ as the vector of stocks of means of production measured in value terms. Then, by substituting into (3.33), we get

$$h^*(C + V + S) = (1 + r)h^*V + h^*C + rh^*K$$

and it follows that

$$r = \frac{h^*S}{h^*V + h^*K}$$

If it is assumed that the rate of depreciation of means of production is uniformly unity ($\delta = I$), which is a case of pure circulating capital, then it follows that $K = C$ and we have Marx's formula. The ratio κ in (3.34) may be interpreted as corresponding to Marx's concept of the *organic composition of capital*. Aggregate quantities of direct labor and means of production in value terms are calculated here at the output composition specified by the standard commodity h^*, which thus serves as a kind of index of aggregation. The composition of h^* is itself related to the composition of workers' consumption and is therefore dependent on the value of labor power.

The rate of profit emerges here in direct correspondence with the rate of exploitation of labor in production and with the conditions of production as represented by the overall organic composition of capital. In

---

[40] Morishima (1973, 1974) derives a similar result linking the rate of profit and the rate of surplus value, which he calls the Fundamental Marxian Theorem. Compare also Medio 1972 and Wolfstetter 1973. The form of this relation differs according to whether it is assumed that wages are paid out of revenue or out of capital. On this, see the Appendix.

our earlier discussion of the price system (pp. 74–79), it was seen that in general the system of prices is related to production conditions, and specifically to labor values, in a determinate way as mediated by the rate of profit. It is now evident that the rate of profit itself can be uniquely related to production conditions and to the value of labor power or rate of exploitation, where the latter is viewed, in Marx's conception, as an expression of "the position of the classes to one another." In this respect, and within the formal terms of this construction, the system of relative prices and income distribution in the capitalist economy may be said to have a definite connection with relations of production or "value relations." This gives a specific sense to Marx's contention that "prices are nothing but transformed values."

In particular, the transformation of values into prices can be seen to involve a precise quantitative deviation between prices and values. That deviation is, however, not arbitrary but systematic. It is associated with the payment of profits in proportion to total capital in price terms. The overall rate of such profits, in turn, bears a definite relation to the amount of surplus value generated through the use of labor in production. In positing the transformation of values into prices, Marx thus points to a systematic divergence between the conditions of production of surplus value and the conditions of appropriation (or distribution) of surplus value—a divergence that is necessarily associated with relations of commodity exchange based on capital and wage labor. He argues further that it is this divergence which creates the appearance that profit is attributable to the amount of capital owned by capitalists (or its technical productivity, or its scarcity) rather than to the exploitation of labor in production. This contradictory character of the relations of capitalist society Marx designated as the *fetishism of commodities* (see *Capital* I: 71–83; III: 826–31).

We see from the foregoing discussion that the Marxian concepts are entirely consistent both among themselves and with the framework assumed here. These concepts take a straightforwardly simple form in the context of our present assumptions. They also carry over, with some modifications, into more complicated settings.[41] These concepts are

---

[41] See, for instance, Schefold 1971, Morishima 1973, and Steedman 1975. It has been shown in the work of these authors that, with the introduction of joint production, special problems arise regarding the existence of positive labor values and positive surplus value;

themselves located in a specifically Marxian theory which seeks to explain the structure and operation of the capitalist economy and the laws of its development. However, this discussion is far from a full statement of that theory and is concerned only with some of its formal aspects, specifically regarding the quantitative relations between price, value, surplus value, and profits. It neglects entirely the qualitative and historical aspects (see Meek 1973, chs. 5, 6; Rubin 1972, ch. 8; Sweezy 1956, ch. 2). It takes as given the available technique of production which must itself be considered to be the determinate outcome of a social process. Furthermore, from the point of view of Marx's abstract conception of the capitalist process as a whole as based on the circuit of capital and involving a unity of production and circulation (see Chapter 10), this analysis may be seen to locate the conditions of determination of the profit rate too narrowly. In particular, it ignores the conditions of "realization" of profits in the sphere of exchange (circulation) of commodities. Correspondingly, by collapsing the forms of the circuit of capital into its particular form as "productive capital," the analysis ignores the movement of capital in its multiple and unified forms as "money capital," "productive capital," and "commodity capital."

Moreover, it is not to be concluded that the preceding analysis, taken by itself, and based as it is on considerations of logical consistency, somehow "proves" the existence of exploitation of labor in capitalism. Clearly, any such claim would have to be rejected. The analysis shows a logical connection between profits and the exploitation of labor, but does not account for how the rate of exploitation itself is determined and at what level. The latter is something which requires to be shown, as Marx himself sought to do, by systematic theoretical analysis of the actual historical process of emergence of capitalism (primitive accumulation) with the creation thereby of a propertyless class of wage laborers alongside the concentration of ownership and control of means of production, as well as the ongoing process of reproduction and expansion of the capitalist economy. Specifically, it needs to be shown what is the process which establishes and sustains the value of labor power at a level con-

---

these problems are essentially concerned with the meaning and interpretation of the logic of more complex models. It would be wholly incongruous to draw any inference from them regarding the causal significance of the Marxian theory. Besides, in the most important case of joint production, i.e. that connected with fixed capital, all of the propositions discussed here continue to hold.

sistent with the continued existence of exploitation. Far from providing such an account, the present analysis simply takes the value of labor power (or rate of exploitation) as given and says nothing about how it may be conceived to be determined. Further elaboration of the structure and content of the theory would therefore seem to be necessary and appropriate.

In this connection, it may be observed that there are substantive problems involved in applying the law of value to the commodity labor power which cannot be ignored or dismissed. These are due essentially to the fact that labor power is not itself the outcome of a process of production like other commodities, that is, it is not produced capitalistically. This means that the equilibrating mechanism that establishes the value of other commodities through the process of competition among different units of capital does not apply to the value of labor power. Some alternative mechanism must therefore be introduced. In Marxian theory this mechanism has been found to lie within the process of capital accumulation.[42] But this mechanism remains to be given a precise theoretical specification recognizing that, in the first instance, wages are paid in the form of money and not directly in commodities. We shall return to this problem in Chapter 10. For the moment, we may note here that it is entirely consistent with the Marxian view to take the value of labor power as given and the wage as equal to it, if it is assumed that conditions of simple reproduction prevail in which there is no accumulation. This is in full recognition that the conditions which determine the wage and the value of labor power are related to capital accumulation and can therefore be considered explicitly only when accumulation is introduced.

Accumulation and Distribution

So far, we have discussed the existence of a surplus product but we have said nothing about how this surplus is utilized. In actual history, a physical surplus in this sense has almost always existed in different societies. It might be used to build pyramids, gilded castles, or rockets to the moon. For present purposes, because of our concern with the implications of accumulation, we need distinguish only between that

---

[42] "The law of capitalistic accumulation . . . states that the very nature of accumulation excludes every diminution in the degree of exploitation of labour, and every rise in the price of labour, which could seriously imperil the continual reproduction, on an ever-enlarging scale, of the capitalistic relation." *Capital* I: 620–21.

part of the surplus which is consumed and that part which is ploughed back for expansion of production.

Assume that a certain amount of output available at the end of the period is added to the existing stock of commodities over and above the mere replacement of commodities that are used up in production. The rest is consumed. Assume further that the increment in the stock of each commodity, or net investment, is uniformly proportional to the existing stock, so that all capital stocks grow at the same rate g. The levels of output, consumption, and employment also grow at this rate. In this sense the economy may be said to be in a state of balanced growth, or a steady state. The purpose of this construction is not to say that in reality capitalist economies actually grow in this way. We know that they do not. Rather, the purpose is to fix the structure of the economy so that we can focus upon the implications of capital accumulation in the context of that given structure.

The output equations can now be written as

(3.35) $$X = \delta A X + ba_0 X + Z, \qquad Z = gAX + C$$

where $C = [C_i] =$ column vector of consumption. For any given vector C the output vector is found by solution of

(3.36) $$X = [I - ba_0 - (\delta + gI)A]^{-1}C$$

Let the vector C be a multiple of the vector of necessary consumption:[43]

(3.37) $$C = \beta ba_0 X$$

By analogy with the definition of the real wage rate $\hat{w}$, β may be regarded as real consumption per man: it is the total number of specified commodity baskets b that are available for consumption. Then, from (3.35) and (3.37) we have

(3.38) $$X = (\delta + gI)AX + \hat{\beta} ba_0 X \qquad \hat{\beta} = 1 + \beta$$

---

[43] This assumption implies that consumption in excess of necessary consumption differs from necessary consumption only by a proportionality factor. There is therefore no variation in the proportion of goods consumed as between necessary consumption and what we might call "excess consumption." It is implied furthermore that the quantity of consumption of each commodity per unit of labor remains the same as total consumption increases. It should be evident from considering these implications that the assumption concerning consumption is very special and cannot be expected to take us very far. We are here bound by the requirement that our assumptions be consistent with a steady state.

and by rearranging terms we get $[I - \hat{\beta}ba_0 - (\delta + gI)A]X = 0$, solution of which requires that

(3.39) $$|I - \hat{\beta}ba_0 - (\delta + gI)A| = 0$$

For a given level of real consumption per man sufficiently low, this condition determines the growth rate as a function of the technical conditions and the given $\hat{\beta}$.[44] Alternatively, for a given growth rate sufficiently small, this condition determines the level of real consumption per man as a function of the technical conditions and the given g. Substituting these values into (3.38) gives the outputs. Since the equations are homogeneous in the outputs, only relative outputs are determined.

To produce outputs X requires stocks of capital goods $M = [M_i]$ and labor L such that $M = AX$ and $L = a_0X$. Associated with a particular solution of relative outputs and the given technique of production there is thus a particular composition of stocks of capital goods and distribution of employment between sectors. The equilibrium structure of the economy, defined in terms of the ratios of outputs, employment of labor, and stocks of capital goods, is therefore fixed. Given either the growth rate g or real consumption per man and the conditions of production, this structure is fully determined and is independent of the price system. The *levels* of the outputs, employment of labor, and capital stocks, as distinct from their ratios, depend on initial conditions that are unspecified.

There is a different economic structure or balanced-growth path corresponding to each possible level of g or of $\hat{\beta}$. We may find the relationship between real consumption per man and the growth rate by rearranging terms in (3.38) so as to get

$$1 = \frac{a_0X}{a_0X} = a_0[I - (\delta + gI)A]^{-1}\hat{\beta}b$$

[44] Algebraically we have

$$I - \hat{\beta}ba_0 - (\delta + gI)A = g\left[\frac{1}{g}I - A(I - \hat{\beta}ba_0 - \delta A)^{-1}\right](I - \hat{\beta}ba_0 - \delta A)$$

The determinant of the expression on the right-hand side is required to vanish. Since the system is productive, the determinant of $(I - \hat{\beta}ba_0 - \delta A)$ cannot vanish if $\hat{\beta}$ is sufficiently small. Therefore the determinant of

$$g\left[\frac{1}{g}I - A(I - \hat{\beta}ba_0 - \delta A)^{-1}\right]$$

is required to vanish. A solution with nonnegative outputs is found by choosing $1/g$ equal to α, where α is the dominant characteristic root of the matrix $A(I - \hat{\beta}ba_0 - \delta A)^{-1}$. Thus, for a given value of $\hat{\beta}$, the equilibrium growth rate is $g = 1/\alpha$.

from which it follows that

$$(3.40) \qquad \hat{\beta} = \frac{1}{a_0[I - (\delta + gI)A]^{-1}b}$$

Call this the growth-consumption curve for the given technique of production. It is evident that this curve has the same mathematical form as the wage-profit curve defined in terms of the commodity basker *b* (cf. equation (3.23a) above). One curve is thus the mirror image of the other.[45]

The level of real consumption per man and the growth rate are inversely related.[46] This result is readily understandable. Given the rates of net reproduction of commodities, the more of the net product that is consumed the less of it is available for expansion, and vice versa. We have here the logical basis of an important idea that was firmly perceived by the Classical economists (see Chapter 1): the growth potential of an economy depends on how the surplus product is divided between consumption and accumulation. It is an idea that can be seen to derive from consideration of the technical possibilities for consumption and accumulation that are consistent with given conditions of production.

We now have to introduce the behavioral conditions under which consumption and accumulation take place in the capitalist economy. This is a substantive problem requiring theoretical treatment on its own terms. But, for the moment, we assume simply that capitalists save a given proportion s_r of the profits they receive and workers save a given proportion s_w out of wages, where $0 \leq s_w < s_r \leq 1$. The rest of profits and wages is consumed.[47] This is a simple rule for representing what is in reality a complex situation, but it is adequate for present purposes.

Taking the price equations (3.18) for a capitalist economy and pre-multiplying by X, we get the "money" value of total income as

$$(3.41) \qquad X'P = X'A'(\delta + rI)P + X'a_0'w$$

Similarly, pre-multiplying the output equations (3.38) by P, we get the money value of total output

---

[45] The existence of this duality relation has been pointed out by Hicks 1965: 318–19; Bruno 1969; Spaventa 1970; Burmeister and Kuga 1970.

[46] We know that the dominant characteristic root of a positive matrix is a monotonically increasing function of each of the matrix elements. An increase in $\hat{\beta}$ increases the elements of the matrix $A(I - \hat{\beta}ba_0 - \delta A)^{-1}$ and correspondingly increases the root α. It follows that g is a monotonically decreasing function of $\hat{\beta}$.

[47] For workers' saving to be positive, it must be assumed that wages exceed the requirements of necessary consumption.

$$(3.42) \qquad P'X = P'(\delta + gI)AX + P'\hat{\beta}ba_0X$$

These are simply the accounting identities for gross product viewed respectively from the side of income and from the side of output. For the overall flow of income and expenditure to balance, it is required that total saving equal investment. This means that

$$P'AXg = s_rX'A'Pr + s_wX'a_0'w$$

which simplifies to

$$(3.43) \qquad g = s_r r + s_w \frac{X'a_0'w}{X'A'P}$$

With the composition of the output vector X and the price system P/w given according to (3.20) and (3.38), we see that equation (3.43) expresses a general relation between the growth rate g and the profit rate r. In the particular case of $s_w = 0$, which is often referred to as the *Classical saving function*, it takes the specific form of a linear relation, $g = s_r r$.

The relation (3.43) is derived from the condition for equilibrium of saving and investment. As such, it is simply an equilibrium condition which is required to hold as a necessary feature of any equilibrium growth path. It must also hold for the economy as a whole, whatever the number of commodities that are produced, and is thus independent of the level of disaggregation of the economy. Taken by itself, it has no causal significance. It acquires such significance only when it is imbedded within a fully articulated theory. Nevertheless, within the overall structure of the scheme of analysis laid out so far, it is a central relationship. It links the relations of prices, wages, and profits with the relations of output as a whole, saving, and investment. In this sense, it provides a direct link between income distribution and capital accumulation.[48] It is necessary to examine the specific way in which this relation is constituted within a complete system of relations for the capitalist economy. This will be a major focus of our attention in considering the specific character of different approaches to a theory of accumulation and distribution.

One last point may be mentioned. On a balanced-growth path, accumu-

---

[48] With reference to this relation, Pasinetti (1962: 267) observes that "it gives a neat and modern content to the deep-rooted old Classical idea of a certain connection between distribution of income and capital accumulation."

lation takes place at a steady rate. As long as the rate of accumulation is positive, some condition must be introduced to ensure that labor is available to match the growing employment. This, as we have seen in Chapter 2, is one aspect of Harrod's problem, and it is formulated there in a specific way. In general, the relation of labor supply to the accumulation process is of central importance for the analysis of the capitalist economy. We shall also have to examine exactly how this relation is constituted in different theoretical approaches.

Conclusion

We have presented in this chapter the elements of an economic model in which the quantitative relations between prices, production, distribution, and accumulation can be clearly identified. These relations express in formal terms the structural interconnections of the economy and thereby constitute the economy as a coherent whole. These are the relations that are consistent with specified conditions which are taken to represent, in highly abstract form, some conditions of the capitalist economy: an economy in which labor power is exchanged on a market, means of production are owned and controlled by capitalists, profits are paid in proportion to the value of owned capital, and competition prevails so as to equalize the rate of profit in different sectors. The conditions of a "subsistence economy" and a "slave economy" serve, as it were, to bring into sharper focus the conditions that are specific to the capitalist economy.

This scheme of analysis thus provides an abstract framework in which a certain limited range of questions concerning the capitalist economy can be discussed, and in terms of which various theoretical approaches to analysis of the capitalist economy can be examined and compared. There is nothing in the foregoing analysis which provides us with a fully articulated theory to answer the relevant questions. For instance, there is no explanation of why capital accumulation should take place at one rate or another or what is the process by which such accumulation occurs. Similarly, why the rate of profit or wage rate or rate of exploitation should be at one level or another is not explained. Various approaches to providing such explanations will be examined in Part Three of this book.

Meanwhile, it is appropriate to regard the scheme of analysis presented here as a statement of the consistency requirements for reproduction of the economy under the specified conditions. In other words, these are the requirements that have to be satisfied if the economy is to be able to reproduce itself from one period to the next. The fundamental problem which remains for subsequent explanation is precisely what is the process by which reproduction occurs in the capitalist economy.

The use of the particular model outlined here is as a vehicle for fixing ideas and concepts, where such ideas and concepts have a theoretical significance going beyond the confines of this particular model. Except for its usefulness in so doing, no special status is claimed for this model, and certainly not that it has any direct correspondence with empirical reality. Other model specifications are also admissible.

Chapter Four

Accumulation and Distribution in a Simple Model

Introduction

This chapter develops further the analysis of a production system in equilibrium with balanced growth, focusing on the relations among prices, production, distribution, and accumulation. The problem of existence of equilibrium growth with continuous full employment of the labor force is examined, with specific reference to Harrod's antinomy that the warranted and natural growth rates cannot be equal except as an accident.[1] We also consider in this context the analytical significance of a measure of the *value* of commodities.

A Simple Model of Production

For the purpose of this analysis we employ a simplified version of the model of production described in the previous chapter. Specifically, it is assumed that there are only two produced commodities ($n = 2$), a capital good and a consumption good. They are produced by means of the capital good and labor, each in a different industry or sector of production.[2] The chief advantage of this specification is that it is the simplest which still retains characteristic features of any real production system, namely, heterogeneity of commodities and circular interdependence in production. It is also the case that many of the results obtained here remain after additional complications are introduced. In particular, the analysis in this chapter can be generalized to a production system, such as that set

---

[1] The underlying argument of Harrod is outlined in Chapter 2.
[2] A division of the structure of production along these lines was first suggested by Marx's two-department scheme. The particular model discussed here has been widely used in recent literature. See, for instance, Hicks 1965; Spaventa 1968, 1970; Jones 1965; Garegnani 1970; Samuelson 1957, 1962; Harris 1967, 1973.

out in the previous chapter, in which any number of commodities is produced. A special feature of the model is that one commodity serves only as capital good and the other only as consumption good.[3] While such commodities can no doubt be found in reality (for example, bulldozers and ice cream), this is clearly a special case. But it is a special case chosen for a specific purpose; namely, that it isolates crucial and relevant aspects of production. These are, first, the "consumptive" aspect: part of production is directed to consumption and such output therefore disappears once it has been produced; and second, the "reproductive" aspect: part of production is directed to the continuation and expansion of production. Furthermore, in Marx's analysis, the division between capital-good industries and consumption-good industries is also considered to reflect a twofold division of capital itself between means of production (constant capital) and workers' consumption (variable capital).

One and only one technique is assumed to be available. For the given technique, we have the matrix of technical coefficients

$$\left[\frac{a_0}{A}\right] = \begin{bmatrix} a_{01} & a_{02} \\ \hline a_{11} & a_{12} \\ a_{21} & a_{22} \end{bmatrix}$$

where a_{0j} are labor coefficients, a_{1j} are capital-good coefficients, and the subscripts $j = 1, 2$ signify respectively the capital-good and consumption-good sectors. Of course, since the consumption good, by definition, does not enter into production, we have $a_{21} = a_{22} = 0$. Otherwise $a_{ij} > 0$.

Let δ = rate of depreciation of the capital good, $0 < \delta \leq 1$. It is assumed that the capital good can reproduce itself with a surplus, and hence $1/a_{11} - \delta > 0$, where $1/a_{11} - \delta$ is the own rate of net reproduction of the capital good.[4] Define the technical parameter

$$\mu = \frac{a_{12}/a_{02}}{a_{11}/a_{01}} \overset{>}{\underset{<}{=}} 1$$

[3] The assumption made here that the capital good is a direct input in its own production is no doubt restrictive. But it is forced upon us by the assumption that there is only one capital good. In a full-blown model of production with many capital goods, there would be no necessity for this assumption.

[4] The own rate of net reproduction of a produced commodity that enters directly or indirectly into its own production can always be found. It is imbedded in the technology. With more than one commodity there would be more than one such rate, one for each commodity. Since this model has only one such commodity, there is only one such rate.

which is the relative proportion of physical capital to labor employed in the two sectors. The concept of a proportion of physical capital to labor has a precise and unambiguous meaning here because of the assumption that there is only one capital good. When there is more than one capital good in use, it would be necessary to have a measure of the various capital goods in terms of a single quantity. Complications associated with this are being avoided with the present assumption. This ratio may be any positive number. A singular case is when $\mu = 1$: the capital-labor proportions in the two sectors are then the same, and the production coefficients can be made the same by appropriate choice of units of measurement. Heterogeneity of commodities in the sense defined above then disappears, and, from the viewpoint of production, there exists only one produced commodity.

Wages and Prices

Consider now a capitalist economy operating with this technique. Firms hire labor and pay wages at the end of the production period. Competition among workers for employment ensures that wages are paid at a uniform rate per unit of labor. Firms are free to invest in any line of production in search of profits. They must therefore obtain, in equilibrium, the same rate of profit on the market value of invested capital. Prices must be such as to cover costs for the given technique—these are the "prices of production" or "normal prices."

These conditions may be expressed algebraically. Let p_1 be the price of the capital good in unit of account, p_2 be the price of the consumption good in unit of account, w be the wage rate in unit of account, and r be the rate of net profit, a pure number per unit of time. In any period, the equilibrium conditions for the price system are

$$(4.1) \qquad p_1 = a_{01}w + a_{11}p_1(\delta + r)$$

$$(4.2) \qquad p_2 = a_{02}w + a_{12}p_1(\delta + r)$$

which state that the price of a unit of output exactly covers its cost of production, equal to wages plus gross profits consisting of depreciation and net profit calculated on the value of invested capital at the ruling rate of profit. (It is assumed that wages are paid out of revenue.) In a monetary economy, the prices of commodities and the wage rate are expressed in terms of money as the medium of exchange. But, for purposes of this analysis, we are free to choose any arbitrary numeraire. Accordingly we choose the consumption good as the numeraire commodity. This means that $p_2 = 1$, and, by this convention, we can interpret the price of the capital good and the wage rate as being expressed in units of the consumption good. In a steady state, the rate of profit is constant over time. Assume also that prices remain constant. With an unchanging technology, the wage rate must therefore be constant.

Note that these conditions give us three equations in the four variables: p_1, p_2, w, r. This means that the system of equilibrium relations between prices, wages, and profits remains open unless one variable is given a predetermined value. To put this another way: once we know either of the two variables w and r, representing the rates at which wages and profits are paid out of the value of net output, then the other variable and the prices of the commodities are fully determined. The prices are uniquely determined by technology and the given distribution of net output and are independent of the level and composition of output. This is a general feature of systems of production of the present type, which shows up no matter how large the number of commodities that are produced and the number of techniques that are available. The reason for this, as we saw in Chapter 3, follows from the assumptions concerning technology and the existence of competition. There remains unanswered, however, a basic question: what determines either the level of the profit rate or the level of the wage rate? We are as yet in no position to provide an answer, but it is a question to bear in mind as we go along. Meanwhile, we can go on to ask: what are the price, wage-rate, and profit-rate configurations that would be consistent with this technique?

In order to show the possible equilibrium configurations of the system, we take one variable as arbitrarily given and solve for the rest in terms of it. Thus, we get from (4.1) and (4.2)

$$(4.3) \qquad w = \frac{a_{11}(R - r)}{a_{02}\xi(r)}$$

$$(4.4) \qquad p_1 = \frac{a_{01}}{a_{02}\xi(r)}$$

where $\xi(r) = \mu - a_{11}(\mu - 1)(R - r) > 0$ and $R = 1/a_{11} - \delta > 0$. Equation (4.3) tells us the various equilibrium combinations of wage and profit rates that are consistent with the given technique. For the wage rate to be positive, it is required that $r < R$. That is to say, there is a maximum level of the rate of profit given by the technologically determined rate at which the output of the capital good can be expanded after providing for replacement. By assumption, R is positive and finite. The meaning of this upper limit on the rate of profit should be clear. The rate of profit must be less than the net output produced per unit of capital input if part of that net output is to be available for meeting wages cost. With a rate of profit equal to the maximum, profits exhaust the whole net product and the only possible wage rate is $w = 0$. At the opposite extreme, with $r = 0$, there is a maximum wage rate W such that

$$(4.5) \qquad W = \frac{1 - a_{11}\delta}{a_{02}[1 + (\mu - 1)a_{11}\delta]} > 0$$

This condition says that the maximum of the wage is equal to net output per unit of labor employed directly and indirectly in producing the consumption good.[5] That this should be so is understandable. If the wage is measured in units of the consumption good, then the wage rate is at a maximum when wages absorb the whole net output of the consumption good per unit of total direct and indirect labor.

Between their two extreme values, the wage rate and the profit rate are inversely related to each other. For a given technique the relation between them can be depicted as a curve in the positive quadrant. This is the wage-profit curve for that technique. As for its shape, Figure 4.1 illustrates three possibilities depending on the technical coefficients of production, in particular, on the relative proportion of physical capital to labor in the two sectors. The curve is concave from below if this proportion is higher in the capital-good sector; it is convex in the opposite case. The

[5] This can be seen by rewriting (4.5) as

$$W = \frac{1}{a_{02} + \dfrac{a_{12}a_{01}\delta}{1 - a_{11}\delta}}$$

Now, consider the terms in the denominator: a_{02} represents labor directly employed in producing one unit of the consumption good. Define z as the amount of gross investment required to replace capital goods used up in producing the consumption good. Then $z = a_{12}\delta + za_{11}\delta$, and employment of labor in producing that amount of gross investment is

$$a_{01}z = \frac{a_{12}a_{01}\delta}{1 - a_{11}\delta}$$

which is the second term in the denominator. The sum of the two terms is total labor directly and indirectly employed to produce one unit of the consumption good.

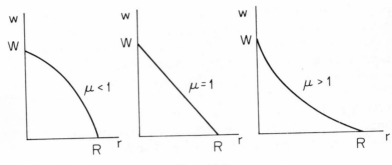

Figure 4.1

curve is a straight line if the proportion is the same in both sectors.[6]

The wage-profit curve is a relation that derives from a given technique of production. As such, it can be found from any technique, once the technical coefficients characterizing it are known.[7] We can obtain from it a remarkable implication: a higher wage rate is necessarily associated with a lower profit rate, and vice versa. This is a basic property of production systems of this type.

Inspection of (4.4) shows that the price of the capital good is positive as long as the profit rate is below its upper limit. The capital-good price may vary either inversely or directly with the profit rate, depending on whether the proportion of physical capital to labor is lower or higher in the capital-good sector.[8] The reason for this seems obvious when it is realized that there are two elements in cost: the wage rate and the profit

[6] From equation (4.3), w is a continuous and differentiable function of r. Its slope is given by

$$\frac{dw}{dr} = -\frac{a_{11}a_{02}\mu}{[a_{02}\xi(r)]^2} < 0$$

Taking the second derivative, we find that

$$\frac{d^2w}{dr^2} = \frac{2\mu(\mu - 1)(a_{11}a_{02})^2}{[a_{02}\xi(r)]^3} \gtreqless 0 \text{ if } \mu \gtreqless 1$$

[7] In characterizing the wage-profit curve in this model, we have made use of the technical coefficient defining the relative proportion of capital to labor in the two sectors. This is a convenience that derives from the assumption that there is only one capital good. When many different types of capital goods are used in production, this simple device is no longer available. There is nevertheless a definite relation between the wage rate and profit rate that can be identified from the technique of production. With many capital goods, the wage-profit curve need not be of uniform curvature; but its slope would be uniformly negative.

[8] From (4.3) we get

$$\frac{dp_1}{dr} = \frac{-a_{01}a_{11}(\mu - 1)}{a_{02}\xi(r)^2} \gtreqless 0 \text{ if } \mu \lesseqgtr 1$$

rate, which vary in opposite directions. With a higher rate of profit (lower wage rate), costs rise more (fall less) in the sector that uses a higher proportion of the capital-good input to labor input. If both sectors have an equal proportion of capital to labor, the change in one element of cost just offsets a change in the other. The relative price is then independent of the level of the profit rate (wage rate), and the price equation becomes simply $p_1 = a_{01}/a_{02}$, which says that the relative price of the capital good equals the relative amounts of labor directly employed in production of the capital good and the consumption good.[9] We thus have, in this case, a condition that satisfies the Labor Theory of Value in its simplest form: price corresponds to labor value. An analogy may be found here with Marx's case of production with a uniform organic composition of capital.

Output, Employment, and Growth

We go on now to introduce the relations governing output, employment, and accumulation in this model. In equilibrium, the total stock of capital goods M and total employment of labor L are adjusted to the technique in use and to the level of output of the two commodities x_1, x_2. Thus

$$(4.6) \qquad M = a_{11}x_1 + a_{12}x_2$$

$$(4.7) \qquad L = a_{01}x_1 + a_{02}x_2$$

The output of the capital good provides for gross investment consisting of depreciation requirements and net additions to the capital stock. Let g be the growth rate of the capital stock or rate of accumulation. Then gross investment is

$$(4.8) \qquad x_1 = (g + \delta)M$$

The overall equilibrium of the system requires that saving equals the value of investment. Firms meet depreciation cost out of gross profits.

---

[9] In this case we could just as well have price equal to the relative quantities of the capital good directly employed in production of the two goods. To see this, we obtain the equation for p_1 in terms of the wage rate. From (4.1) and (4.2) this equation is

$$p_1 = \frac{a_{11}}{a_{12}} + \frac{\mu - 1}{\mu} a_{01}w$$

Setting $\mu = 1$ leads to $p_1 = a_{11}/a_{12}$. The essential point is that, when the conditions of production of the two goods are the same, their relative price is technologically determined, and by appropriate choice of units of measurement, this price can be set equal to unity.

The saving that finances net investment comes out of the incomes derived from net profits and from wages. A simple way of representing saving behavior is to assume that a given proportion s_r is saved out of net profits and a given proportion s_w out of wages, where $0 \leq s_w < s_r \leq 1$. We shall later consider, as an alternative to this, the case of $s_w = s_r = s$, which assumes that the same proportion is saved out of net income regardless of its distribution between wages and profits. Valuing net investment at the relative price of the capital good and assuming there is no time lag between investment and saving which finances it, we get the saving-investment equilibrium condition

$$(4.9) \qquad p_1 g M = s_r p_1 M r + s_w w L$$

which implies $g = s_r r + s_w(wL/p_1 M)$. The value of net output (per unit of total employed labor), measured at numeraire prices, is obtained from the accounting identities

$$(4.10) \qquad y = \frac{x_2}{L} + g p_1 \frac{M}{L} = c + gk$$

$$(4.11) \qquad y = w + rk$$

where $c = x_2/L$ is consumption per man and $k = p_1 M/L$ is the value of the stock of capital per man.

It is worth pausing here to examine the structure of the model. Consider first the relations represented by (4.6), (4.7), and (4.8). For a given growth rate, these can be solved to get

$$(4.12) \qquad \frac{x_1}{M} = g + \delta$$

$$(4.13) \qquad \frac{x_2}{M} = \frac{a_{11}(G - g)}{a_{12}}$$

$$(4.14) \qquad \frac{M}{L} = \frac{a_{12}}{a_{02}[\mu - a_{11}(\mu - 1)(G - g)]}$$

where $G = 1/a_{11} - \delta = R$. Nonnegativity of (4.13) obviously requires $g < G$ (which implies $M/L > 0$), where G represents the maximum rate of growth and is equal to the technologically determined rate of net reproduction of the capital good. Next, substituting (4.3), (4.4), and (4.14) in (4.9), we get

$$(4.15) \qquad g = \frac{(s_r - s_w)\mu r + s_w R \xi(r)}{\mu(1 - s_w) + s_w \xi(r)}$$

which gives the rate of growth that is consistent in equilibrium with the given saving proportions, the technical coefficients, and the rate of profit.

The system of equations thus dichotomizes neatly into two sets of relations. One set, consisting of (4.12), (4.13), and (4.14), gives the ratios of output, capital stock, and labor employed in relation to the technical coefficients and the growth rate. The other, represented by (4.3) and (4.4), gives the relative price of the commodities and the wage rate in relation to the technology and the profit rate. The link between them is the saving-investment equilibrium condition (4.9), which yields in (4.15) a direct relation between the growth rate and the profit rate. This is the growth-profit relation, which, as we have seen before (p. 94), occupies a central place in this scheme: it provides a direct link between income distribution and capital accumulation.

These relations can be represented on a diagram in order to bring out the nature of the interdependencies that are involved. For this purpose, observe that, from equations (4.13) and (4.14), consumption per man is

$$(4.16) \qquad c = \frac{x_2}{L} = \frac{a_{11}(G - g)}{a_{02}[\mu - a_{11}(\mu - 1)(G - g)]}$$

For a given technique of production this equation defines a relation between consumption per man and the growth rate, or a growth-consumption curve. It is the mirror image of the wage-profit curve, as can be seen by comparing equations (4.16) and (4.3). One such growth-consumption curve is drawn in quadrant IV of Figure 4.2 and the matching wage-profit curve in quadrant I. In quadrant II is drawn a growth-profit curve corresponding to the given technique and given saving proportions in accordance with equation (4.15). Quadrant III contains the 45° line.

Starting from an arbitrary point on any one of the curves, such as point P in quadrant I, we find the associated values of the variables w, r, c, and g. The value of capital per man and output per man can also be obtained from the diagram. Note that, from the accounting identities (4.10) and (4.11) we have $k = (c - w)(r - g)$. Thus, the value of capital is measured by the slope of the line joining the points P and Q in the diagram. The corresponding level of net output per man is given by the point y^*, where the line through PQ cuts the vertical axis.

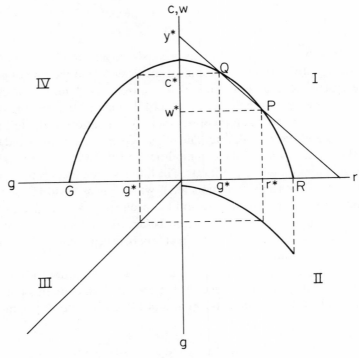

Figure 4.2

The diagram thus displays the configuration of equilibrium relations appropriate to a particular growth equilibrium. Of course, the system of relations remains open in the sense that, given the technique in use, there are more variables to be determined than there are independent equations. Or, in other words, the point from which we start in Figure 4.2 remains indeterminate.

Existence of a Golden Age

Suppose now we assume that the labor force grows over time at a constant rate which is exogenously determined and that there is full employment of labor. This implies that $L_t = L_0(1 + n)^t$, where L_0 is the given initial labor force, n its rate of growth, and t the index of time. In the absence of technical change, maintenance of full employment over time requires that the capital stock grow at the same rate as the labor force. Thus we must have

(4.17) $$g = n$$

As it now stands, the model has a straightforward economic inter-pretation. From (4.17) the rate of accumulation necessary to keep full employment over time is externally given by the rate of increase of the labor force, that is, by the "natural" rate of growth. This rate of accumula-tion determines the ratios of the physical quantities on the steady-state path, whereas the levels of output and the equilibrium stock of capital follow from the condition that the existing labor force is fully employed with the given technique. Given the proportion of saving from each type of income and the technique in use, there is one rate of profit such as to make the equilibrium value of saving per unit of capital equal to the predetermined rate of accumulation. The rate of profit is therefore deter-mined by the rate of accumulation. This rate of profit and the given technique then determine the wage rate, the relative price of the capital good, and the value of the stock of capital. The ratio of this value of capital to total net income constitutes the capital-income ratio corres-ponding to the given rate of profit and the technique of production.

With this specification, we are now in a position to examine further one side of the problem that Harrod posed: the occurrence of a singular value of the "warranted" rate of growth, which could equal the natural rate only by accident.

Equation (4.15) shows that, corresponding to each possible rate of profit, there is a particular value of g and path of warranted growth. We know, from our analysis of the wage-profit relation, that the technically feasible range of r is $0 \leq r \leq R = 1/a_{11} - \delta$. There is therefore a cor-responding range of values of g obtained from (4.15). At one extreme, with r at its maximum, we have one value. At the other extreme, with $r = 0$, we have another value.[10] Between these two extremes there is a range of possible values. Within this range there may exist one value such as to satisfy condition (4.17) or there may exist none at all, depending on the size of the relevant parameters.

---

[10] Checking (4.15) for $r = R$, we find that $g = g' = s_r R$, and for $r = 0$,

$$g = g'' = s_w R \frac{\mu - (\mu - 1)a_{11}R}{s_w[\mu - (\mu - 1)a_{11}R] + (1 - s_w)\mu}$$

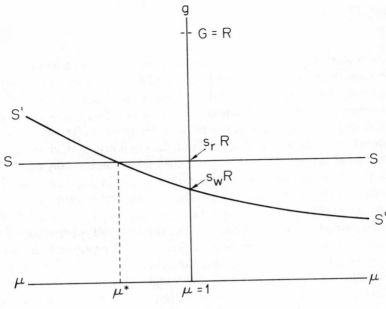

Figure 4.3

The possibilities are illustrated in Figure 4.3. The curve $S'S'$ plots the value of g at $r = 0$ for different values of μ, given the value of other parameters. The horizontal line SS gives the value of g at $r = R$. Points between $S'S'$ and SS represent the range of possible growth rates. The range is widest when $s_r = 1$ and $s_w = 0$, for then the growth rate can be any number between zero and the maximum technically feasible rate G. The range narrows down to a single possibility at a point where $\mu = \mu^*$.[11] If, in addition, it is assumed that $s_w = s_r = s$, this condition reduces to $\mu = 1$ and the single warranted growth rate becomes $g = sR$. R is the net output per unit of input of the capital good in the production of itself. When $\mu = 1$, this ratio must be the same for the production of the consumption good.[12] R then measures net output per unit of capital, or the inverse of the capital-income ratio for the economy as a whole. This result is

[11] From the previous footnote, by equating g' and g'' we obtain

$$\mu^* = \frac{s_w(s_r - 1)Ra_{11}}{s_w(s_r - 1)Ra_{11} - (s_r - s_w)}$$

If $s_w = s_r$, this reduces to $\mu^* = 1$.

[12] As we saw above, when $\mu = 1$, we have $p_1 = a_{11}/a_{12}$. It follows that $R = 1/a_{11} - \delta = 1/p_1 a_{12} - \delta$.

therefore the same as Harrod's formula for the warranted growth rate.[13]

Harrod's formula can thus be seen to follow from *two* conditions. The first says that the proportion of saving to income is the same for different categories of income. The second relates to technology and states that the proportion of physical capital to labor is the same in each sector. A consequence of this is that the price of the capital good, and hence the ratio of the value of capital to income, is fixed.[14] Once either or both of these conditions are dropped, the problem of a singular value of *g* disappears. There are correspondingly two sets of circumstances in which that problem would not arise.

The first is when the proportion of income saved is different for wage and profit incomes. The average ratio of saving to income is then dependent on the distribution of income. With a given capital-income ratio there are different shares of profit (and wages) corresponding to each possible level of the rate of profit. The average saving rate varies accordingly. Within this range it may be possible to find one saving rate that, at the given capital-income ratio, provides just enough saving to match the investment corresponding to the natural growth rate.

The second is when the conditions of production of the two goods are different. Their relative price is then dependent on the profit rate. The value of the capital good, and hence the capital-income ratio, therefore varies according to the rate of profit. Within this range it may be possible to find a capital-income ratio that, with a given uniform ratio of saving to income, makes the warranted rate equal to the natural rate.

In either of these circumstances the distribution of income is made to accommodate the independently determined rate of accumulation. What if the rate of profit itself (or the wage rate) were somehow independently given? This would fix the relative price of the capital good, the overall capital-income ratio, and, for given saving ratios, the warranted rate of growth. Anything that restricted the range in which *r* (or *w*) is free to vary would, of course, restrict *a fortiori* the range of possible growth rates. This would be so, for instance, if we were to take account of a minimum

---

[13] Compare equation (2.2) in Chapter 2.

[14] To avoid confusion, it should be emphasized that the technological condition underlying this argument has nothing to do with the assumption that there is a single technique of production. It has to do rather with the assumption that the conditions of production of the two goods are the same. Prices could of course be fixed for different reasons. But the assumption of a single technique is, by itself, neither a necessary nor a sufficient condition for the existence of a single warranted growth rate.

floor of "subsistence" or "necessary consumption." But apart from the purely technological factors so far discussed, we have not yet indicated any reasons why this should be so. To do this requires introduction of appropriate behavioral conditions, and we therefore leave this question open for the moment.

Meanwhile, a further consequence of the dual conditions that $s_r = s_w = s$ and $\mu = 1$ should be noted. This is that the link between the rate of profit and rate of accumulation is broken. Hence there remains nothing in the model to determine the rate of profit. These are the conditions under which Harrod's problem of uniqueness of the warranted growth rate arises. It should now be apparent that what is missing under these conditions is an explanation of what determines the distribution of income. Once either or both of the above conditions are dropped, not only does the problem of uniqueness of g disappear, but we are also provided with one possible way of supplying this missing link.

There is, of course, no guarantee that, within the technically feasible range of values of the profit rate and under given conditions of saving behavior, a warranted growth rate would exist such as to correspond to the growth rate of the labor force. We could therefore still have the same sort of impasse as Harrod indicated, namely inequality of the warranted and natural growth rates. One way out of this that has been suggested is to let the growth of the labor force itself be a variable which is dependent on some other variable in the model, such as the wage rate.[15] This approach moves in the direction of the Malthusian theory of population.

Even if it is technically or physically possible to do so, why should the rate of accumulation be set equal to the rate of increase of the labor supply? In a capitalist economy, investment decisions are generally made by individual firms, and there is no reason to expect that the total amount of planned investment arrived at in this way must necessarily correspond to, or be limited by, the amount of investment required to keep full employment over time. To this extent it would appear that this construction is completely arbitrary.

What kind of alternative investment behavior we should specify is not very clear. One case of interest is that of "animal spirits," a concept introduced by Joan Robinson (1956: 99), following Keynes, to describe

[15] This possibility is suggested in models constructed by Haavelmo 1954, Nelson 1956, Leibenstein 1957, and Niehans 1963. A special case of this is when the labor supply is in perfectly elastic supply at a given wage rate. On this see Lewis 1954, Robinson 1956, and Hicks 1965.

the complex of forces that govern investment decisions in a capitalist economy. Once investment is specified as a function of some such independent element as animal spirits, this has the effect of introducing an additional equation into the system without an additional variable. The system of equations therefore becomes overdetermined, and it is impossible in general for all of them to be satisfied, including equality of the warranted and natural rates of growth. Overdeterminancy in this case is designed to show the inherent inconsistency of the warranted and natural rates of growth except as an accidental feature of a "mythical" golden age. Outside of such a golden age, growth may still be conceived to take place at a steady rate, but there is then no guarantee of continuous full employment. The point to see here is that full employment is itself an arbitrary assumption for which there may be no justification whatsoever. Once this assumption is given up, it is possible to make the unemployment rate a variable, as with Marx's "industrial reserve army." When the rate of accumulation is high enough, the system may run up against a scarcity of labor. Even then, there may be a way out, as Marx noted, which is through technical change that raises the ratio of capital to labor.[16]

Finally, it may be noted that no mechanism has been specified that would show whether an economy could achieve the golden-age path even if it existed. This relates to the other side of the problem posed by Harrod, i.e. that there is no automatic self-adjusting mechanism in a capitalist economy to ensure steady growth at full employment. This now appears all the more clearly when we have seen that the problem of uniqueness of the warranted growth rate can be avoided even on the most simple assumptions.

Comparative Equilibrium Analysis

Our next task is to compare different equilibrium positions of the system. This procedure was earlier referred to as comparative equilibrium analysis. In this context we shall often refer to changes in one variable connected with changes in another or in a parameter. It should be remembered throughout that we are only concerned with comparison between different equilibrium positions or, as it were, between economies with permanently different characteristics and not with processes of change through time.

As between any two economies or equilibrium positions the technique

---

[16] A similar argument is presented by Robinson (1962a: 15, 110) and by Kaldor (1957).

of production is the same by assumption. Two economies that are alike with respect to the growth rate and the saving proportions will also have exactly the same distribution of income, price ratio, and ratios of physical quantities, even though differing in scale. This follows naturally from the assumption of constant returns to scale. A difference with respect to any of these quantities, however, is likely to be associated with differences in the rest. We are interested in the pattern of such differences and isolate for consideration the relations between the wage rate, profit rate, and share of profits in net income.[17] Since only one technique is assumed to exist, these relations can be represented as continuous and differentiable functions. We can therefore have recourse to differential calculus for making comparisons of equilibrium positions with infinitesimal differences between them.[18]

For the share of profits in net income we take the ratio of net profits to wages, which is

(4.18)
$$\pi = \frac{rk}{w}$$

where k is the value of capital per man. This is only a definition of the profit share and says nothing about what its actual magnitude might be. To examine the relation between π and its constituent elements, we differentiate equation (4.18) with respect to r.[19] This leads to

(4.19)
$$\frac{r}{\pi} \cdot \frac{d\pi}{dr} = 1 + \frac{r}{k} \cdot \frac{dk}{dr} - \frac{r}{w} \cdot \frac{dw}{dr}$$

which indicates that the relation between the profit share and the profit rate can be expressed in terms of two other relations: (1) that between the value of capital per man and the rate of profit, (2) that between the wage rate and rate of profit. The equality (4.19) holds *in general*, following as it does from what is a definition of the profit share. It is expressed in terms of proportional changes ("elasticities"). The magnitude and sign of these elasticities would depend on the specific conditions underlying the various relations. In particular, the wage-profit relation is derived from the technical conditions of production. It was shown on pp. 100–102 to

---

[17] This analysis is meaningful so long as the missing equation determines one of the variables in terms of exogenous parameters.

[18] This is a convenience we shall not be able to use when we come to examine the case of many techniques of production, except under very special conditions.

[19] Notice also that this says nothing about what might be the direction of dependence between the constituent elements of the profit share.

take the form of a wage-profit curve with negative slope. The relation between value of capital per man and the profit rate remains to be examined.

For the value of capital per man we have

(4.20)
$$k = \frac{p_1 M}{L}$$

Differentiating with respect to r, we get:

(4.21)
$$\frac{r}{k} \cdot \frac{dk}{dr} = \frac{r}{p_1} \cdot \frac{dp_1}{dr} + \frac{r}{M/L} \cdot \frac{d(M/L)}{dg} \cdot \frac{dg}{dr}$$

From this result it appears that there are two distinguishable components of the difference in value of capital per man between different equilibria. The first is simply a difference in the price of the capital good associated with a difference in the profit rate. Call this a *price effect*. The reason for this, as we saw on p. 102, is that prices are likely to differ in accordance with a difference in costs depending on the technical conditions of production. The second component involves a more complex set of relations. With given saving proportions, when the profit rate is different the growth rate is likely to be different. This follows from the equilibrium condition for saving and investment. In addition, the difference in growth rate calls for a difference in the stock of physical capital per man. This arises because, when the two commodities are produced by different methods, a different stock of capital goods is required to produce the different composition of output that the difference in the growth rate entails. Call this set of relations a *composition effect*. The overall difference in the value of capital per man is the outcome of both the price and composition effects.

From the equations specifying the economic system set out in this chapter, we can determine the sign of these relations.[20] The results for

----

[20] The relations for price, wage rate, and profit rate were derived on pp. 100–103. For the rest, we get from equation (4.14)

$$\frac{d(M/L)}{dg} = \frac{a_{12}a_{11}(\mu - 1)}{a_{02}[\mu - a_{11}(\mu - 1)(G - g)]^2} \gtreqless 0 \text{ if } \mu \lesseqgtr 1$$

and from (4.15)

$$\frac{dg}{dr} = \frac{\mu[(s_r - s_w)\mu + s_w(1 - s_r)(\mu - 1)Ra_{11}]}{[(1 - s_w)\mu + s_w\xi(r)]^2} \gtreqless 0 \text{ if } \mu \gtreqless \mu^*$$

where

$$\mu^* = \frac{s_w(s_r - 1)Ra_{11}}{s_w(s_r - 1)Ra_{11} - (s_r - s_w)}$$

various cases are summarized in the accompanying table. It can be seen that, whatever the conditions regarding saving and technology, the wage rate is inversely related to the profit rate. This is the only relation for which there is a single unambiguous sign in all cases. The sign of the price effect is positive or negative depending only on the relative proportions of physical capital to labor. The sign of all other relations may be negative or positive in some of the cases shown; in other cases (with a question mark) the sign is ambiguous and can be found only by specifying particular numerical values of the coefficients.

Comparison of Equilibria: Sign of d_x/d_r

	$\mu > 1$			$\mu < 1$		
x	$0 < s_w < s_r$	$0 = s_w < s_r$	$s_w = s_r = s$	$0 < s_w < s_r$	$0 = s_w < s_r$	$s_w = s_r = s$
w	−	−	−	−	−	−
p	−	−	−	+	+	+
g	+	+	+	?	+	−
M/L	−	−	−	?	+	−
k	−	−	−	?	+	?
π	?	?	?	?	+	?

A clear-cut case is when $\mu < 1$ and there is no saving out of wages, so that $s_w = 0$. The sign of all the relations, excepting the wage-profit relation, then becomes positive. This is also the only case, among those shown in the table, when the relation between the profit share and profit rate is unambiguous in sign (the sign is positive).

When the proportion of physical capital to labor is greater in the consumption good sector ($\mu > 1$), we also have unambiguous results under all conditions of saving and for all relations excepting the profit-share relation.

Mention should be made of three particular cases, each characterized by the fact that net output of the economy consists of only one commodity. These are as follows:

(1) $s_r = s_w = 1$, where net output consists of the capital good,

(2) $s_r = s_w = 0$, where net output consists of the consumption good and the economy is in a stationary state, and

(3) $\mu = 1$, where, except for physical units of measurement, there is no technical difference between the two goods.

In all of these three cases the composition effect disappears. In the first two only a price effect remains, and the value of capital per man varies accordingly. In the third case, the price effect also disappears; the value of capital per man becomes simply a technological parameter ($k = a_{11}/a_{02}$) and the profit share is $\pi = (r/w)(a_{11}/a_{02})$, variations in which are described entirely by the wage-profit curve.

Another special case arises if it happens that $g = r$. This would be the case if the saving proportions were such that $s_r = 1$ and $s_w = 0$. In this case we find that

$$k = \frac{a_{11}}{a_{02}[\xi(r)]^2} = -\frac{dw}{dr}$$

which indicates that the value of capital per man is equal to the slope of the wage-profit curve of the single technique. Multiplying this relationship by r/w, we then get

$$\pi = \frac{rk}{w} = -\frac{r}{w}\cdot\frac{dw}{dr}$$

which says that the share of profits is uniquely related to the elasticity of the wage-profit curve at any point on that curve.

Value and Distribution

From the foregoing discussion we see that—with one exception, the wage-profit relation—it is not possible to establish any general rule about the pattern of differences between one equilibrium situation and another. The fact that we are able to make a general statement concerning the relation between the wage rate and profit rate—that is, they are inversely related—is of course an interesting one. It points to a basic characteristic of the production system with which any relevant theory must be consistent. But about the overall distribution of the product between wages and profits we are unable to say unambiguously to what extent and in what direction these shares of the product are different between one situation and another when the profit rate (or the wage rate) is different.

The reason for this is evident from the preceding analysis. In general, when we compare two situations in which the rate of profit (or the wage rate) is different, there are likely to be associated differences in the relative prices of the commodities (the price effect), in the composition of the product (the composition effect), and therefore in the quantity of capital and of output when both are measured at the numeraire prices or exchange values corresponding to the two situations. We can make no general statement about the direction of these effects, and hence about the difference in distribution of the product. The problem is due to the fact that, measured in terms of exchange values, the quantity of the product itself and the quantity of capital on which the amount of profits is calculated are different when the wage rate or profit rate is different.

This problem is an important one from the point of view of a theory of distribution, such as that of the Classical economists, which conceives of wages and the share of wages in the social product as being determined at a definite level independent of the level of the product itself and independent of the prices in which the product is measured. Within this theory, the magnitude of wages and that of the social surplus (as the difference between the social product and the amount of wages) are conceived to undergo definite quantitative variation from one situation to another in accordance with changes in the determining conditions. From the viewpoint of such a theory it is therefore important to have a measure of these magnitudes so as to be able to assign an unambiguous quantitative meaning to them and to differences which occur in them from one situation to another, independently of associated differences in prices and in the physical composition and uses of the product.

This is a problem which worried Ricardo and which he sought to solve in his quest for an "invariable standard of value." For the purposes of a Ricardian theory, the heterogeneous commodities constituting the aggregate of wages and social product must be reduced to a common standard. That standard could not itself be an exchange standard, that is, the prices at which commodities exchange, because it would then be dependent upon distribution. To be capable of providing an independent measure of distribution, the measuring standard would itself have to be independent of distribution. What is needed is a measure of the value of commodities. In this way, a connection is established in Ricardian theory between the theory of value, as an analysis of what regulates the value of commodities, and the theory of distribution, as an analysis of the determination of relative shares in the social product.

What if we adopted the quantity of labor embodied in each commodity as the standard of value? As we have seen from earlier discussion (pp. 82–83), this quantity can be determined once the technical conditions of production are given. It is equal to the amount of labor directly and indirectly required per unit of output of each commodity. In the case of our simple model of production we have

$$(4.22) \qquad \lambda_1 = a_{01} + a_{11}\delta\lambda_1 = \frac{a_{01}}{1 - a_{11}\delta}$$

$$(4.23) \qquad \lambda_2 = a_{02} + a_{12}\delta\lambda_1 = a_{02} + \frac{a_{12}a_{01}\delta}{1 - a_{11}\delta}$$

Then, $1/\lambda_2$ is output per unit of direct and indirect labor employed in production of the consumption good. The wage rate, measured in units of the consumption good, is w. Therefore, the surplus product in production of this commodity is $1/\lambda_2 - w$. This can be rewritten as $(1 - \lambda_2 w)/\lambda_2$. Here, $(1 - \lambda_2 w)$ is the difference between one unit of labor and the amount of labor embodied in the wage. In other words, it is the surplus labor obtained from employing a unit of labor in production. Dividing this quantity by the labor embodied in the wage gives $\epsilon = (1 - \lambda_2 w)/\lambda_2 w$, which is an equivalent expression, in the simple model, for the rate of surplus value or rate of exploitation as defined in Chapter 3 for the case of a general production model.

As long as the same uniform wage is paid throughout the system, this latter ratio must be the same in the production of every commodity and hence throughout the entire system of production. It therefore gives us a unique, independent, and unambiguous measure of distribution in the sense of the relative share of the labor expended in production which goes to the workers as against that going to the owners of capital. We can also say that, in general, it is inversely related to the level of the wage, $d\epsilon/dw < 0$. Thus, within the scheme of labor values, we have a basis for dealing with the problem in terms of the rate of surplus value or rate of exploitation.

The relevant relationships are exhibited in Figure 4.4. The wage-profit curve is represented in the right-hand quadrant and the exploitation curve in the left-hand quadrant. The intercept of the wage-profit curve on the vertical axis (or the maximum wage rate W) is equal to the inverse of the labor value of the numeraire commodity. This can be set equal to unity by appropriate choice of physical units—one physical unit of the numeraire commodity embodies one unit of labor. Accordingly, a wage of w in terms of the numeraire commodity contains w units of embodied labor. Corresponding to a given wage, say $\bar{w}$, there is a rate of exploitation equal to the ratio $(W - \bar{w})/\bar{w}$ measured on the vertical axis, or to $\bar{\epsilon}$ in

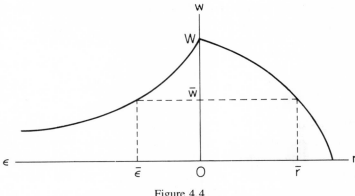

Figure 4.4

the left-hand quadrant. The associated profit rate is $\bar{r}$. In general, when the wage rate is higher (lower) the rate of exploitation is lower (higher) and so is the profit rate.

We may consider in this context the meaning of the solution proposed by Sraffa (1960) to Ricardo's problem of an invariable standard of value. Sraffa proposes to use the net output of the standard system as the basis upon which to measure the share of wages and its variations. The standard system consists entirely of "basic" commodities, defined as those commodities which, in the given system of production, enter directly or indirectly into the production of all commodities including themselves. In the simple model of production, the capital good is the only basic commodity in this sense. It therefore constitutes the standard commodity.

Now, assume that all labor is employed in production of the standard commodity—thereby making production of this commodity into a sort of miniature model of the economy. This implies that

$$(4.24) \qquad a_{01}gM + a_{01}a_{11}\delta gM = L$$

or $a_{01}(1 + a_{11}\delta)gM = L$, where the left-hand side represents direct and indirect requirements of labor in production of the standard commodity. Taking the net output per man of the standard commodity as numeraire, we have

$$(4.25) \qquad P_1 g \frac{M}{L} = 1$$

It follows from (4.24) and (4.25) that

$$(4.26) \qquad P_1 = a_{01}(1 + a_{11}\delta)$$

Thus, the price of the capital good is equal to labor employed directly and indirectly in its production. It is, then, independent of the wage rate (or profit rate). Substituting this condition into equation (4.1) and rearranging terms, we get

$$(4.27) \qquad r = \frac{1 - a_{11}\delta}{a_{11}} \left(1 - \frac{wa_{01}}{a_{01}(1 + a_{11}\delta)(1 - a_{11}\delta)} \right)$$

$$= R(1 - v)$$

where v is the share of wages in the standard net output and R is the rate of net reproduction of the standard commodity or maximum rate of profit.

We thus obtain a linear relation between the rate of profit and the share of wages in the standard system. It depends only on the technical conditions of production. With a given share of wages in terms of the standard system we get a unique rate of profit and vice versa. The rate of profit varies inversely with the share of wages.

We note a similarity of the standard system with the labor value scheme to the extent that the former is also based on a labor measure of value. However, in the former case, the level of wages is measured in terms of units of the standard commodity and, as such, can have theoretical significance only if it can be assumed that workers bargain in terms of the standard commodity (here, the capital good). The labor value measure, on the other hand, has theoretical significance as an expression of a real social-production relation: the division of the labor time of the workers or the division of the "working day."

The standard system is a miniature model of the economy and provides a measure of distribution in the form of a simple linear relationship between wages and profits. However, this particular relationship does not in general carry over to the economy itself even when all relevant variables are measured in terms of the standard commodity. This feature further limits the theoretical significance of the standard system. Moreover, in a context of change in technical conditions of production, the standard commodity must itself be considered to vary, so that comparisons in terms of the standard commodity are then ruled out.

Chapter Five

Many Alternative Techniques

Introduction

In this chapter we present an analysis of the problem of choice of technique when it is assumed that many alternative techniques of production exist in a given state of technical knowledge. A comparative equilibrium analysis is developed in this context for economies in a stationary state. The logic of the analysis, as we shall see, is quite straightforward. The problem is to determine what theoretical significance, if any, it has. We consider this problem at the end of the chapter.

Accumulation and Technical Change

Throughout the analysis presented in the previous two chapters it is assumed that only one technique of production exists—one method of producing each of the commodities, consisting of a fixed complement of capital goods and labor. Within the context of the assumed condition of a given state of technology this is an entirely reasonable assumption to make. Moreover, it may not be so far removed from reality as might be supposed.[1] Insofar as different techniques of production are actually observed, their availability and the transition from one technique to another should properly be viewed as the outcome of a process of technical change which brings those techniques into existence as viable alternatives and a simultaneous process of accumulation which enables their incorporation into new outfits of capital equipment. This was

[1] Kaldor (1960: 104) observes: "It is a significant fact of modern technique that *given the type of equipment in existence* there is a relation of strong complementarity between them; that is to say, the extent to which the proportions of these factors can be varied in production is highly limited."

certainly the view of the Classical economists and of Marx.[2] In recent times this view has also received expression in the works of Kaldor (1960: ch. 13), Robinson (1962), and Salter (1966), among others.

In accordance with this view, the assumption of one technique of production may be considered a way of abstracting from the process of technical change. This procedure recognizes fully that analysis of the process of technical change is a matter which requires to be confronted in its own right but which can be left out at this level of abstraction. In so doing there is no necessary implication that technical change is a phenomenon which occurs in isolation from and outside of the economic process. It only requires us to accept that it makes sense to consider, as is done here, the process of accumulation in the absence of technical change. The rationale for doing this is to be found in the insights that can be obtained from the analysis, at this level of abstraction, into the relations between accumulation, distribution, the structure of production, and the demand for and supply of labor.

Alternatively, one could base this procedure on a hypothesis that the particular technique adopted in an economy, except for its connection with the process of accumulation and technical change, is independent of the particular relations included in the analysis at this level. Specifically, the hypothesis would be that the technique adopted is independent of the prevailing configuration of prices and distribution of income. The assumption of a given technique could be taken to reflect this hypothesis. Such a hypothesis may perhaps seem strange, especially in the light of a specific and familiar theoretical framework, namely, neoclassical theory, which views changes in technique as a matter of technical "substitution" between factors in response to changing factor prices. However, this hypothesis would not be entirely meaningless. It may have validity if, for instance, there is an association between particular techniques of production and a minimum size of firm.[3] It seems consistent also with a view of the process of technical change from a long-run perspective as

---

[2] When he discusses the problem of "substitution of machinery for human labor," Ricardo (*Principles*, ch. 31) makes it clear that the problem occurs *in the context of accumulation*: "I have been supposing that improved machinery is *suddenly* discovered and extensively used; but the truth is that these discoveries are gradual, and rather operate in determining the employment of the capital which is saved and accumulated than in diverting capital from its actual employment." For Marx's analysis, see *Capital* I, ch. 15.

[3] This point is argued by Levine (1973) in an analysis of the relation between evolution of techniques of production and the size of firms.

involving, not incremental changes in a single process or sector of production, but a "switch" of technique encompassing a change in many sectors or, in the extreme, in the whole matrix of the production system. Such a switch may prove to be profitable over a wide range of market prices and wage rates (or profit rates).

Even if the choice among alternative techniques, when such alternatives are assumed to exist, is considered to depend on market prices and on the ruling rate of profit, the assumption of one technique would be the *logical* one to make within the context of the steady-state assumptions and a given state of technical knowledge. For, with a given and constant rate of profit, the technique chosen in accordance with the ruling conditions remains the same on a particular steady-state path (though, as we shall see, the choice may not be unique). Thus, from the point of view of characterizing the properties of particular steady-state paths, it is completely irrelevant whether there exist many alternative techniques, an infinite number of them, or just one. If there is more than one technique available, the technique in use is selected from among the available alternatives on the principle of minimizing costs or maximizing profits. That the coefficients of that technique are invariant with respect to the scale of output is a reflection of the assumption of constant returns to scale.[4] That the coefficients are unchanging over time reflects the assumptions that the profit rate is constant and technical knowledge is given. In these various ways, it may be said that technical coefficients of production are "fixed." That technical coefficients are "fixed" in this sense has nothing to do with the number of techniques that are assumed to be available. Whatever that number might be, there is no sense in which technical coefficients can be considered to be "variable" or techniques "substituted" one for another in a particular steady state.

As between one steady state and another there may be a difference in the technique in use. This would be because the ruling conditions are different. In particular, there must be a difference in the rate of profit such as to make one technique most profitable in one situation and another

---

[4] The assumption of constant returns to scale is also a reasonable one to make under the assumed condition of a given state of technical knowledge. If we were to assume that the level of output is fixed, as in a stationary state, and there is no change in the composition of output between different stationary states, then it would not be necessary to make any assumption whatsoever regarding the nature of returns to scale. This is the procedure adopted by Sraffa (1960).

technique most profitable in the other. Each of the techniques must be considered to have its own particular mix of reproducible capital goods, some or all of which may be specific to that technique. For this reason, one cannot conceive of a changeover occurring from one technique to the other in the absence of a simultaneous process of accumulation and technical change (at least through depreciation and gross investment). To go further in the direction of explaining how such a changeover might occur requires a theory of the process involved. This serves as a forceful reminder that the analysis presented here abstracts from that process. It may also be safely said that at this time no such theory exists—only the outlines of possible approaches to the problem.

Choice of Technique

For the purpose of analysis of the choice of technique it is useful to conceive of the technology as consisting of a *book of blueprints*. Each page in the book gives the specification of a particular technique. The contents of the book represent the state of technical knowledge, which we continue to assume is fixed.

Without loss of generality, the analysis is carried out here for the case of the simplified model of production described in the previous chapter. It is assumed that the same consumption good is produced with the different techniques.[5] The capital good is different from one technique to another, and there are as many techniques as there are different capital goods. Each type of capital good can be employed with specified amounts of labor to produce either itself or the consumption good (but not other types of capital goods). Each has its own physical rate of depreciation independent of use and its own particular rate of net reproduction. Each technique is thus represented by a particular set of production coefficients:

$$\left[\frac{a_0^i}{A^i} \right] = \left[\begin{array}{cc} a_{01}^i & a_{02}^i \\ \hline a_{11}^i & a_{12}^i \\ a_{21}^i & a_{22}^i \end{array} \right]$$

The rate of depreciation is δ^i, a scalar.

A difference in the capital good from one technique to another implies

---

[5] It could be assumed instead that there is a fixed bundle of consumption goods common to all techniques. This would make no difference to the results presented here.

a difference in all the production coefficients. However, because of the difference in the physical specification of the capital good, the coefficients of one technique are not all directly comparable with those of another. It would be possible to conceive of a technology in which the capital good is the same for different techniques. This case could be represented in a number of ways. One is to have the production coefficients in the capital good sector remain the same. The difference between techniques then consists only of a difference in the coefficients of the consumption good sector. Alternatively, the production coefficients in both sectors could be made to differ while the ratio of input proportions in the two sectors remains the same. However, the assumption that one technique differs from another only in using more or less of the same capital good in proportion to labor is obviously a very special one. We need not limit ourselves to such a special case.

Which of the many techniques will be employed in equilibrium? The principles governing the choice follow from the condition that firms seek to maximize profits and from the existence of competition. This can be shown as follows.

Start with one technique, say α. Let the wage rate be given at $w = \bar{w}$ and assume that $\bar{w}$ is less than the maximum wage rate for that technique —otherwise it would not be eligible. For the given technique, the wage rate $\bar{w}$ is associated with a definite profit rate $r = \bar{r}$ and a relative price of the capital good $p_1 = \bar{p}_1$. These can be found, as we saw in the previous chapter, by setting price equal to unit costs for each of the commodities and solving the price equations, which, for technique α, are

(5.1) $$p_1^\alpha = a_{01}^\alpha \bar{w} + a_{11}^\alpha p_1^\alpha (\delta^\alpha + r)$$

(5.2) $$p_2^\alpha = a_{02}^\alpha \bar{w} + a_{12}^\alpha p_1^\alpha (\delta^\alpha + r)$$

(5.3) $$p_2^\alpha = 1$$

where the consumption good is taken as numeraire.

Let there be another technique, say β. Use the wage rate $\bar{w}$ and the profit rate $\bar{r}$ to evaluate the costs of production with technique β. We get

(5.4) $$p_1^\beta = a_{01}^\beta \bar{w} + a_{11}^\beta p_1^\beta (\delta^\beta + \bar{r})$$

(5.5) $$p_2^\beta = a_{02}^\beta \bar{w} + a_{12}^\beta p_1^\beta (\delta^\beta + \bar{r})$$

Now compare the two techniques.[6] If $p_2^\beta < 1$, technique β is cheaper than technique α, which is to say that

$$\frac{1 - a_{02}^\beta \bar{w} - a_{12}^\beta p_1^\beta \delta^\beta}{a_{12}^\beta p_1^\beta} > \bar{r}$$

Thus, a firm could employ technique β and, in the price situation corresponding to technique α, make greater profits. Alternatively, at the profit rate $\bar{r}$, it could sell at a lower price and still cover costs. If one firm could, so could all the rest. Competition ensures that, in equilibrium, technique β would be employed. If on the other hand $p_2^\beta > 1$, technique β is less profitable and would be rejected. Whichever technique is more profitable would be selected. If the two are equally profitable, firms would employ either of them or both in combination.

Suppose there were a third technique available. A similar comparison could again be made, and from this the most profitable technique would be selected. If there were more still, a further comparison could be made, continuing to the next, and the next, and so on, for the entire book of blueprints. In the end, the technique would be selected that, at the given wage rate, yields the highest profit rate.[7] By the same reasoning it can be shown that, given the profit rate, firms would choose the technique that yields the highest wage rate.

The choice of technique can be illustrated with a familiar diagram. As indicated by our analysis in the previous chapter, various equilibrium combinations of wage and profit rates are possible with a given technique. These can be represented by a wage-profit curve in the positive quadrant.

---

[6] Note that it would make no sense to compare two techniques in terms of the price of the capital good when the capital good used in each is different. This limitation would not arise in a production system with many capital goods, for different techniques are then likely to have one or more capital goods in common. Except for this qualification, the argument presented here is independent of the number of capital goods and consumer goods in the system.

[7] It needs to be shown that, as the comparison continues in this way, no technique that proved less profitable in one price situation could prove more profitable in another. Otherwise it would be possible to go back and forth endlessly without coming to one most profitable technique. In general, however, such a possibility can be ruled out. To see this, go back to techniques α and β. Suppose β is cheaper ($p_2^\beta < 1$) when evaluated at the rate of profit corresponding to technique α and the given wage rate. Then, with the same wage rate, technique β will break even ($p_2^\beta = 1$) at a higher profit rate. Technique α, which was dearer at the same wage rate and a lower profit rate, must be dearer still at the higher profit rate. The same can be shown for any other pair of techniques and therefore for all of them. For a proof, see Levhari 1965: 101–2.

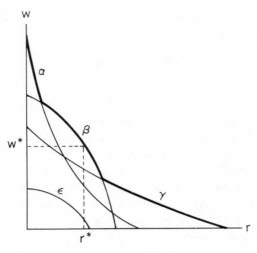

Figure 5.1

The curve will slope downward, will cut both axes, and, in general, will be either concave or convex to the origin. Now, there will be as many such curves as there are alternative techniques in a given book of blueprints. Each curve is described by the technical coefficients of the technique it represents. Since the wage rate is always measured in terms of the same consumption good, all the individual wage-profit curves can be drawn on the same diagram. Given the level of the wage rate, provided it is feasible,[8] firms will choose the technique that yields the highest profit rate, or the wage-profit curve that is furthest to the right. Alternatively (which comes to the same thing) given the profit rate, the technique will be chosen that yields the highest wage rate. This is shown in Figure 5.1 for a case of four techniques. At the wage rate w^* (or the profit rate r^*) technique β is chosen as the most profitable.

We may go on now to note that, at different levels of the wage rate (or profit rate), either the same or a different technique will be selected— whichever has the wage-profit curve furthest out along a line from the given w or r. Of course, no technique can ever be chosen unless it is most profitable at some wage or profit rate. For instance, technique ϵ in Figure 5.1 is completely dominated at every profit rate and is therefore

---

[8] For a given wage rate (profit rate) to be feasible, it is necessary that there be at least one technique with a maximum wage rate (profit rate) greater than the given one.

irrelevant. The wage-profit curves corresponding to the techniques that are chosen at different wage or profit rates will generate an outer envelope as depicted in Figure 5.1. Let us call this envelope the wage-profit frontier.[9]

With a finite number of alternative techniques, as in Figure 5.1, the wage-profit curve of each technique contributes a segment to the frontier. In this case the frontier therefore has corners. Each corner represents a point of intersection of two wage-profit curves. The corresponding techniques are equally profitable at the associated wage and profit rates and can therefore coexist. The larger the number of techniques, the smaller would be each segment on the frontier. In the limit, with an infinite number of techniques, it is possible to generate a smooth frontier which is tangent at each point to one wage-profit curve.[10] This would obviously require very special conditions on the technology. In general, since the frontier is derived from wage-profit curves that are negatively sloped, it must itself be negatively sloped. Its curvature depends on the structure of the underlying technology. Where the component curves are either convex to the origin or straight lines, the frontier must be convex or a straight line. Where the curves are concave, the frontier must be concave. The frontier may therefore have any curvature, possibly with convex and concave segments alternating.

The wage-profit frontier provides a useful tool for characterizing the relation between the available techniques of production and the equilibrium wage-profit configuration corresponding to particular steady states. Given any profit rate, we can find from the frontier the technique that would be in use. Associated with that technique and the given profit rate would be a particular wage rate. Knowing, in addition, the relative price of the commodities, the composition of output, and the physical stock of capital goods appropriate to that technique and to the growth rate of the economy, we can calculate the value of capital and of output at the given price and profit rate, and hence the overall share of wages (and profits) in the net product. Knowing the labor value of the commodities, we can calculate the rate of exploitation.

[9] The envelope is sometimes called a "factor-price frontier." Cf. Samuelson 1962. The present terminology is preferable because it does not foreclose the issue of whether profit is the price or reward of a "factor" of production. See Chapter 1 for a discussion of this issue.

[10] It is possible that the frontier could be tangent to more than one curve at a given point, regardless of whether the number of techniques is finite or infinite. For present purposes, this possibility can be ruled out.

A Profitability Curve

The problem of choice of technique can be approached from another direction so as to bring out certain properties of the problem and the solution to it.

For this purpose we assume here, without loss of generality, that the economy is in a stationary state.[11] This implies that the rate of net accumulation is zero, production of the capital good is just sufficient for replacement, and net output consists entirely of the consumption good. Accordingly, in our simple model of production, net output per man is $y = x_2/L$. For a given technique, we get from equation (4.16), after setting $g = 0$ and taking account of equation (4.5),

$$y = \frac{1 - a_{11}\delta}{a_{02}[1 + (\mu - 1)a_{11}\delta]} = W$$

Thus, in a stationary state, net output per man is equal to the maximum wage rate for the given technique.[12] This considerably simplifies matters. We can now calculate directly from the technical conditions the relationships that are relevant for this analysis. This is shown in Figure 5.2, where the wage-profit curve of a single technique is drawn.[13] Net output per man for that technique in a stationary state is $\bar{y}$. At the wage rate $\bar{w}$ the corresponding profit rate is $\bar{r}$, and vice versa. The difference $\bar{y} - \bar{w}$ measures the amount of net profit per man. Capitalizing this infinite stream of profits at the profit rate $\bar{r}$ gives the value of capital per man as $\bar{k} = (\bar{y} - \bar{w})/\bar{r}$, which says that $\bar{k}$ is given by the slope of the line $Q\bar{y}$ or the tangent of the angle $\bar{w}Q\bar{y}$. At a given wage rate we thus have, for a particular technique, a determinate value of capital and distribution of the net product between wages and profits. The same holds for other techniques in the book of blueprints at any wage rate or profit rate that is feasible.

[11] Assuming an economy in steady-state growth would mean that net investment is positive and must be included in the net product. Complications arising from this are being avoided with the present assumption. They will be taken up in the next chapter.

[12] It is easy to see why this is so. In a stationary state, net output consists entirely of the consumption good. Recall that, in the previous chapter, we found that the wage rate, measured in units of the consumption good, is at a maximum when wages absorb the whole net output of the consumption good per unit of total direct and indirect labor employed in its production. It follows that in a stationary state net output per man equals the maximum wage rate measured in terms of the consumption good.

[13] This geometrical construction is due to Bhaduri (1969) and Garegnani (1970).

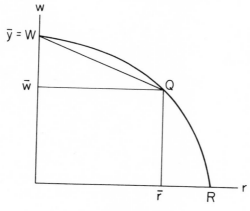

Figure 5.2

Now, let the profit rate be given at, say, r_0. Compare two eligible techniques, say α and β. From the income-accounting identity we have, for the two techniques, $y^\alpha = w^\alpha + r_0 k^\alpha$ and $y^\beta = w^\beta + r_0 k^\beta$. By subtraction we get

$$\frac{y^\alpha - y^\beta}{k^\alpha - k^\beta} = r_0 + \frac{w^\alpha - w^\beta}{k^\alpha - k^\beta}$$

The left-hand side is the ratio of the difference in the infinite stream of net output for each technique to the difference of the value of the capital invested in each. We may call it the *ratio of profitability* for the two techniques. A ratio such as this could be computed for any arbitrary pair of techniques at any profit rate that is feasible. In general, of course, it would not be equal to the profit rate. A difference between the two magnitudes is accounted for by the difference between the two techniques in the amount that would be left over from the net product for paying wages after deducting profits at the given rate on the value of the respective capitals. One technique is more (less) profitable than another according as the ratio of profitability is greater (less) than the profit rate. When the respective amounts available for paying wages are equal ($w^\alpha = w^\beta$), the ratio of profitability turns out to be equal to the profit rate. The corresponding techniques are then equally profitable.

Comparison of the profitability ratio with the rate of profit thus provides a basis for evaluating the relative profitability of different techniques and, therefore, for determining the technique that is most

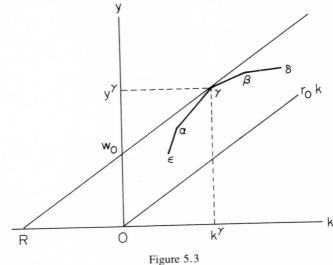

Figure 5.3

profitable. The procedure involved here can be shown on a diagram. Let
the profit rate be given at r_0, represented by the slope of the ray $r_0 k$ in
Figure 5.3. The points $\alpha, \beta, \gamma, \delta, \epsilon$ represent the values of net output per man
and capital per man for the eligible techniques at the profit rate r_0. The
ratio of profitability between techniques is the slope of the line joining
any two adjacent techniques. The resulting locus formed from the entire set
of techniques may be called a *profitability curve*.[14]

Now, compare the ratio of profitability for successive pairs of techniques
on the profitability curve with the given profit rate. Start at ϵ and compare
this technique with technique α. The slope of the line joining these two
points is greater than the profit rate. Therefore technique α is more
profitable. Next, compare techniques α and γ. Technique γ is more
profitable. Repeating this procedure for the remaining techniques, we
find that β is less profitable than γ and δ less profitable than β. It follows
that γ is the most profitable of all the techniques. At the profit rate r_0,
technique γ yields the highest wage rate measured by the vertical distance
$0w_0$ between $r_0 k$ and the line parallel to $r_0 k$, which is tangent to the
profitability curve at γ.

[14] This construction was introduced by Robinson (1956: 412), who called it a "productivity
curve" and referred to the ratio of profitability as the "marginal product of investment."
She has indicated to the author that use of these terms was misleading.

The same procedure could be carried out no matter how large the number of available techniques or the number of commodities.[15] The profitability curve (or its segments) would be positively sloped and display diminishing ratios of profitability between techniques going from left to right.[16] There is one point on the curve to the left of which the ratio of profitability between techniques is greater than the given profit rate, to the right of which it is less. The technique represented there is the most profitable at the given profit rate.

That a single technique is the most profitable seems the likely case when there are a finite number of discrete techniques. However, it may happen that two techniques are equally the most profitable.[17] It will be found, in this case, that the ratio of profitability for the two techniques is exactly equal to the given profit rate. This equality means that the difference in the value of output per man for the two techniques is just sufficient to yield profit at the given rate on the difference in the value of capital per man. It is a necessary implication of the condition that the two techniques are equally profitable. It obviously does not provide a criterion for determining the profit rate, since the latter is, so to speak, given in advance. The whole procedure is only a way of representing the choice of technique.

[15] To represent the value of capital and of output for the different techniques on the same diagram, the commodities must be evaluated at the same set of prices in terms of the same numeraire. The representation would differ according to which set of numeraire prices is chosen. In the particular case assumed here, all of the relevant magnitudes are uniquely defined in terms of units of the single consumption good. Note, furthermore, that at one profit rate (and corresponding set of prices) there is one profitability curve. At a different profit rate, the wage rate, relative prices of commodities, and value of capital per man would in general be different for each technique. Thus, at each and every profit rate there would be a different profitability curve. For an analysis of some aspects of the general *n*-commodity case, see Morishima 1964: 122–30.

[16] This shape is a consequence of economic rationality, not of any special feature of the technology, as might be suggested, for instance, by the notion of "diminishing marginal rates of substitution between factors" to be found in marginal productivity theory. The reason is straightforward. Any technique that, taken with another, had both a lower value of output and a higher value of capital (that is, a negative ratio of profitability) would be irrelevant. Similarly, if between any three adjacent techniques the ratio of profitability were higher between the second and third than between the first and second, the second would be ruled out and comparison made directly between the first and third.

[17] This would be the case at a point of intersection of two wage-profit curves on the wage-profit frontier. This case seems more likely the larger the number of relevant techniques. It has been suggested by Solow (1970: 427) that, in the limiting case of an infinite number of techniques, every point on the frontier becomes a point of intersection in this sense. This may well be so, but the interpretation that one puts upon this feature of the problem is quite another matter. See Robinson 1971b.

The ratio of profitability relates to a comparison of two techniques, with technically different capital goods, output, and capital for each technique being evaluated on a uniform basis in terms of numeraire prices and a common profit rate and growth rate (equal to zero in a stationary state). In general, it has no meaning or significance as a measure of technical "productivity" of the different capital goods, or the "marginal productivity of capital," which could bear interpretation as an independent determinant of the rate of profit. Similarly, Solow ([1967], [1970]) has shown that at a point such as that discussed here, where two techniques are equally profitable, one can define a "rate of return" that is equal to the profit rate. Like the ratio of profitability, this notion of rate of return provides no independent basis for determining the level of the profit rate.[18]

The Ordering of Techniques

A question which can now be posed is whether, in comparing different equilibrium positions within a given technology, it is possible to order the associated techniques uniquely by the rate of profit. More fundamentally, is there a unique correspondence between the value of capital or net product per man of the techniques so ordered and the rate of profit? These questions arise in the context of neoclassical capital theory, where it is a basic postulate that (a) techniques of production can be uniquely ordered in relation to the rate of profit, and (b) the ordering is such that more "capital-intensive" (or more "mechanized," or more "roundabout") techniques are adopted at lower rates of profit. It is now known that this postulate has no general validity.[19] This section provides an analysis of the problem in the framework of our simple model of production.[20]

In the special case constructed in Figure 5.4, a unique ordering of techniques is evidently possible. As the rate of profit varies from its maximum value to zero, there is a switch from one technique to another, no single

[18] For a discussion of this point, see Pasinetti 1969, 1970.

[19] Reference may be made here to the earlier notion of an "average period of production" put forward by Bohm-Bawerk (1959). It was thought that the "average period of production," in some quantifiable sense, would have an inverse relationship to the rate of profit. But this relationship was also shown to be invalid. For a discussion of this problem, see Blaug 1968: 510–30.

[20] The possibility of "reswitching" of techniques was conclusively demonstrated by Sraffa (1960, ch. 12). For subsequent discussion of this result, see Pasinetti 1966c; Levhari and Samuelson 1966; Morishima 1966; Bruno et al. 1966; Garegnani 1966; Samuelson 1966; Robinson and Naqvi 1967.

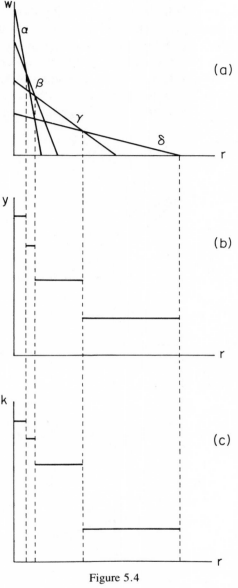

Figure 5.4

technique within the whole spectrum appearing more than once. Since each successive technique is characterized, in a stationary state, by a higher net output per man, it follows that there is a unique, inverse relation between net output per man and the profit rate. Moreover, taking the value of capital for any two adjacent techniques at the rate of profit corresponding to the switch point, it is evident that the switch is always to the technique with the higher value of capital per man as the rate of

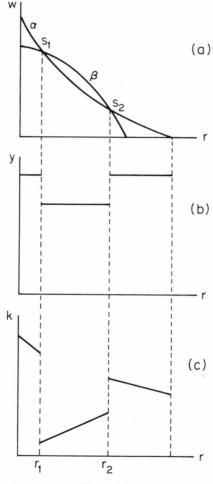

Figure 5.5

profit is lowered. Since this is true for the whole spectrum of techniques, it follows that there is a unique inverse relation between the value of capital per man and the rate of profit. Thus, a higher "capital intensity" (in this sense) is associated with a lower rate of profit.

Now take the case of Figure 5.5, with two techniques. The two wage-profit curves intersect twice, at s_1 and s_2. At s_2, with r falling, the switch is from technique α to technique β. At s_1, when r becomes less than r_1, there is a switch back to α. Technique α is profitable for two different ranges of the profit rate, and therefore the two techniques cannot be uniquely ordered. At s_2, moreover, as r falls, the switch is to the technique with a lower net output per man and lower value of capital per man evaluated at r_2. We therefore find in this instance a positive relation between r and the value of capital per man or net output per man. At s_1 there is an inverse relation like that of the previous case.

What accounts for the difference in these results? Comparing Figure 5.4 with Figure 5.5, we can see that an essential difference between the two cases relates to the curvature of the wage-profit curves. This curvature, as we have seen, depends on the ratio of capital-labor proportions in the two sectors. The coming back, or reswitching, of techniques is due to the difference in this ratio that occurs from one technique to another, reflecting the technical difference between the production processes using the respective capital goods. Indeed, a sufficient condition for absence of reswitching is that the ratio should be the same for all techniques represented on the wage-profit frontier.[21] This condition may be taken to mean that the capital goods of different techniques are technically the same; techniques differ only with respect to the quantity of the capital good employed per unit of labor. The case in which all wage-profit curves are straight lines ($\mu = 1$) is simply a special case of this condition, implying in addition that the consumption good *and* the capital good are technically the same.

Other related conditions for absence of reswitching in this model, and hence for a unique ordering of techniques, can be found.[22] All of these

---

[21] This was shown by Hicks (1965: 154).

[22] One condition that is sufficient, though not necessary, is that for each successive technique represented on the frontier the maximum wage rate W (or the intercept of the wage-profit curve on the vertical axis) should rise and the maximum profit rate R (the intercept on the horizontal axis) should fall as the rate of profit falls. See Bruno et al. 1966. Another condition has been worked out in terms of variations in the composite coefficient $a_{12}a_{01}$, representing the amount of indirect labor required per unit of consumption-good output. See Brown 1969.

conditions imply specific restrictions on the pattern of variation of the technical coefficients describing the available methods of production, and hence on the technology of the system. There would seem to be no theoretical basis for restricting technology in such ways, and they must therefore be regarded as completely arbitrary conditions.[23]

It appears, from our simple production model, that it is the variation in the ratio of capital-labor proportions from one technique to another, and hence the heterogeneity of production processes using capital goods, which accounts for the existence of reswitching. This result therefore holds *a fortiori* in more complex models of production with many capital goods. We conclude that, in general, the reswitching of techniques cannot be ruled out. Except under very special conditions, techniques of production cannot be uniquely ordered by the rate of profit.

The existence of reswitching of techniques among those represented on the wage-profit frontier draws attention to the possibility that a unique inverse relation between the rate of profit and the value of capital per man or output per man may not exist. But it is important to realize that no such unique relation may exist even when there is no reswitching, that is, even if techniques can be uniquely ordered by the rate of profit. A simple case of this is illustrated in Figure 5.6. Values of capital per man in the range k_0 to k_1 recur at different levels of the profit rate in the absence of reswitching of techniques. Once this possibility is recognized, then a striking conclusion emerges. There is in general no reason to expect that the ordering of techniques on the scale of variation of the rate of profit should necessarily correspond to the ordering, on the same scale, of the values of capital per man and net output per man for those techniques.

There is a further point to be noted. It was indicated above that, as the number of techniques increases, the segment contributed by each to the frontier becomes smaller. In the limit, with an infinite number of techniques, it is possible to generate a frontier that is tangent at each point to a single wage-profit curve. Now, at any such point, an infinitesimal variation in the profit rate is associated with a switch from one technique

[23] We might also quote here the conclusion of Robinson and Naqvi (1967: 591): "Evidently multiple switching is the general case, and Samuelson's straight lines the most restricted. But there is no point in discussing which is most 'likely to be found in reality.' First, the argument concerns comparisons of equilibrium positions with different rates of profit and the same 'state of technical knowledge.' These are not found in nature and cannot be observed. Second, the argument is concerned with a point of logic, to which the number of instances has no relevance one way or the other. The benefit of the discussion is only to dispel illusions."

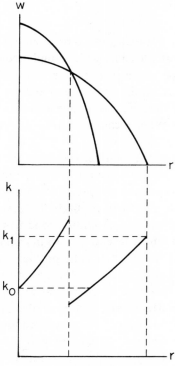

Figure 5.6

to another. In this sense there is continuous variation of techniques with respect to the profit rate. But this does not imply that the differences in the value of capital per man and output per man between two neighboring techniques necessarily become smaller. These differences may remain large regardless of how close to each other two techniques might be on the frontier.[24] It follows that continuity in the variation of techniques with respect to the profit rate does not imply continuity in the variation of values of capital per man and net output per man with respect to the profit rate.[25]

[24]This is evident from the fact that the intercepts of two wage-profit curves could be far apart no matter how close their respective points or segments on the frontier might be. The difference in the technical coefficients determining the intercepts accounts for the difference in the values of output and capital per man.

[25]This was pointed out by Pasinetti (1969: 523), who concluded: "This in fact seems to be one of the most important results emerging from the reswitching of techniques discussion. It seems to reveal capital theory as a field unsuitable to the application of calculus and infinitesimal analysis, and thus of marginal analysis."

Conclusion

A wage-profit curve is a relationship between the wage rates and profit rates that are technically feasible with a single technique. A wage-profit frontier is an envelope of wage-profit curves for all techniques. A profitability curve is a relationship between output per man and value of capital per man for all techniques at a given profit rate (or alternatively, at a given wage rate). What meaning is to be attached to these relationships?

In a particular steady state the technique in use is chosen so as to be appropriate to the particular wage rate (or profit rate) which is ruling on that path. All other wage rates (or profit rates) would be irrelevant. One meaning it is possible to give to the profitability curve is as a representation of the alternatives that firms in a capitalist economy would face in choosing the concrete forms in which to embody an investment of finance that is being planned. It may be noted that the problem is formulated in terms of differences in profitability calculated for the entire matrix of the production system. It must therefore be conceived to apply *at the level of the economy as a whole*. Furthermore, each type of capital good is specific to a particular technique and cannot be transferred to another. The problem must therefore be conceived to refer to a comparison of investment projects in advance of the actual investment. Once the finance to be invested is committed to a particular form, there is no possibility of shifting to another, or of "substituting" one technique for another, without going through a process of change. This point serves to remind us, once more, that this whole analysis is devoid of any conception of the *process* of change.

There is also an obvious question here of what the form of the problem of technical choice is and the analysis of it *at the level of the individual firm*. For the present analysis, it is assumed that all firms face the same set of investment opportunities and that the capital of the firm, as a sum of exchange value, is free to move from one line of production to another. (This is the meaning of the assumption of competition, and this condition ensures a uniform rate of profits in equilibrium.) But the distribution of firms across different lines of production and their scale of operation in each line are matters that are left open. Similarly, when two techniques coexist, the particular combination of techniques adopted and their pattern of allocation among different firms are indeterminate. What is missing here is a theory appropriate to analysis of the individual firm in the context of accumulation and technical change.

So far as the comparative analysis of different stationary states with different techniques of production is concerned, it could be said that "the comparison of different economies with the same technical possibilities and different rates of profit is an exercise in pure economic logic, without application to reality" (Robinson 1962a: 33). The exercise is nevertheless enlightening. It warns us to be wary of assumptions concerning these relations that are of seeming generality when they are in fact based on very restrictive conditions and when those conditions have no particular theoretical justification. The important conclusion we reach is that there is, in general, no such thing as a hierarchy of techniques of production ranked in terms of their "capital intensity" such that higher degrees of capital intensity are associated with lower rates of profit. In general, also, there exists no unique ordering of technical methods of production in relation to the rate of profit. These conclusions are reached by considering a simple model of production with one consumption good and one capital good. They hold *a fortiori* in more complex models of production with many capital goods. What is the possible significance of these conclusions and the analysis underlying them? This problem can be resolved only when we come to consider the specific theory—namely, the neoclassical theory of distribution and growth—which assigns a particular role to the relations between technology and distribution that are discussed here.

In the next chapter we extend this analysis to deal with situations in which the economy is expanding over time. In addition to the problems of growth which then arise, we shall be able to reexamine the propositions developed in this chapter in a broader context.

Chapter Six

Accumulation with Differences in Technique

Introduction

We seek now to extend the analysis developed in the previous chapter to consider problems of growth in the context of many alternative techniques of production. In particular, we consider once more the question of existence of a golden age and examine the properties of steady-state paths, comparing one with another. We also develop the meaning in this context of the neoclassical "one-commodity model" and evaluate its analytical significance for a theory of distribution.

A Golden Age Once More

In the previous chapter it was shown that there are as many wage-profit curves as the number of alternative techniques of production in a given book of blueprints. The outer envelope of these curves constitutes the wage-profit frontier, which defines the equilibrium wage-profit configurations that are consistent with the given technology. With a finite number of alternative techniques, the frontier is made up of segments of the contributing curves and therefore has corners. With an infinite number of techniques, the frontier may become a smooth curve tangent to one wage-profit curve at each point. In general, there may be reswitching of techniques such that a single curve contributes more than one segment (or point) to the frontier.

Consider now the implications for the warranted growth rate g. From Chapter Four, the equation for g when there is a single technique is

$$g = \frac{(s_r - s_w)\mu r + s_w R \xi(r)}{\mu(1 - s_w) + s_w \xi(r)}$$

Thus, for any given technique, say α, and given saving proportions, we have a relation between the growth rate and the profit rate, or a growth-profit curve. Its shape depends on the technical coefficients of production and on the saving proportions. A similar relation would hold for techniques $\beta, \gamma \ldots$, given the magnitude of their respective technical coefficients and the relevant saving proportions. The whole spectrum of techniques thus generates a set of different growth-profit curves, one such curve for each technique. The range of possible growth rates now consists of those rates corresponding to the level(s) of r at which each technique is selected. The overall growth-profit configuration which emerges depends on the pattern of saving and on the nature of the underlying technology.

Figure 6.1 illustrates a number of possible features. Panel (*a*) represents the wage-profit curves of the available techniques. Panel (*b*) gives the corresponding growth-profit curves for the case of saving behavior represented by a uniform saving proportion, $s_w = s_r = s$. Each technique contributes a segment to the range of possible growth rates corresponding to the segment of its wage-profit curve included in the wage-profit frontier. It is evident that the same growth rate may be associated with more than one profit rate, each corresponding to a different technique. When there is reswitching of techniques, as with technique α, two discrete ranges of profit rates and corresponding growth rates are associated with the same technique. At a switch point, where two different techniques coexist at the same profit rate, different growth rates are associated with the two techniques at the same saving rate. Any growth rate between these two could prevail, depending on the particular combination of the two techniques that is adopted. With a technique such as γ, represented by a linear wage-profit curve, there is a single growth rate associated with the range of profit rates at which that technique would be selected.

Similar features could be derived for the case of saving behavior represented by $s_r > s_w > 0$. Considerable simplification is achieved if it is assumed that $s_r > 0$ and $s_w = 0$, as in panel (*c*) of Figure 6.1. The growth-profit relation now becomes independent of the technology, being represented by a continuous straight line from the origin up to the maximum profit rate for that technology. Every possible growth rate is associated with a unique rate of profit and, except at a switch point, with a single technique. At a switch point, the two coexisting techniques have the same growth rate. As in the case of panel (*b*), when there is reswitching, two discrete ranges of profit rates and growth rates are compatible with

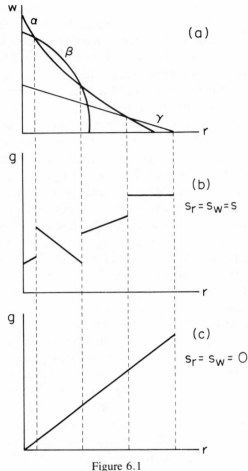

Figure 6.1

the same technique. We find in this case, however, that there is a range
of possible growth rates associated with technique γ represented by a
linear wage-profit curve.

From this analysis it follows that, when more than one technique is
available, there exists more than one possible growth rate (or a range of
possible growth rates) corresponding to the available techniques, to the
given saving proportions, and to the profit rates at which those techniques are eligible. Even if, for any one technique, the technical conditions
and saving proportions are such that only one warranted rate of growth

exists, still there may be other possible growth rates corresponding to other techniques at the profit rates which make those techniques eligible. Among these possible growth rates there may exist one such as to satisfy the condition of a golden age or there may exist none at all. Thus, there is still no guarantee that a golden age exists.

What can we now say of Harrod's problem concerning the existence of a singular value of the warranted rate of growth? On the basis of this analysis we can isolate the following set of conditions, which, taken together, are sufficient for the existence of a singular value of the warranted growth rate: (1) there exists a single technique of production, (2) that technique is such that the conditions of production of both commodities are the same (the wage-profit curve is linear), and (3) there is a uniform saving proportion for all categories of income. These conditions are, of course, *only* sufficient and *not* necessary.

Another condition that would give rise to Harrod's problem of a single value of g is if the rate of profit (or the wage rate) were taken as fixed at a particular level. In that case, there would be just one relevant growth rate (except at a switch point) regardless of the number of available techniques and the pattern of saving.

Clearly, in both of these cases what is missing is an explanation of what determines the level of the profit rate (or wage rate). In the first case the profit rate is simply left suspended between zero and the maximum feasible level. In the second case, it is taken as somehow fixed.

Comparison of Steady States

We proceed next to a comparative analysis of different growth equilibria within the possible range. Such an analysis was carried out in Chapter 4 for the case of a single technique. When there are a finite number of techniques, the same analysis holds for each technique within the range of profit rates corresponding to the segment of its wage-profit curve included in the frontier. The additional feature that now concerns us relates to the comparison of equilibrium positions between which the technique of production is different.

Given, say, the growth rate or profit rate, we can identify the entire configuration of equilibrium relations appropriate to a particular growth equilibrium. At a different growth rate or profit rate, corresponding to a different growth equilibrium, either the same or a different technique would be in use. The associated equilibrium quantities would be different. These can be calculated and the two situations compared. When the technique of production is the same, the differences between equilibria can be separated into a price effect and a composition effect, as shown in Chapter 4. When the technique of production is different, the problem becomes more complicated.

Call the difference in technique associated with a difference in the profit rate between two equilibria a *substitution effect*. There is no implication here of a process of change from one equilibrium to another. Different equilibria are to be regarded as if they were different planets with no connection between them. The presence of the substitution effect means that the composition and price effects are no longer as sharply distinguishable as in the single-technique case. This is because the capital good may be different when the technique of production is different. No quantitative expression in technical units of the capital good can then be given to the difference in the physical stock of each capital good associated with each equilibrium.[1] Neither can any meaningful comparison be made of the price of each capital good when they are different goods.[2] Instead, comparison could be made of the exchange value of capital and output expressed in terms of the numeraire commodity common to the different techniques. This difference would, however, incorporate all three effects. Here, again, it would be possible to express the underlying differences uniquely and unambiguously in terms of labor value.

In comparing the various equilibria that are possible within the given conditions of technology and saving behavior, the same technique might be found in two different ranges of the profit rate. This reflects the existence of reswitching or non-uniqueness in the ordering of techniques. The exchange values of capital and net output per man for that technique in one range of the profit rate may be uniformly higher or lower than in the other range. These values may even be the same.[3] The result depends on the particular pattern of price and composition effects for that tech-

---

[1] This is the particular form of the problem in a simple production model with one capital good for each technique. But the problem itself is obviously a general one, as appears from considering it in the context of a production system with many different capital goods for each technique.

[2] This particular limitation would not arise in a production system where each technique has many capital goods, for different techniques are then likely to have one or more capital goods in common.

[3] For example, take the case of a technique with a straight-line wage-profit curve that is tangent to the frontier over two discrete segments. For any two points, each on a different segment, both price and composition effects are zero so that the exchange value of capital is the same.

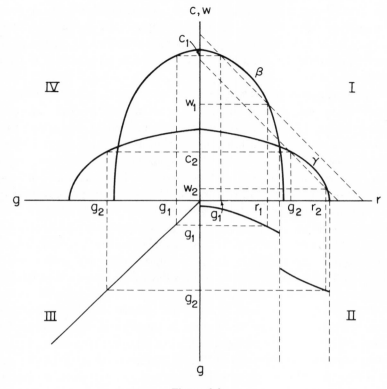

Figure 6.2

nique. There is, in this sense, no necessary inverse relation or one-to-one correspondence between "capital intensity" and the rate of profit.

But it is equally clear that no such correspondence may exist even in the absence of reswitching. An example of this is shown in Figure 6.2, using a construction discussed on pp. 105–6. At r_1 and r_2 we have

$$k^\beta = \frac{c_1 - w_1}{r_1 - g_1}, \qquad k^\gamma = \frac{c_2 - w_2}{r_2 - g_2}$$

respectively. It follows, by construction, that $k^\beta = k^\gamma$. We have here a recurrence of the same value of capital per man associated with two different techniques at two different levels of the profit rate. Thus, in this case, the relation between quantity of capital, measured in terms of prices, and the rate of profit is not unique. It is easy to construct similar cases under different conditions. It is also easy to show that, as between a higher and a lower level of the profit rate, each associated with a different technique, the value of capital for the technique in use at the lower profit rate may be higher or lower than that for the technique in use at the higher profit rate. This too can be shown under a variety of different conditions.

Without adequate theoretical justification, there can be no meaningful restriction on the range of admissible conditions. Therefore such cases as are pointed out here cannot simply be ruled out of existence. All of them have a basic implication: any presumption that a unique inverse relation exists in general between the quantity of capital, measured in terms of prices, and the rate of profit is untenable. The substantive meaning of this formal argument will be considered when we come to discuss the neoclassical theory of growth and distribution.

Finally, consider the case of a switch point where two techniques may coexist. The associated equilibrium magnitudes can be identified for each technique separately, using the common profit and wage rates. It will be found that the difference in the value of output per man between them is just sufficient to yield profit at the given rate on the difference in the value of capital per man, or, in other words, that the ratio of profitability between the two techniques is equal to the profit rate. This finding, as we saw before, is a necessary implication of the condition that the two techniques are equally profitable. If the saving rates are the same for the two techniques, the growth rate associated with each is different. The reason for this is straightforward. Since the wage rate is the same, the technique with the higher net output per man has a higher level of profit per man. The value of capital per man must be correspondingly higher so as to keep the rate of profit the same. This leaves unaltered the rate of growth financed by saving out of profits at the same saving rate. With saving out of wages the same and the value of capital per man higher, the rate of growth financed by saving out of wages is lower. It follows that the overall rate of growth of capital must be lower for this technique. For the growth rate to be the same, the saving rates associated with the two techniques must be different. If the economy is in a stationary state, consumption out of profits is greater with the technique that has the higher net output per man.

The Case of Infinite Techniques

Beyond what has been said so far, there is little that can be added regarding the properties of steady-state equilibria. The main conclusions we have reached continue to hold regardless of the number of available techniques and the number and types of commodities characterizing each technique. Nevertheless, we go on in this section to examine the limiting case of an infinite number of techniques, if only for the sake of logical completeness. This exercise also serves the purpose of establishing the point of contact between the preceding framework of analysis and that of a "neoclassical model" based upon the assumption of one produced commodity and an infinite number of techniques. This aspect of the matter will be taken up in the next section.

We can approach the case of an infinite number of techniques by conceptually arranging the techniques in the order in which they become eligible as r varies and by considering the coefficients of the techniques so arranged as functions of r. For this purpose we need only the coefficients a_{11}, a_{02}, μ, and the intercepts (W,R) of the corresponding wage-profit curves. Thus we write

(6.1) $\qquad a_{11} = a_{11}(r), \quad a_{02} = a_{02}(r), \quad \mu = \mu(r), \quad W = W(r), \quad R = R(r)$

There is no a priori reason to expect these functions to have any particular form. Reswitching of techniques implies that the ordering is not unique. Particular restrictions can be placed on the technology so as to ensure a unique ordering. These must of necessity be arbitrary. One such condition that is sufficient but not necessary is that, for each successive technique represented on the frontier, W should fall and R rise as r rises.[4] Assuming $W(r)$ and $R(r)$ to be differentiable, this says that

(6.2) $\qquad\qquad \dfrac{dW}{dr} < 0, \dfrac{dR}{dr} > 0 \text{ for all } r$

Even with this restriction, there is no logical necessity for the coefficients a_{11}, a_{02}, and μ to vary in any particular way with r.[5] The restriction is satisfied in the special case when μ is the same *for all techniques*.

[4] Cf. Hicks 1965: 154 and Bruno et al. 1966: 534. A related condition has been worked out by Brown (1969) in terms of variations in the composite coefficient $a_{12}a_{01}$ representing the indirect labor requirements per unit of consumption-good output.

[5] If it were to be assumed that δ is the same for all techniques, $dR/dr > 0$ implies $da_{11}/dr < 0$, so that the quantity of physical capital per unit of output in production of the capital good varies inversely with the profit rate. But no definite implication can be drawn for variation of a_{02} and μ. In the special case of $\delta = 0$ (the capital good lasts forever), $dW/dr < 0$ implies $da_{02}/dr > 0$, so that output per unit of labor in production of the consumption good varies inversely with the profit rate. Needless to say, these conditions tell us nothing about the quantity of aggregate capital per man or the quantity of aggregate output per man.

The equation of the envelope constituting the frontier can be found from the functions in (6.1) and from the equation for the wage-profit curve. Write this as

(6.3)
$$w = \varphi[a_{02}(r), a_{11}(r), R(r), \mu(r), r]$$

The frontier represented by (6.3) is negatively sloped and may have any curvature. Thus, where differentiable,

(6.4)
$$\frac{d\varphi}{dr} < 0, \frac{d^2\varphi}{dr} \gtrless 0 \text{ for all } r$$

Similarly, substitute the functions of (6.1) into the growth-profit relation and into the equation for the value of capital per man.[6] The resulting relations may be written as

(6.5)
$$g = g[s_r, s_w, a_{11}(r), R(r), \mu(r), r]$$

(6.6)
$$k = k[a_{02}(r), a_{11}(r), R(r), \mu(r), g(.), r]$$

The assumption of an infinite number of techniques does not necessarily imply that k and y become differentiable functions of r. However, for ease of exposition, it will be convenient to make the arbitrary assumption that these functions are continuously differentiable with respect to r. We can therefore characterize the difference between one equilibrium and another by taking the total derivatives as follows:[7]

(6.7)
$$\frac{dg}{dr} = \left[\frac{\partial g}{\partial a_{11}} \cdot \frac{da_{11}}{dr} + \frac{\partial g}{\partial \mu} \cdot \frac{d\mu}{dr} + \frac{\partial g}{\partial R} \cdot \frac{dR}{dr} \right] + \frac{\partial g}{\partial r}$$

(6.8)
$$\frac{dk}{dr} = \left[\frac{\partial k}{\partial a_{02}} \cdot \frac{da_{02}}{dr} + \frac{\partial k}{\partial a_{11}} \cdot \frac{da_{11}}{dr} + \frac{\partial k}{\partial \mu} \cdot \frac{d\mu}{dr} + \frac{\partial k}{\partial R} \cdot \frac{dR}{dr} \right]$$
$$+ \frac{\partial k}{\partial g} \cdot \frac{dg}{dr} + \frac{\partial k}{\partial r}$$

(6.9)
$$\frac{dy}{dk} = \left(\frac{d\varphi}{dr} + k \right) \frac{dr}{dk} + r$$

Various components of the difference between equilibria appear from these relationships. Take the value of capital per man, k. With the tech-

---

[6] See equations (4.4), (4.14), (4.15), and (4.20).
[7] It is assumed here, for simplicity, that different equilibria have the same savings proportions.

nique held constant, the last two terms on the right-hand side of (6.8) represent respectively the composition effect and price effect. When the technique of production is different, a substitution effect also exists. One might think of this as being represented by the bracketed terms in (6.7) and (6.8).[8]

Given the respective magnitudes for each equilibrium, the ratio (dy/dk) of the difference in value of net output per man to the difference in value of capital per man can be expressed in terms of the various components identified by equation (6.9).[9] An apparent similarity may be observed between this ratio and that called above the ratio of profitability. Nevertheless, the two should be clearly distinguished. The ratio of profitability is computed for different techniques evaluated *at the same rate of profit*, reference being made either to a switch point between two techniques (in which case the ratio is equal to the profit rate) or to a profitability curve representing all the available techniques. It provides a way of representing the choice of technique through comparison of its magnitude with the given rate of profit. In the case of the ratio dy/dk, not only is the technique different, but the rate of profit is also different in the two situations compared. Moreover, this ratio is in general not equal to the profit rate. For what purpose can this ratio be used? The ratio in equation (6.9) has meaning only as a comparison of different growth equilibria or steady states. It can be used, so to speak, for accounting purposes, that is, to measure the difference between equilibria. We may therefore call it the *accounting ratio*.

No general rule can be laid down concerning the sign and magnitude of these relations and therefore the direction of the overall difference between equilibria. The reason for this is obvious enough; it is impossible to obtain a unique form of the functions (6.1) that would be valid for all conceivable technical conditions. This remains so even when the sufficiency conditions (6.2) for absence of reswitching are assumed to hold.

---

[8] When the capital good differs from one technique to another, it makes no sense to compare prices. It is therefore not economically meaningful to draw a strict separation between the difference in capital per man due to the difference in prices (the price effect) and that due to the technical difference in the capital good (the substitution effect).

[9] A similar formula was used by Bhaduri (1966), who called it "the marginal product of capital." But, as we shall see, it can be regarded as the marginal product of capital, signifying thereby a purely technical relation, only in a very special case. In the finite-techniques case, this ratio is one of finite differences. It is expressed in terms of infinitesimal differences in the present case because of the assumption of differentiability in the underlying relationships.

Particular results can be obtained under particular conditions of saving and/or technology. In the next section we examine some special cases and evaluate their analytical significance.

A "One-Commodity Model"

Consider now two hypothetical cases distinguished by particular assumptions concerning, in the one case, the pattern of saving, in the other, the technical conditions of production.

Case 1: $s_w = 0$; $1 \geqq s_r > 0$. In this case the growth-profit relation is independent of the technology. In particular, $g = s_r r$ for all r.[10] One technique may be associated with more than one profit rate because of reswitching. The variation of value of capital and net output in relation to the profit rate may take any form. It depends on the exact pattern of price, composition, and substitution effects.

If we take the special case of $s_r = 1$, this implies that $g = r$.[11] By setting $g = r$ in the equation for the value of capital per man, we then get

$$(6.10) \qquad k = \frac{\mu a_{11}/a_{02}}{\xi(r)^2} = -\frac{dw}{dr}$$

which says that the value of capital is equal to the slope of the wage-profit curve corresponding to the technique in use at a given level of r. The same condition holds for every level of r, given the associated technique and its wage-profit curve. Since the wage-profit frontier is tangent to the wage-profit curve at every such point, their slopes are identical. It follows that, for all r,

$$(6.11) \qquad k = -\frac{d\varphi}{dr}$$

Multiplying (6.11) by r/w leads to

$$(6.12) \qquad \frac{rk}{w} = \frac{d\varphi}{dr} \cdot \frac{r}{\varphi}$$

which defines the ratio of total profits to wages, or the distribution of net product, in terms of the elasticity of the wage-profit frontier. We also

---

[10] Under the particular conditions of the Pasinetti Theorem (to be considered in the next chapter), a similar relation holds without the special assumption that $s_w = 0$.

[11] Some implications of this case were pointed out by Bhaduri (1966: 288) and Spaventa (1970: 137).

have from (6.11) and (6.4)

$$(6.13) \qquad \frac{dk}{dr} = -\frac{d^2\varphi}{dr^2} \gtreqless 0$$

which says that the value of capital may be increasing or decreasing in r depending on the curvature of the wage-profit frontier. Finally, by substituting (6.11) into (6.9) we get, for all r,

$$(6.14) \qquad \frac{dy}{dk} = r$$

so that the accounting ratio is in this case equal to the rate of profit.

Case 2: $\mu(r) = 1$ for all r. Here the growth-profit relation becomes, for all r,

$$g = (s_r - s_w)r + s_w R(r) \text{ if } 0 < s_w < s_r$$

or

$$g = sR(r) \text{ if } s_w = s_r = s$$

In either case of saving behavior, this relation is dependent on the technology through the function $R(r)$, which, in this case, represents the output-capital ratio for the economy as a whole. Though in general nothing can be said about the form of $R(r)$, under the special conditions of this case we know that techniques can be uniquely ordered so that $dR/dr > 0$ for all r. It follows that g is a continuous, monotone-increasing function of r. Thus there exists a unique relation between the growth rate, rate of profit, and technique of production over the entire range of available techniques.

By setting $\mu = 1$, the value of capital per man at a given rate of profit becomes $k = a_{11}/a_{02} = -dw/dr$. As in Case 1, it is defined by the technical coefficients representing the slope of the wage-profit curve corresponding to the technique in use. The results (6.11), (6.12), and (6.14) therefore hold also in this case. A special feature of this case is that the wage-profit curves of all techniques are straight lines. This implies that $k = -dw/dr = W/R$. Since the condition (6.2) for unique ordering of techniques is fulfilled in this case, it follows that the value of capital per man is a monotone-decreasing function of the profit rate.

The characteristics of Case 2 can be readily explained. When $\mu = 1$, there is no difference in the technical conditions of production of the two goods. Being technically the same, they can be regarded as one and the same good (except for units of measurement). Therefore their relative price is equal to unity (by appropriate choice of units) and is independent of the profit rate. This means that the price effect disappears. Furthermore, any composition of output can be produced with the same physical stock of the capital good. Thus the composition effect also disappears. There remains only a substitution effect, which takes a special form. In particular, all the available techniques can be ranked according to the increasing quantities of the consumption good required (as capital good) in production and according to the increasing quantity of net output of the consumption good produced. This ranking is unique and corresponds to the ordering of the techniques in relation to the profit rate. The quantity of capital per man, being equivalent here to a physical quantity of the consumption good, also follows the same ordering.

All of this can be understood by reference to the concept of a profitability curve. In general, as we saw in Chapter 5, there exists one profitability curve describing the relation between value of capital and value of output for all of the (noninferior) techniques at one rate of profit. There is a different curve for different rates of profit. For reasons of economic rationality, the curve is positively sloped and characterized by diminishing ratios of profitability between techniques, going from left to right. It can be used to represent the choice of technique at an appropriate equilibrium profit rate. The special feature of Case 2 is that, with the particular technology assumed, there exists one and only one profitability curve for all techniques at all profit rates. Owing to the assumption of an infinite number of techniques, corners are ruled out. At any level of the rate of profit there is a single point on the curve corresponding to the technique that is most profitable. Any difference in the rate of profit, no matter how small, is associated with a different technique represented by a different point on the same curve. The curve itself becomes a relation between homogeneous physical quantities. Room is thereby created for viewing it as if it were a purely technical relation between physical quantities of input and output, or a "production function" for the whole economy (producing a single commodity).

Thus, a relation that is constructed to represent the choice of technique at a given profit rate corresponding to a particular growth equilibrium comes to represent all the equilibria that are possible within a particular technology at different rates of profit and to represent also a description of the technology itself. Case 2 corresponds to what has come to be called the "neoclassical one-commodity model." It also constitutes the basis for Samuelson's concept of a "surrogate production function," which will be discussed in Chapter 9.

The result that the accounting ratio (referring to two neighboring equilibria) equals the rate of profit is common to both Cases 1 and 2 and is similar to the result we found at a switch point in the finite-techniques case. In Case 2, however, this result is susceptible of a further interpretation. Note, in particular, that in this case the difference in output per man and capital per man between two neighboring techniques consists entirely of a difference in their technical coefficients of production (a pure substitution effect). The ratio of these differences (that is, the accounting ratio) is thus a technical datum independent of the rate of profit.[12] Since it is also equal to the rate of profit, it would appear, in comparing the two economies, *as if* a rate of profit existed for purely technological reasons. Furthermore, since the profit share is equal to the elasticity of the wage-profit frontier, the distribution of income would appear to be uniquely related to the technology. These appearances would exist no matter what other explanation for the rate of profit and distribution of income might be offered by a theory relevant to the situations being compared. The technological reasons might even be made themselves to constitute such a theory. The point is, however, that those reasons and any such theory would have no applicability outside the framework of the special assumptions of this case and would therefore be, in general, of little or no interest whatsoever.

The fact that the same result (that the accounting ratio equals the rate of profit) is found in Case 1 reflects the peculiar circumstances of saving behavior in that case and, beyond that, has none of the significance attached to Case 2. In particular, it does not mean that a higher value of capital is necessarily associated with a lower rate of profit. Neither is the accounting ratio susceptible of being interpreted as a technical datum which explains the rate of profit.

The common feature of both of these cases is that the quantity of

---

[12] From this the possibility also arises of regarding the accounting ratio as if it were the "marginal product" of the capital good itself. For one equilibrium differs from another only by the addition of an infinitesimal quantity of the same capital good and by an associated increment in output. But when the capital good is different, and in the general case of many capital goods, no such interpretation is possible. For then the difference in capital per man and output per man has to be expressed as a magnitude of exchange value involving prices and the rate of profit.

capital is uniquely defined in relation to the technology.[13] The results of each case can be seen to follow directly from this condition. In the one case this condition is an incidental feature of a particular pattern of saving. In the other it is an incidental feature of a particular type of technology. Because, in Case 1, nothing is implied concerning the nature of technology, no general statement can be made about the form of the relation between capital per man and the rate of profit. Because, in Case 2, a particular type of technology is assumed, there are particular implications for the way in which the quantity of capital varies: it varies inversely with the profit rate.

There is no reason for assuming one or the other case as more likely to be found in reality than other conceivable possibilities. Indeed, in the present context, the conditions of the problem are sufficiently remote from reality to make any such statement meaningless. However, at the present level of abstraction, what we can see is that particular assumptions concerning the technology are sufficient to give an inverse relation between value of capital and rate of profit. The restrictive nature of such assumptions and of the relation derived from them is evident from the fact that that relation no longer holds as soon as some slight change is made in those assumptions. Therefore, no theory based upon such foundations can lay claim to validity or generality or even to any significance as a "parable" or illustration of what exists in reality.

Conclusion

This discussion almost completes the analysis of the purely formal problem regarding the properties of steady-state equilibria. By whatever means the differences between equilibria are expressed and however simple or complicated the underlying assumptions, the question still remains: what accounts for the particular rate of profit and distribution of net product which prevail in a capitalist economy? And what accounts for the economy's particular rate of growth? For an answer, comparisons of equilibria are not enough. This is the role of a theory. We are still far from considering any such theory and we must try to get to that. But before doing so a number of other formal problems must be got out of the way. This is done in the next chapter.

---

[13] Note that, in either case, this feature is in no way related to the assumption of an infinite number of techniques. It could as well be found in a system with only one technique. See Chapter 4, p. 115.

Chapter Seven

Saving, Income Distribution, and Social Class

Introduction

   This chapter is concerned primarily with the implications of alternative assumptions concerning saving behavior for the properties of steady-state equilibria. We go into the possible meaning of this analysis regarding the role of social class in a theory of growth and distribution. We consider also the meaning and significance of certain propositions regarding the relation between accumulation, consumption, and profits in steady states. It is evident from this analysis that there is no basis in production for the presumption of a necessary relation between "thrift" or "abstinence" and the rate of profit.

Saving Behavior in a Golden Age

   Two polar types of conditions concerning saving behavior have been considered in our analysis so far. In one case, saving behavior is represented by different saving proportions for profit and wage income: $1 \geqq s_r > s_w \geqq 0$. In the other, saving behavior is represented by a saving proportion that is uniform for all incomes: $s_r = s_w = s$. Let us consider, in the context of a golden-age equilibrium, the implications of these alternatives for the exact form of the growth-profit relation and the structure of the equilibrium solution.

   From the condition of saving-investment equality and the golden-age condition we get directly

(7.1) $$n = g = (s_r - s_w)r + s_w \frac{y}{k} \text{ if } s_r > s_w > 0$$

or

(7.2) $$n = g = s\frac{y}{k} \text{ if } s_r = s_w = s$$

Both the rate of profit and a capital-income rate (k/y) corresponding to that rate of profit are determined to satisfy equation (7.1) at the given rate of accumulation (n). In this sense, the rate of profit and capital-income ratio are obtained by simultaneous solution of the system. Depending on the technology, there may be one or many combinations of profit rate and capital-income ratio, or none at all, which yield a solution. Equation (7.2), on the other hand, determines a unique capital-income ratio appropriate to the given rate of accumulation and the uniform saving proportion. The rate of profit has to be consistent with that capital-income ratio and with the existing technology. There may be many such profit rates, just one, or none at all, depending on the technology.

The difference in the structure of the solutions is clearly related to the difference in saving behavior. Equation (7.2) says simply that, with a uniform saving proportion for all categories of income, there is one ratio of income to the value of capital that makes saving equal investment at the given rate of growth of capital. However, when there is a higher saving proportion for profit income than for wage income, saving from all income exceeds what would be saved at the saving proportion for wage income only. This leads to a different condition for equilibrium of saving and investment. In particular, the rate of profit must be such that the excess of saving from profits just matches the difference between investment and the amount that would be saved out of all income at the saving proportion for wage income. Thus, in this case, the rate of profit and the capital-income ratio have to be mutually consistent. This is what equation (7.1) expresses.

Matters are a bit different in the special case of saving behavior represented by the condition $s_w = 0$, $s_r \leq 1$. For, in that case, the system dichotomizes, which is to say that the growth-profit relation is independent of the technology. The profit rate is then determined uniquely by the rate of accumulation and the proportion of saving out of profits (s_r). Nevertheless, the distribution of income is still dependent on the technical conditions of production by way of the capital-income ratio.[1] This case is also understandable. Since there is only one saving rate, one that is associated with profit income, there can be only one profit rate, one that makes saving out of profits equal investment.

---

[1] Similarly, Kahn (1959: 147) concludes: "Even . . . when the rate of growth can be isolated as an independent factor . . . it is only the rate of profit which can be imputed solely to it and to the savings coefficients. If we are interested in how wages and the distribution of income are determined, the technical conditions have to be brought in."

Technology enters this general picture in a rather ambiguous fashion. When there is a uniform saving proportion for all categories of income, the capital-income ratio is independent of the technology but the rate of profit has to be consistent with this ratio and with the technology. When there is a different saving proportion for different categories of income, the rate of profit and capital-income ratio are jointly determined so as to be consistent with saving behavior and with technology. The rate of profit is independent of technology only when it is assumed that the Classical saving function holds.

Differences of Income and Class

The assumption that there is a uniform rate of saving ignores all possible differences in saving behavior as between, say, different sectors of the economy or between different categories of income. By contrast, the assumption that there are different saving proportions for profit and wage income makes the aggregate savings in the economy dependent on the distribution of income between wages and profits. This assumption also receives empirical support from the observed high rates of saving from corporate profits.[2]

Let us consider further the meaning of the latter assumption. In particular, it is assumed that a given proportion of profits is saved which is greater than the proportion of wages saved. One meaning that has been given to this assumption is that it involves an underlying conception of firms in capitalist economies as autonomous institutions with a certain degree of control over the disposal of profits.[3] Of crucial significance in this connection is the profit-retention rate, or its inverse, the pay-out rate.[4] The firms, on this view, retain a certain proportion of profits to finance investment and distribute the rest. Whatever the proportion of distributed profits and wages saved by individuals, say, s_r^* and s_w, we get for total saving and investment

$$(7.3) \qquad I = [\lambda + s_r^*(1 - \lambda)]rK + s_w wL$$

[2] See, for instance, Burmeister and Taubman 1969: 87.

[3] See Kaldor 1966; Robinson 1956: 405–6. This conception has been presented more explicitly by Kregel (1971, 1973).

[4] Under monopolistic conditions, what is important also is the size of the markup above costs, which governs the total of available profits and hence the amount of saving from profits at a given retention rate. This connection between the profit margin and the savings that go to finance investment is central to the analysis developed by Kalecki (1971b) and Steindl (1952). For a further development of some aspects of this relation see Eichner 1976.

where I is net investment and λ is the retention ratio. The saving proportion for total profits is thus $s_r = \lambda + s_r^*(1 - \lambda)$. It is then the case that $s_r > s_w$, provided only that

$$\lambda > \frac{s_w - s_r^*}{1 - s_r^*}$$

A different approach to specification of the underlying conditions of saving behavior has been suggested by Pasinetti [1962]. This is based on the assumption that there are two different *classes* with different saving proportions. One class consists of individuals whose income and therefore saving are derived solely from their ownership of capital and hence from profits. These are the "pure" capitalists. The other is the class of workers who derive income from labor services and from the profits they obtain by saving and lending to the capitalists.[5]

There is a real difference between these two approaches. The second is based on the assumption of an identifiable class of savers and property owners distinguished by the fact that they derive income solely from their ownership of capital and occupy a position in the process of production and accumulation different from that of workers.[6] In the first formulation no role is assigned to any such class. Indeed, the conditions of ownership are left completely unspecified.[7] What matters is control over the disposal of profits by the managers of the corporations. In this regard Kaldor (1966: 310) asserts: "It is the enterprise, not the particular body of individuals owning it at any one time, which finds it necessary . . . to plough back a proportion of the profits earned as a kind of 'prior charge' on earnings." On the other hand, Pasinetti's assumed conditions are consistent with the view of Kalecki (1971b: 107) that "a joint-stock company is not a 'brotherhood of shareholders' but is managed by a controlling

---

[5] Since, in this formulation, all workers are assumed to be also *rentiers*, they might be more correctly called *worker-rentiers*. Cf. Robinson 1970b. It would be possible to introduce a subcategory of "pure" workers who do not save and hence own no capital without making any difference to the results. The essential distinction between workers (or worker-rentiers) and capitalists remains that, apart from their different saving propensities, the former obtain income from labor services (as well as ownership of some capital) whereas the latter obtain income exclusively from ownership of capital.

[6] See Pasinetti 1962: 274–75. Kregel (1973, ch. 11) seeks to base the distinction not so much on considerations of class position in this sense as on a difference between the forms of income as such, that is, between "quasi-contractual incomes" (wages, fixed interest, rent) and "residual incomes" (corporate profits).

[7] Pasinetti (1962: 270) pointed to this omission as a "logical slip", but it is evident that specification of those conditions is a matter of substance that makes considerable difference for the analysis itself.

group of big shareholders while the rest of the shareholders do not differ from holders of bonds with a flexible rate of interest." The difference between the two formulations can thus be seen to relate to quite different conceptions of the structure and operation of the firm with regard to its conditions of ownership and control. What is at issue is the precise character of those conditions and their significance for the process of capital accumulation as it occurs within and among firms.[8]

The two formulations also have quite different implications for analysis of the steady-state properties of the economy. Consider the implications of introducing the two different classes of savers. To the extent that workers save, they must come to own some capital and receive profits on the amount of capital they own. Distinguishing the amount of capital owned by workers and by capitalists, K_w and K_c, respectively, we have for the total value of capital: $K = K_c + K_w$, and for total income: $Y = wL + r(K_c + K_w)$, where it is assumed that the rate of profit on invested capital is the same for each class.[9]

Now, let workers save a given proportion, s_w, of their income regardless of its source and capitalists a proportion, s_c, of theirs. Then the increment of capital owned by each class is

$$(7.4) \qquad I_c = s_c r K_c$$

$$(7.5) \qquad I_w = s_w(Y - rK_c)$$

For steady-state growth it is required that the capital owned by each class grow at the same rate, which is the overall growth rate $g = n$. Thus

$$(7.6) \qquad \frac{I_c}{K_c} = \frac{I_w}{K_w} = \frac{I}{K} = n$$

Substituting into (7.6) from (7.4) and (7.5) and solving leads to

$$(7.7) \qquad s_c r = n$$

---

[8] The thesis of a "managerial revolution" in contemporary capitalism, involving emergence of a managerial group distinct and separate from the owners of firms to a controlling position within firms, has been advanced variously by Berle and Means (1932), Burnham (1941), and Galbraith (1967), among others. There is an abundance of available evidence and systematic critique that casts considerable doubt on this thesis. See, for instance, Larner 1970; Burch 1972; Nichols 1969; and Miliband 1969, ch. 2. The arguments for "managerial control" and their implications for a theory of accumulation are developed by Marris (1964) and Williamson (1970).

[9] This assumption can be modified to allow for the possibility that workers receive a lower rate of profit on their capital than do the capitalists. See Laing 1969.

(7.8)
$$\frac{K_c}{K} = \frac{s_c rv - s_w}{(s_c - s_w)rv} \qquad v = \frac{K}{Y}$$

(7.9)
$$\frac{K_w}{K} = \frac{s_w(1 - rv)}{(s_c - s_w)rv}$$

From (7.7) follows the result that the rate of profits is $r = n/s_c$. Given this rate of profit and the capital-income ratio v (hence the overall share of profit rv) and the respective saving proportions, the share of each class in total capital is determined according to (7.8) and (7.9).

Equation (7.7) states that the equilibrium rate of profit is uniquely determined by two parameters: the rate of accumulation (n) and the capitalists' saving proportion (s_c). This is the Pasinetti Theorem.[10] It has a striking implication, which is that the rate of profit is independent of the saving propensity of the workers as well as of the technology. To this extent it gives a result similar to that obtained previously for the Classical saving function, in which there is no saving out of wages. The present result, however, is obtained without making any such special assumption about saving from wages, and it is interesting to consider why this is so.

The answer can be seen in a number of ways. Rewrite (7.8) to get

$$s_w\left(1 - rv\frac{K_c}{K}\right) = s_c rv\left(1 - \frac{K_c}{K}\right)$$

or

$$s_w(Y - rK_c) = s_c rK_w$$

From these equations it is clear that, in golden-age equilibrium, whatever the rate of profit and overall share of profit (rv) may be (as long as rv falls within certain limits to be discussed below), the workers' share of capital $(1 - K_c/K)$ always turns out to be such that workers' saving from their total income $s_w(Y - rK_c)$ exactly matches what the capitalists would save out of workers' profits ($s_c rK_w$) if it accrued to them instead of to the workers. Alternatively, from (7.9) we have

$$s_w\left(\frac{1 - rv}{v}\right) = (s_c - s_w)r\frac{K_w}{K}$$

which says that workers' saving out of wages equals the gap between their saving out of the profits they receive and what the capitalists would save

---

[10] See Pasinetti 1962. For an extended discussion of the meaning of this theorem, see Meade 1963; Pasinetti 1964; Meade and Hahn 1965; Pasinetti 1966a,b; Meade 1966; Samuelson and Modigliani 1966a,b; Robinson 1966; Kaldor 1966; Sato 1966; Stiglitz 1967.

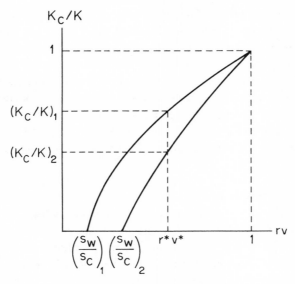

Figure 7.1

out of the same profits. Thus, from the point of view of aggregate saving, what matters is the saving propensity of the capitalists out of *total* profits, that is, their own profits *plus* that of the workers; workers' saving does not matter. It is as if the capitalists themselves were to determine the total value of the workers' saving by reinvesting a portion of the workers' profits and distributing the rest to them for consumption.[11]

It follows from this theorem that, for the purpose of a theory of the rate of profit and distribution of income between profits and wages, no hypothesis is necessary concerning the saving behavior of workers. Whatever that behavior might be, equation (7.7) gives us a unique profit rate and, corresponding to it on the wage-profit frontier, a unique wage rate. Given this profit rate and wage rate together with the growth rate and technology of the system, the value of capital per man and capital-income ratio can then be determined. Hence the share of profits (or wages) in income is determined.

It should be evident from equations (7.8) and (7.9) that what the saving propensity of workers determines is their share in a predetermined total

[11] In this connection Pasinetti notes (1962: 274): "These conclusions ... shed new light on the old Classical idea ... of a relation between the savings of that group of individuals who are in the position to carry on the process of production and the process of capital accumulation."

value of capital and profits. The higher their saving proportion, the higher that share is as between different equilibria (see Figure 7.1). That this is a statement involving only comparisons of equilibria should be emphasized. It says nothing about what would happen if the workers should attempt to change their saving proportion when the economy is already adjusted to the equilibrium appropriate to a particular saving proportion.

Thus, workers' saving behavior does matter. It matters, however, for determination of the share of each class in property and income from property and not for determination of wage and profit shares in the net product.[12]

Saving and Property Relations

The results of the Pasinetti Theorem hold only within certain well-defined limits. These will now be identified. It should then be possible to draw out certain broader implications of the preceding analysis.

For the results to be economically meaningful, it is necessary that the share of capital owned by each class be positive. From (7.8) and (7.9), this can be seen to require three conditions: first, $1 - rv > 0$; second, $s_w < s_c$; third, $s_w < s_c rv = nv$. The first condition states that the share of wages (rv being the share of profits) in income should be positive. This is natural enough since, if there are no wages, then there are no workers. The second says that the saving proportion of workers should be less than that of the capitalists. The third is a condition on the saving proportion of workers in relation to the equilibrium rate of investment (nv) and is worth considering further.

Rewriting (7.8) and substituting from (7.7) we have

$$(s_c - s_w)r\frac{K_c}{K} = n - \frac{s_w}{v}$$

which has a straightforward interpretation. If golden-age investment exceeds what workers would save out of aggregate income ($n - s_w/v > 0$),

---

[12] The analysis can be extended to allow for the existence of many different categories of workers and capitalists, each with a different saving proportion. The result is that the equation for the profit rate is expressed in terms of the saving proportion of the category of capitalists with the highest saving proportion. The rate of profit remains independent of the workers' saving proportion and of the technology. The relative share of each class in total capital is dependent on the maximum saving proportion of the capitalists and a weighted sum of the saving proportions of the different categories of workers. The share of capital owned by each category of workers is dependent on their own saving proportion and on the fraction of workers who belong to that category. See Samuelson and Modigliani 1966a: 283 and Vaughan 1971.

then there exist a share of capital owned by capitalists (K_c/K) and a corresponding share of profits that make the excess of capitalists' saving over that of workers

$$(s_c - s_w)rK_c/K$$

just match the gap between golden-age investment and workers' saving. The higher the saving proportion of workers relative to that of capitalists, the lower is the required share of capitalists in total capital and in profits. There is one value of the workers' saving proportion high enough so that workers' saving alone is sufficient to meet investment requirements. The critical point is where $s_w = s_c rv = nv$. Equilibrium is then inconsistent with a positive share of capitalists in capital and profits. The reason for condition (3) thus lies in the effect of the saving proportion of workers upon the share of workers' saving in total investment, and hence upon the required share of capitalists in capital. In other words, condition (3) is crucial if there is to be any economic rationale for the ownership of property by capitalists. The specific rationale implied by this analysis may be seen to lie in the difference between the saving proportion of workers and that of capitalists. In particular, capitalists by their higher saving proportion contribute an amount of saving to fill the gap between golden-age investment requirements and workers' saving. Their ownership of property is required in order to enable them to make this contribution.

Figure 7.2 illustrates the point. Quadrant I describes the relation between the capital-income ratio (v) and the profit rate for a particular technology and at a given growth rate of the system (n). The corresponding relation between the profit share (rv) and profit rate for the same technology and growth rate is represented in quadrant II.[13] The curve in quadrant III gives the share of capitalists in capital in relation to the profit share for a given ratio of capitalists' and workers' saving proportions (s_w/s_c). Now, according to the Pasinetti Theorem, the ratio n/s_c determines a particular profit rate $\bar{r} = n/s_c$, associated with which is a capital-income ratio $\bar{v}$ and profit share $\bar{r}\bar{v}$. Workers' saving proportion is such that $s_w/n < \bar{v}$. Equilibrium therefore requires a share of capital $(K_c/K)^*$ owned by capitalists. With a higher saving proportion of workers, the ratio s_w/n is higher. The curve in quadrant III shifts (its intercept s_w/s_c is higher) and equilibrium requires a smaller share of capitalists in capital. At the

---

[13] The capital-income ratio can also be found in quadrant II as the slope of a ray from the origin to any point on the rv curve.

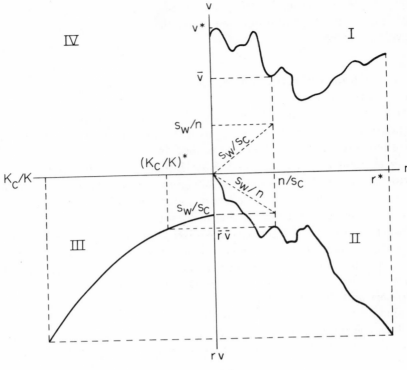

Figure 7.2

critical point where $s_w/n = \bar{v}$, the implied share of capitalists in capital is equal to zero: capitalists' saving is redundant and so is their ownership of property. For an equilibrium to exist, a regime in which there is a single class of savers and property owners, i.e. the workers, must come into existence. The equilibrium in this case resembles a Harrod equilibrium in which there is a knife-edge balance between the single saving proportion (s_w), the capital-income ratio $(\bar{v})$, and the growth rate (n).

What if the workers' saving proportion were higher still (that is, $s_w/n > \bar{v}$)? In such a case, a golden-age equilibrium is not necessarily ruled out. It requires, as in the knife-edge case, a regime in which all capital is owned by the workers. The saving proportion (s_w) and the growth rate (n) then determine a unique capital-income ratio: $v = s_w/n$.[14]

[14] Samuelson and Modigliani (1966a,b) show that, under certain assumptions, when the saving of workers is such that $s_w > s_c r v = nv$, starting from any position the share of

With the technology shown in the diagram, such an equilibrium is evidently possible as long as $\bar{v} < s_w/n < v^*$. The equilibrium in this case corresponds to the one we have analyzed before, in which there is a single uniform saving proportion for the economy as a whole.

A Regime of Classes and a Classless Regime

The preceding analysis thus brings to light two possible economic regimes: one in which there are two classes, workers and capitalists; another in which no class distinction exists. In the two-class regime the distinction between classes is related to their saving propensity and to their role in production. Ownership of property is not a distinguishing characteristic when workers save. When it is assumed that workers do not save, wages and profits accrue to different classes, which are clearly distinguishable in terms of their saving behavior, ownership of property, and role in production. The *class position* of workers and capitalists then emerges, so to speak, in its "pure" form. In the classless regime, on the other hand, there is no distinction between individuals either in terms of their saving behavior, their role in production, or their ownership of property. The only distinction is that between different categories of income, and there is no special significance to be attached to this, apart from the strictly technical distinction between the different inputs or factors to which these categories of income correspond.

The difference between the two regimes is manifested in a difference in the equilibrium configuration of the system and in the interpretation (or the "story") that can be associated with each. In the two-class regime, the rate of profit is uniquely determined by the rate of growth and the capitalists' saving propensity and is independent of technology and of workers' saving propensity. There is a corresponding wage rate determined from the wage-profit frontier. The share of profits (or wages) may or may not be unique, depending on the technology. In general, however, a higher (lower) growth rate, other things being equal, entails a higher (lower) profit rate whatever the form of the technology, and a correspondingly lower (higher) wage rate. Accordingly, it might be said that greater accumulation brings a greater "return" to the capitalists. But the

capital owned by workers is continuously growing relative to that of capitalists. The capitalists are gradually "squeezed out," so that eventually there is effectively only one class of savers, the workers. The corresponding golden-age equilibrium is, appropriately enough, that in which $v = s_w/n$. The underlying assumptions have been critically examined by Pasinetti (1966b) and Kaldor (1966).

"abstinence" from consumption is borne by the workers in the form of a lower wage rate, so that the return to the capitalists in this case cannot be a reward for abstinence on their part. For the same growth rate, if the capitalists should be thriftier (that is, s_c is higher) the rate of profit would be lower and the wage rate higher. Here greater "abstinence" on the part of capitalists yields a lower "return" to them while the workers experience an increase of consumption (or a reduction of their "abstinence"). Greater thrift on the part of workers entails a greater share for them in capital *as property* and in profits, but their wage income remains the same. In this sense, the amount of the net product which workers get *as workers*, that is to say, the payment for their services in production, is independent of their own saving. But the quantitative division of property ownership, and hence of profits, between workers and capitalists is definitely connected with their relative rates of saving.

By contrast, in a classless regime, the single uniform saving propensity and the growth rate determine a unique capital-income ratio. The associated profit rate is one that is consistent with the technology and with the given capital-income ratio. There may be one or many such profit rates (and corresponding share of profits), depending on the technology. A higher growth rate with the same saving propensity (or less thrift with the same growth rate) entails a lower capital-income ratio. The associated profit rate may be higher or lower. It follows that the equilibrium rate of profit bears no necessary relation either to thrift or to the quantity of capital.

Thus, the analysis presented here shows, at a formal level, that there are certain definite implications and interpretations associated with an analysis which gives explicit recognition to the existence of different social classes in the capitalist economy. These implications and interpretations are quite different as between an analysis of this type and one in which the existence of classes is denied or ignored.

Social class is strictly identified here with differences in saving behavior, which are implicitly associated with the status of property owners and with the status of being a worker. However, although giving recognition in this way to the existence of a class structure in capitalist society, this particular manner of specification of the class structure remains essentially ad hoc and tentative. Beyond the assumed connection of class with differences in saving behavior, no systematic theoretical account is given of the class relation itself. There is no grounding of the class relation in the relations of production involving, as in Marx, the wage-labor relation and in the historical process of development of those relations such as to account for differentiation and stratification among workers, on the one hand, and different groups of capitalists, on the other. In the absence of such a theoretical determination, social class becomes a matter of a purely quantitative difference in saving behavior. Room is then left for interpreting divisions of property ownership between workers and capitalists, and hence their relative positions in production, as being somehow derived from their relative degree of thrift.

In the controversy surrounding the Pasinetti Theorem, attention has been directed to statistics on the saving proportion of workers and on ratios of investment to income as a basis for determining which of the two regimes is a more "reasonable" representation of the capitalist economy.[15] However, argument on these terms would appear to miss the point. For it is evident that the issue, such as it is, cannot be settled by an appeal to statistics. It is a far jump from the formal and abstract level at which this analysis is set out to any real capitalist economy and to any particular set of statistical data for a particular economy. As Joan Robinson (1966, p. 308) pointed out in this connection: "Before appealing to reality and claiming support from statistics ... we need to allow for some further complications, including the fact that no period of actual history is a golden age."

Accumulation, Consumption, and Profits

We may round off our discussion in this chapter by examining the form of the relation between capital accumulation and the level of consumption per man for the economy as a whole. This will enable us to consider the meaning and significance of certain propositions that have been developed concerning this relation.

In our model economy, consumption per man (c) for a given technique is as follows:

$$(7.10) \qquad c = \frac{a_{11}(G - g)}{a_{02}[\mu - a_{11}(\mu - 1)(G - g)]}$$

Thus, c depends on the technical coefficients (a_{11}, a_{02}, μ, G) and on the growth rate of the economy (g). Call this a growth-consumption curve.

[15] See Samuelson and Modigliani 1966a,b, Pasinetti 1966b, Kaldor 1966.

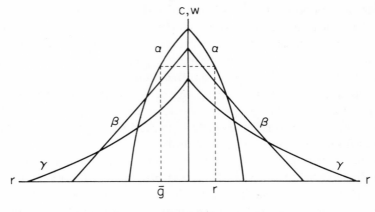

Figure 7.3

Being negatively sloped, it has the implication that a higher rate of accumulation is necessarily associated with a lower level of consumption per man, and vice versa. An interesting feature of this relation, as was noted above, is that it is the mirror image of the wage-profit curve: the two curves are identical except for the replacement of c by w and g by r.[16] Just as the wage-profit curve is a property of the production system, so is the growth-consumption curve. Both relations are derived from a given technique of production and can be found from any technique once its production coefficients are known. There are as many such curves as there are alternative techniques in a given book of blueprints. The envelope of the individual curves forms a wage-profit frontier in one case and a growth-consumption frontier in the other. One frontier is the mirror image of the other. These relations are illustrated in Figure 7.3.

Suppose now that the growth rate of the system is set exogenously at some level, say $\bar{g}$ in Figure 7.3. Given the alternative techniques available, we know from the growth-consumption frontier that there is one technique which, at that growth rate, would provide the highest level of consumption per man.[17] In the diagram, it is technique α. What profit rate would allow that technique to be chosen as the most profitable one? From the symmetry of the relations it is easy to see that, at any particular growth rate,

---

[16] For a discussion of this "duality relation" and its construction from more complex technologies, see Hicks 1965: 318–19; Bruno 1969; Burmeister and Kuga 1970.

[17] At a switch point, two techniques would be equally eligible.

the profit-maximizing technique corresponds to the one that maximizes consumption per man *if the rate of profit is equal to the rate of growth,* that is, if $r = \bar{g}$. This result is known as the neo-neoclassical theorem or golden rule of accumulation.[18]

With the technology represented in Figure 7.3, the condition that $r = \bar{g}$ is sufficient but clearly not necessary for the consumption-maximizing technique to be the most profitable. This is because there is actually a range of profit rates (including the point at which $r = \bar{g}$) at which technique α is the most profitable. This range corresponds to the segment of the wage-profit curve included in the wage-profit frontier. The existence of such a range of profit rates is in this case a consequence of the discreteness in the technology. It is likely to occur in any technology with a finite number of techniques. It would not occur in the infinite-techniques case because the frontier is, in that case, tangent to a point and not a segment of the wage-profit curve.

An additional reason why the condition that $r = \bar{g}$ is not necessary for maximizing consumption can be seen if we take account of the possibility of reswitching of techniques. For then the consumption-maximizing technique may be compatible with profit maximization at more than one profit rate (or more than one range of profit rates) because of reswitching. This may occur whether the number of techniques is finite or infinite.

The golden rule tells us what technique of production permits the highest maintainable level of consumption for an economy that is growing at a steady rate. Specifically, it tells us that this technique is the one selected from the available alternatives at a profit rate equal to the rate of accumulation of capital. As such, the golden rule is a proposition concerned entirely with a technical property of the production system. That this is so can be seen from the fact that, in deriving this proposition, nothing has been said about saving behavior and the distribution of income and property in the economy.

We may go on now to ask: what saving behavior, if any, would be consistent with the conditions of the golden rule? To answer this, we consider first the characteristics of an equilibrium path with arbitrarily given saving behavior. For this purpose we add to the technology represented in Figure 7.3 the growth-profit relation corresponding to a saving

[18] For this theorem, see Robinson 1962b, Phelps 1961. The proof sketched here follows Spaventa 1970.

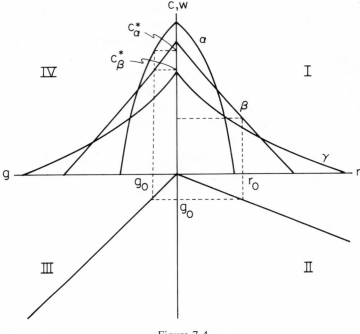

Figure 7.4

function of the form $0 = s_w < s_r < 1$. This is shown in quadrant II of Figure 7.4. The ray from the origin in quadrant III is the 45° line. Given this saving function and a particular growth rate (g_0), the rate of profit corresponding to it in steady-state equilibrium is r_0. At that profit rate, technique β is chosen as the most profitable. The level of consumption per man obtainable with that technique at the growth rate g_0 is c_β^*. But at the same growth rate a higher level of consumption could be obtained with technique α. Choice of technique β therefore involves a lower level of consumption than the maximum for that growth rate.

For a given growth rate and arbitrary saving function, maximization of consumption is compatible with profit maximization if the corresponding growth-profit relation happens to pass through the appropriate point ($\bar{g}, r = \bar{g}$) or through the relevant range of profit rates. This could only be the result of a fluke. Equality of g and r at any predetermined level of g or r is guaranteed if the saving function is such that $s_r = 1$, $s_w = 0$, for then equality of g and r holds at every level of g or r.

The conditions of the golden rule relate entirely to a property of technology. However, the achievement of those conditions in a capitalist economy places specific requirements on saving behavior and the associated distribution of income and property on the steady-state path (cf. Sato 1966). Consider, for instance, the case of the two-class regime discussed in the last section. Fulfillment of the golden rule requires, in this case, that the saving proportion of the capitalists should be equal to unity and that the capitalists own a corresponding share of property.[19] In the case of a one-class regime, it is required that the equilibrium profit share should be equal to the uniform saving proportion.[20]

By contrast, in a socialist economy, investment decisions are carried out by the state and the saving to finance investment comes from the surplus accruing to the state (through the budget) and from loans to the state by individuals.[21] Achievement of the golden rule requires that the rate of interest applied in the process of pricing and in the payment of interest on loans to the state be set equal to the rate of growth. Fulfillment of this condition automatically ensures that total saving exactly matches the steady-state rate of investment regardless of what the saving decisions of individuals may be.[22]

If saving behavior in a capitalist economy is such that the equilibrium growth-profit configuration does not correspond to the golden rule, then consumption per man is not being maximized.[23] There is nothing in the

---

[19] It is the relative size of capitalists' and workers' saving proportions that matters for the distribution of income and property. Since the workers' saving proportion does not enter into the determination of the equilibrium profit rate, that proportion could be any number within the prescribed limit for that regime.

[20] Recall that the equilibrium condition is $s_w/n = v$. Adding the golden-rule condition ($n = r$) gives $s_w = nv = rv$.

[21] To the extent that individuals save by lending to the state, it might be said that there is property in loans and a distribution of such property according to the saving proportion of individuals. But it must be assumed that the means of production are owned directly by the state.

[22] This was pointed out by Pasinetti (1962: 277) as a counterpart to the theorem discussed on pp. 159–62, above. It follows directly from the equilibrium equation (7.7) when s_c is set equal to unity. Here s_c is interpreted as the saving proportion of the state out of the surplus accruing to it, and all of this surplus is reinvested by assumption. Over and above the investment it is carrying out, the state may also provide social services and income transfers. Transfers of income through taxation cancel out, and social services can be included as part of the wage bill paid to workers. In this way the assumption that $s_c = 1$ remains intact (cf. the objection of Samuelson and Modigliani (1966a: 286) to this assumption). For a discussion of the meaning of the golden rule in the context of socialist economy as compared with capitalist economy, see Nuti 1970.

[23] Nuti (1970: 54) associates this situation with a form of exploitation under capitalism that is quite different from that analyzed by Marx: "the other more subtle form of exploitation is the lower average level of consumption per head associated with a sub-optimal technical choice, whenever consumption out of profit prevents the fulfilment of the Golden Rule."

previous analysis to show how it would be possible for such an economy to move from an existing position to one in which consumption per man is maximized.

For the more limited purpose of making equilibrium comparisons, is it possible to say in general how consumption per man varies between one equilibrium and another? Specifically, what is the form of the relation between consumption per man and the rate of profit? For a single technique, this relation depends on a composition effect that may be of any sign.[24] When more than one technique is available, we have in addition a substitution effect related to the particular ordering of techniques in relation to the rate of profit. This effect may also be of any sign. It follows that there can be no presumption about a uniformly negative relation between consumption and the profit rate. It also follows from this and earlier analysis that there can be no general presumption about a specific sign of the relations between consumption per man, the value of capital per man, and the rate of profit: a higher rate of profit may be associated with more or less capital, and greater capital with more or less consumption.

Conclusion

A number of conclusions follow from the analysis presented in this chapter. It is evident that different formulations of saving behavior have different implications for the properties of steady-state equilibria. Furthermore, different implications follow from the existence of social classes, when distinctions of social class are associated with differences in saving behavior. The analysis shows also that there is nothing in the nature of production to support the presumption of a necessary relation between thrift or abstinence on the part of capitalists and the rate of profit. Moreover, in the capitalist economy, maximization of consumption per man is incompatible with profit maximization except under conditions that could only be the result of a fluke.

Saving behavior is represented here by some simple rules applied to the economy as a whole. Although this procedure may be adequate as

---

[24] By differentiation of (7.10) we get

$$\frac{dc}{dr} = \frac{-a_{11}\mu}{a_{02}[\mu - a_{11}(\mu - 1)(G - g)]^2} \frac{dg}{dr}$$

and from Chapter 4 we know that $dg/dr \gtreqless 0$ if $\mu \gtreqless \mu^*$.

a first step, it cannot be expected to take us very far. For this purpose it would be necessary and useful to carry out a further analysis of saving in the capitalist economy as related, for instance, to the conditions of operation of the large modern corporation, sectors of small ("petty") capital, and workers' saving schemes, as well as to the activities of the state.

The existence of social class is strictly associated here with quantitative differences in saving behavior between different groups of individuals. This may be considered an inadequate theoretical specification of the nature of class relations in capitalist society. Lying behind this ad hoc and tentative introduction of social class are considerations related to the structure of ownership and control of the corporation in modern capitalism and to the differentiation and stratification existing both within the working class and among different sectors of capitalists. These are, in turn, associated with historically changing production relations and technology and with the attendant process of concentration and centralization of capital. A proper theoretical treatment of these relations is called for on their own terms.

The present analysis is of course entirely based on examination of the properties of golden-age equilibria and is, to that extent, of limited theoretical significance.

Part Three. Alternative Approaches

Chapter Eight

The Neo-Keynesian Formulation

Harrod's Problem

In Harrod's formulation of the problem of economic growth in the capitalist economy, the warranted rate of growth is regarded as fixed at a unique level given by the overall rate of saving out of income and a predetermined level of the capital-income ratio. This is the problem of uniqueness of the warranted rate of growth. From this, it is argued that there could exist only by accident a state of steady growth wherein the warranted growth rate equals the maximum feasible or "natural" rate given by growth of the labor force and technical change.

It could be said that this argument points to the existence of a *contradiction* in the operation of the capitalist economy.[1] Specifically, this contradiction is such that the aggregated acts of investment undertaken by capitalist firms as a whole, even though proving to be "warranted" from the point of view of the firms themselves taken individually, turn out to either exceed or fall short of what is required to maintain steady growth with full employment. The contradiction implies the impossibility of a state of steady growth with full employment in the capitalist economy except as the result of a fortuitous accident.

In this light, our search for the conditions that would give rise to uniqueness of the warranted growth rate can be seen as an attempt to examine the logical basis of the argument and to discover, through this examination, the sources of that contradiction. As a result of our inquiry we found one set of sufficient conditions for the existence of a unique warranted rate of growth: (1) there is a uniform saving proportion for all income classes, (2) there exists a single technique of production, and

---

[1] Harrod himself did not present the problem in these terms.

(3) the technical conditions of production are the same for all commodities. The source of the problem in this case is seen to lie in the nature of the technical conditions of production as well as in the pattern of saving. Alternatively, a sufficient condition is that the profit rate (or wage rate) is somehow fixed at a particular level. In this case, the source of the problem lies in the forces governing the rate of profit and hence the distribution of income between profits and wages.

Any of these conditions would be sufficient to establish a determinate limit on the rate at which firms can expand consistent with equilibrium of saving and investment, and hence to account for lack of equality of the warranted and natural rates of growth. The other side of the coin is, of course, the assumption that the rates of growth of the labor force and of labor productivity due to technical change are themselves fixed exogenously at a unique level.

Given these sources of the problem as identified at a theoretical level, it follows that the contradiction would be manifested either in the investment plans of firms running up continually against the barrier of labor force and productivity growth or in chronic unemployment of available labor and excess capacity of plant and equipment. Such situations being observed in capitalist economies, one could then seek to explain them within the framework of this analysis. In this way the analysis could be said to offer a specific explanation of actual periods of chronic stagnation or boom in capitalist economies. That explanation would be rooted in one or other of the particular conditions we have identified.

In Harrod's analysis, an additional aspect of the problem is located in an inherent instability due to the nature of the forces governing investment decisions of firms. This is the problem of the business cycle. In the present work we have not gone into this aspect of the matter at any length.

Needless to say, such explanations of the problem of growth in capitalist economies as this analysis suggests have to be viewed only as first approximations. This is due, in the first place, to the simplified level at which the analysis is set out. In addition, it is due to the fact that major elements of the problem have been left out of the analysis. These have to do, for instance, with the process of technical change, with monetary factors, with foreign trade and investment, and with the role of the state. Nevertheless, even if they are viewed only as first approximations, it must be granted that these explanations do not go very far. For instance, the supply of labor needs to be brought within the orbit of the analysis instead of being treated as an exogenous condition imposed upon the system. Similarly, savings decisions are treated simply as an exogenous constant applied to the overall level of national income. No explanation is offered of the forces governing these decisions at the level of firms as the basic unit through which such decisions are made in capitalist economies. Moreover, it seems from this analysis that the investment plans of firms are bound within limits imposed upon them by the amount of savings put at their disposal. Instead, one might conceive of firms as having a degree of control over the amount of savings through their allocation of the profits they receive.

Our investigation into the logical structure of the argument makes it clear also that, at a theoretical level, a crucial element is missing. This is an explanation of what determines the distribution of income.[2] In particular, we saw that in one case a possible link between accumulation and distribution is broken, so that the rate of profits is left, as it were, hanging in the air. In the other, the question of what determines the rate of profits is simply left open by taking the rate of profits as given from outside the system.

Fundamentally, what is missing here is an analysis of the structure and operation of the capitalist economy at the level of production and the relations of production. This basic implication can be drawn from the set of sufficiency conditions for Harrod's problem that we have isolated as related to saving and technology. Even if these conditions are viewed only as first approximations, it must be noted immediately that they are such as to ignore entirely characteristics of production related, for instance, to differences in production conditions between sectors. This is quite apart from any consideration, which may itself be regarded as of dubious relevance, concerning technical substitution between alternative methods of production. When differences in production conditions between sectors are recognized, an analysis of prices arising out of those production conditions would have to be introduced. In turn, the analysis of prices, as we have seen in previous discussion, presupposes a theory of distribution. Recognition of the need for a theory of distribution, viewed as a matter of distribution between wages and profits, comes also out of prior recognition of these categories of income as tied up with the ownership and control of capital and with the employment of wage labor

[2] This point was noted by Robinson (1965: 50).

in production, that is to say, with the existence of capital and wage labor as two sides of a social relation. This would in turn have consequences, among other things, for the analysis of the forces determining saving and consumption.

Instead of all this, what we find, within the set of conditions identified as constituting the source of Harrod's problem, is that there is no room for prices. This is so as long as the technical conditions of production are assumed to be the same for all commodities. Capital and labor are distinguished as technical inputs into production, and categories of income are associated with each. But the social classes associated with a distinction between work and property are not identified. They can therefore play no role in the analysis, even in the limited area of the disposal of income between saving and consumption. As Joan Robinson (1970b: 735) puts it: "The awkward appearance of this model is due to the fact that it reflects some features of a capitalist system but not others."

Discussions of Harrod's problem, starting with that of Solow (1956), have tended to emphasize the set of conditions relating to technology—in particular, the existence of a single technique of production—as constituting the main causal factor underlying that problem. In this way, attention has been directed toward the essentially neoclassical principle of (unlimited) substitutability among technical methods of production as a way out of the contradiction that Harrod posed. Eisner (1958) has tried to shift the balance by pointing to behavioral limits on the profit rate arising, for instance, from the existence of "a floor to the interest rate." Similarly, Matthews (1960) and Sen (1965) examine a case in which the rate of profit on capital is tied to a fixed rate of interest on money. But how the rate of profit could be determined in this particular way is not explained. Harrod himself has not developed an explicit formulation relevant to this matter, though the discussion by him (1948: 19, 22), based as it is on "the hypothesis that the rate of interest does not change," would seem to point in the same direction.[3]

Accumulation and the Rate of Profits

One way out of the problem of uniqueness of warranted growth, as we have seen from our analysis in previous chapters, is to recognize that

---

[3] See the exchange between Robinson (1970a,b) and Harrod (1970) on this question. Harrod calls attention to the fact that he had "dealt very extensively with the mutual influence of growth rates and profit rates" in his earlier work (1936: 65–93).

there are different rates of saving associated with different categories of income (or with different social classes). The overall rate of saving then depends on the distribution of income between such categories (or classes). There is a range of profit rates consistent with the given technology and, corresponding to this and to the given saving rates, a range of possible warranted growth rates. The problem of uniqueness of the warranted rate thus disappears. Existence of a golden age can then be viewed as a matter of finding the appropriate distribution of income—the particular distribution that, at the given rates of saving for the different categories of income, makes the overall rate of saving such that the warranted rate is equal to the natural rate, whatever the technique of production and corresponding capital-income ratio might be.

Significantly, we found that the problem of uniqueness of warranted growth disappears even if there is only one known technique of production. This is because there is a range of technically feasible profit rates and corresponding distribution of income for any one technique. A *sufficient* condition for a range of growth rates to exist is that the overall rate of saving depend on the distribution of income. But this condition is not *necessary*. A range of possible growth rates may exist even if there is one technique of production *and the rate of saving is uniform for all incomes*. A sufficient condition in this case is that there is a difference in the conditions of production of the capital good and consumption good with the given technique. For, as long as the conditions of production are different, the relative price of the two commodities will differ according to the level of the rate of profit. The difference in relative price is what matters in this case. Note also that what matters is the price of the capital good in terms of the consumption good. It does not matter how many consumption goods there are and which of them is taken as numeraire. Nor does it matter how many capital goods there are as long as their prices vary with the profit rate. In isolating this price relation, we are able to identify a basic relationship that has not been given much attention in the literature. It matters because the magnitude of the capital-income ratio is dependent on the relative price of capital and consumption goods. Given the range of possible values of the capital-income ratio, there may exist one relative price and associated profit rate that makes the saving corresponding to the single uniform saving rate exactly match the rate of accumulation required for a golden age, or there may not. There is still no logical necessity that a golden-age solution exist.

The distribution of income is here made to accommodate the rate of accumulation appropriate to a golden age. This is achieved either through the direct dependence of saving on income distribution or through the relation between saving, relative prices, and distribution, or through both of these relations. In general the link is provided by what we have called the growth-profit relation.

This connection between accumulation, saving, and distribution emerges most clearly in the context of an analysis of steady-state growth such as that carried out in previous chapters. In this respect, we could say that the steady-state model is a useful analytical device for isolating this relationship. But the significance of the relationship goes beyond the confines of this simple model. This relation constitutes an essential element of the neo-Keynesian approach to a theory of distribution and growth in capitalist economies, as developed by Robinson (1960: 145–58), Kaldor (1956, 1957), Pasinetti (1962), and others.

The basic idea in this theory is that, if the overall rate at which firms are planning to expand (whether equal to the "natural" rate or not) is taken as given, there is within certain definite limits a distribution of income between profits and wages to ensure that saving matches investment and demand absorbs output produced with the growing productive capacity. As Robinson (1962a: 82–83) notes: "The Keynesian models are designed to project into the long period the central thesis of [Keynes'] General Theory, that firms are free, within wide limits, to accumulate as they please, and that the rate of saving of the economy as a whole accommodates itself to the rate of investment that they decree." The nature of these limits will be examined presently. Within these limits and for a given technology, the distribution of income is determined by the given rate of accumulation and by the respective saving propensities associated with wage and profit incomes. According to this view, saving adjusts to match investment, not the other way around. Investment is taken as given only in the sense that the overall rate is independent of distribution and of the various saving propensities. That rate itself remains to be explained. On this Kaldor (1956: 95) writes: "The interpretative value of the model (as distinct from the formal validity of the equations or identities) depends on the 'Keynesian' hypothesis that investment . . . can be treated as an independent variable, invariant with respect to changes in the two savings propensities."

Whether—and if so, how—the rate of accumulation planned by firms could come to coincide with the "natural" rate required for a golden age is another matter. Robinson argues, in this connection, that the golden age is a purely "mythical" construction. The various approaches to this question within the neo-Keynesian framework of analysis will be discussed in the next section. The point to see meanwhile is that, within this framework, the obstacle to achievement of a golden age does not necessarily arise from the side of saving, pricing, distribution, and technology as it does in Harrod's analysis. To put the point another way, these are not seen as the basic sources of the contradiction. The source is to be found elsewhere—in particular, in the decisions governing accumulation itself: in the "animal spirits" of capitalists (Robinson) or in the "technical dynamism" of the capitalist economy (Kaldor).

The growth-profit relation, viewed simply as an equilibrium condition, is of course consistent with any theory of growth and distribution. What gives causal significance to this relation in the case of the neo-Keynesian theory is the proposition that the rate of accumulation is an independent variable and there is a relation of *dependence* of the rate of profit on the rate of accumulation. This is one proposition about which all varieties of neo-Keynesian theory are in full agreement and one distinguishing that framework of analysis from others. The differences within this framework are located elsewhere—for instance, in the explanation of what determines the rate of accumulation and in the treatment of the problem of unemployment in a growing economy and the process of technical change.

The growth-profit relation is derived from the macroeconomic condition of saving-investment equality.[4] As such, it is a *macroeconomic* relation which holds independently of the level of disaggregation of production sectors. It is also a *general* relation in the sense that it is independent of any specific hypothesis concerning the nature of technology and the structure of markets for commodities. Indeed, under the simplifying assumption that saving out of wages is zero or negligible, a theory of the rate of profits could be entirely divorced from any specific proposition

---

[4] It was from this condition that Keynes (with R. F. Kahn) derived the investment multiplier, based on an average propensity to consume, to explain the determination of the level of income and employment. A major difference between the original Keynesian formulation and the neo-Keynesian lies in the emphasis of the latter on the role of the share of profits in the propensity to consume. The introduction of this idea (initial responsibility for which is due to Kalecki) leads directly to a link between investment and distribution both in the context of a theory of income and employment and in the theory of growth.

concerning technology and market structure. In other words, a theory of the rate of profits could, in that case, be consistent with many different configurations of technology and with market structures of different degrees of competition or monopoly. This is the full significance of the relation $g = s_r r$ when placed within the context of the neo-Keynesian analysis.

This is no doubt a rather powerful result to hang on such a seemingly special assumption as that of $s_w = 0$. But it is not an unreasonable or implausible assumption to make at this level of analysis. The reason commonly given for this assumption is the *empirical* one that, in practice, saving from wage income goes to finance purchases of durable consumption goods and can therefore be ignored when dealing with investment in capital goods and growth in production (see Kaldor 1966). But this assumption might also be considered the appropriate *theoretical* starting point for an analysis which focuses upon the class relation between workers and capitalists in its pure form. The same result holds, moreover, under the conditions of the Pasinetti Theorem, where the assumption that there is zero savings out of wages is not strictly necessary. On the other hand, without the assumption that $s_w = 0$ or the conditions of the Pasinetti Theorem, the growth-profit relation would also incorporate the capital-income ratio, which depends on technology and prices. In this case, the rate of profit, prices, and the capital-income ratio would therefore have to be consistent with each other and with the technology. To determine the rate of profit, it would not be enough to know only the rate of accumulation and saving proportion for profit income. Whatever the case, it is evident that there is no room in this formulation for viewing the rate of profits as being tied to the productivity of "capital" viewed as a technical input in production or varying in accordance with the "capital intensity" of production.

Of course, regardless of whether or not the rate of profits depends on technology and prices, the share of profits is itself dependent on the capital-income ratio and hence on technology and prices. This means that the neo-Keynesian theory of distribution, *as a theory of distribution*, cannot be formulated independently of the specification of technology and prices even though the corresponding theory of the rate of profits might be so formulated.

It is interesting to note, however, that the neo-Keynesian formulation holds whether there is just one technique or many, that is to say, regardless of the possibility of choice among alternative techniques. In this sense, the existence of more than one technique is not a necessary condition of this formulation. The starting point of the formulation is the overall rate at which firms plan to grow. Even with one technique there may be a rate of profit consistent with this growth rate and with the saving proportions for the different income classes. In this connection we may say that the relation between accumulation and distribution is in the forefront of the analysis; the problem of choice of technique is a subsidiary matter. If more than one technique is assumed to exist in a given state of technical knowledge, a choice can be incorporated into the analysis. The choice is made so as to maximize profits (or minimize costs) on the investment being planned. An analysis of this was set out in Chapter 5. However, this problem could itself be regarded as having little or no real significance. In particular, Robinson views the notion of an *ex ante* profitability curve, or "pseudo-production-function," only as a logical construction with no application to reality. In the neo-Keynesian analysis, what is considered to be far more significant than the problem of choice of technique as such is the interdependence between accumulation and technical change. This idea is formally expressed in Kaldor's conception of a "technical progress function."

There is an obvious question here of what determines the growth of individual firms. This is being left open, although there is a presumption that the basic objective of the individual firm is to grow, that is, to expand the size of its capital.[5]

What if the rate of accumulation is zero? This is the hypothetical case of a stationary state, and it may well be asked how the rate of profit is determined in this particular case. Within the framework of the neo-Keynesian theory the rate of profit depends on the rate of accumulation and on the saving propensity of different income classes. In a stationary state the rate of accumulation is zero and there is no net saving. It would appear that the rate of profit should then be zero. To explain the existence of a positive rate of profit in this case, within the framework of this theory, one must refer to the habits of consumption of the class of rentiers who receive profits for *owning* capital (see Robinson [1956], p. 413). It is then evident that it is the *ownership relation* which accounts for the existence

---

[5] For a development of the neo-Keynesian theory along these lines, see Marris 1964; see also Robinson 1971a, ch. 7.

of profits in the first place. In this respect the theory must be seen to start from a recognition of the prior existence of capital as property, a class of owners of such property, and a class of workers. These social relations of production can be seen to play a definite role in the theory insofar as the determination of the rate of profits is concerned, but only through the activities of investment and consumption.

What needs to be recognized here is that *the neo-Keynesian theory solves the problem of distribution from the side of the demand for output*, in particular, in terms of the demand for investment and the propensities to consume out of profits and wages. Specifically, this formulation shows that as long as the owners are spending at a certain rate, on investment or consumption, then they are able to sustain or "realize" through sales of the product a certain share of the product in the form of profits. This is what Marx called the problem of "realization," and in the Marxian view, it is only one side of the problem of distribution. The other side is the exploitation of labor *in production*. This side of the matter is missing from the neo-Keynesian analysis. There is lacking, in this sense, a *theory of exploitation* such as is found in Marxian theory (see the discussion in Chapter 3).

There is, at the same time, no room in the neo-Keynesian theory for a conception of profits as being associated with the "abstinence" or "sacrifice" of consumption on the part of savers, as is to be found in neoclassical theory. This is seen most sharply in the comparison of steady states with workers' saving equal to zero or with a two-class regime of the Pasinetti type. For then a higher growth rate is associated with a higher profit rate and, correspondingly, wfth a lower wage rate. Here, the burden of "abstinence" is clearly seen to fall on the workers, not on the savers.

The Rate of Accumulation

"The question of what governs the rate of accumulation that firms undertake is one on which there is no agreed doctrine in orthodox economics." On this note Robinson (1962a: 36) proceeds to consider and reject various approaches and to suggest a plausible alternative of her own.[6] In this section we consider this and other alternatives. The reasons given by her for rejecting other approaches are interesting in and of themselves and are also worth mentioning here.

[6] The question is also considered at length in Robinson 1956, ch. 5.

One condition introduced into the analysis of previous chapters is that the rate of accumulation (the "warranted" rate of growth) is equal to the growth rate of the labor force. When it is assumed that the growth rate of the labor force is independently determined, this implies that the rate of accumulation is somehow adjusted to that growth rate. It is then possible to interpret this condition as saying that the autonomous growth rate of the labor force determines the general rate of accumulation in the economy as a whole.

There are two main elements involved in this approach. One is the supposed existence of a mechanism for adjusting accumulation to the growth of labor.[7] Robinson argues that there is no such mechanism in the capitalist economy. She appeals here to the familiar arguments of Keynes's *General Theory* and to an analysis of investment behavior, to be presented below. The other element is the implication that the growth of labor sets a limit to the rate of accumulation. Robinson rejects this for the reason, she argues, that capitalist economies normally operate with a considerable margin of unemployed labor. The rate of accumulation can therefore exceed the growth of labor for some time by absorbing this pool of unemployed. Conversely, accumulation at a rate below the growth rate of labor causes the pool to increase.[8]

Another approach to the determination of investment is based on the view that accumulation, under conditions of labor scarcity, takes the form of "capital deepening" in response to a rise in the relative price of labor and capital. Specifically this view, which might be called the neoclassical theory of demand for capital, holds that, in full employment equilibrium under competitive conditions, the marginal products of capital and labor are equated respectively to the rate of profit and the wage rate. The ratio of marginal products is uniquely related to the "capital intensity" of production. The latter is accordingly related to the wage-profit ratio. A rise in this ratio calls for an increase in capital intensity (or capital deepening) if equilibrium is to be restored. Because of diminishing returns in production, capital deepening ensures that the marginal product of labor rises (the marginal product of capital falls) so as to equal the higher wage rate (lower profit rate). This construction, it may be noted, provides a theory of the demand for capital and does not by itself explain either the rate at which investment (the addition to capital)

---

[7] It is usually assumed that this situation is brought about by the monetary and fiscal policies of a more or less omniscient government.

[8] Compare Marx's conception of the role of the "reserve army."

occurs or the process by which adjustment takes place between one equilibrium and another. Furthermore, it does not say anything about the rate at which the stock of capital grows in equilibrium. It is as consistent with a stationary state in which the stock of capital is fixed as with an equilibrium of steady growth with a constant ratio of capital to labor.

The idea of technical substitution underlying this view may be rejected on grounds that there exists at any moment only one or a few "best-practice" techniques that are eligible for investment.[9] Robinson rejects this view also as a dubious application of the idea of a profitability curve.[10] The point here is that the profitability curve, as a logical construction, represents the eligible techniques at a given set of prices for a period during which technology is taken as given. The investment undertaken in that period embodies the most profitable of those techniques. But the actual process of accumulation is such that as time goes by "the eligible techniques change, and there is not the smallest reason to identify the succession of techniques chosen with points on the productivity curve existing at one particular date" (Robinson 1962a: 15, n.1). Furthermore, even if it is assumed that there are many alternative techniques in a given state of technical knowledge, we saw in our earlier analysis that there is no necessary reason why the technique that is selected at, say, a higher wage rate should be characterized by a higher value of capital per man. It could very well be characterized by a lower value of capital per man.[11] Whatever the case, it is not evident how this construction, set out in terms of comparisons of steady states, carries over to a process of accumulation with technical change.

What then determines the rate of accumulation? According to Robinson (1962a: 37): "To attempt to account for what makes the propensity to accumulate high or low we must look into historical, political and psychological characteristics of an economy." To this complex of characteristics she gives the name "animal spirits."[12] For a given state of animal spirits, the rate of accumulation planned by firms can be expressed as an increasing function of the expected rate of profit. This is Robinson's investment function. The idea here is that firms require a higher level of profits in

[9] This conception of the nature of technical alternatives has been developed by Salter (1966). See also Leon 1967.

[10] For the concept of a profitability curve, see Chapter 5.

[11] On this see Chapter 5, pp. 132–37

[12] The term orginated with Keynes, who used it with reference mainly to the uncertainty involved in investment decisions. See Keynes 1936: 161–62.

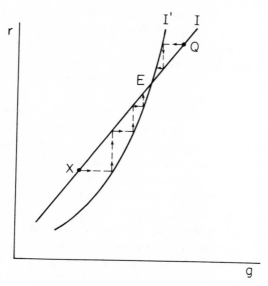

Figure 8.1

order to sustain a higher rate of accumulation. The higher the level of expected profits, the higher therefore is the rate at which they will plan to grow. This is both because greater profits offer greater compensation for the risks attached to investment and because greater profits make a greater pool of internal funds available for further investment. In this connection it is emphasized that "profits are desired for the sake of growth rather than growth for the sake of profits" (Robinson 1962a: 45).

When this investment function is combined with the earlier discussed relation of dependence of the rate of profit on the rate of accumulation, what we get is a "double-sided relationship" between the rate of accumulation and the rate of profit. The nature of this relationship is illustrated in Figure 8.1. The *I* curve represents the rate of profit that would be realized at any rate of accumulation within the possible range. We may call this the *profit-realization curve*. When there is no saving out of wages, it starts at the origin. Its slope depends on the saving propensity associated with profit income. Some assumption must be made on what determines the expected rate of profit. It is simplest to assume that "expectations are based upon a simple projection of the current situation" (Robinson 1962a: 47). Thus, the expected rate of profit is equal to the actual rate. The *I* curve therefore gives the expected and the actual rate of profit as a function of the actual current rate of accumulation. The planned rate of accumulation is in turn a function of the expected rate of profit on investment. The I' curve describes this relation. It is positively sloped. The position of this curve reflects the state of animal spirits: when animal spirits are low, a higher expected rate of profit is required to induce any given rate of accumulation, and vice versa.

Given the conditions that determine the slopes and positions of the curves in the diagram, there is one possible position consistent with equilibrium. This is at the point of intersection of the two curves. For all positions to the left of this point, as at X, the rate of profit generated by the current rate of accumulation and expected to continue into the future is such that the planned rate of accumulation exceeds the current rate. Firms as a whole are planning to increase the rate of accumulation. For positions to the right, as at Q, the planned rate of accumulation is less than the current rate: firms are planning to reduce the rate of accumulation. At the point E the realized rate of profit is just that required to induce firms to maintain the same rate of accumulation as they are currently undertaking, neither more nor less. The process by which an economy might adjust to this position in historical time, starting from a different initial position, cannot be shown on this diagram. This is because the technical and behavioral conditions involved in the process remain to be specified, or, as Robinson puts it, "time is at right angles to the page." With this diagram and assuming that investment plans are realized, we can trace the logically necessary sequence involved. This is shown by the arrows. In general, however, analysis of a dynamic process of change would require taking account of the "short-period limits to investment." These have to do with (1) the existence of an "inflation barrier" due to a spiral of money wages and prices when real wages cannot be further reduced, (2) the availability of plant and equipment in the capital goods industries and, at full employment, the ability of those industries to draw workers away from consumption goods industries, (3) the amount of outside finance that firms can organize, (4) the supply and cost of monetary balances, and (5) the state of the balance of payments. (See Robinson 1956: 48–53.)

Thus, this analysis gives us the equilibrium rate of accumulation and, along with it, the equilibrium rate of profit appropriate to the given conditions. Robinson calls this the "desired" rate of accumulation "in the sense that it is the rate which makes the firms satisfied with the situation in which they find themselves" (1962a: 49). It should be distinguished from Harrod's "warranted rate of growth." It is obviously based on a rather different set of determining conditions from those involved in Harrod's analysis. One should note that the conditions may be such that no equilibrium is possible. This occurs, for instance, when the curve I' lies above I for all levels of the profit rate. The curves may also intersect more than once, thus giving rise to the existence of multiple equilibria.

Even if there is an equilibrium appropriate to a given set of conditions, this does not ensure that it would persist indefinitely. For changes may occur in the nature of the underlying conditions. There is nevertheless a special set of conditions under which development of the economy could be conceived to occur, with an approximately constant rate of accumulation and corresponding rate of profit being maintained over time. This is when "tranquillity" prevails, so that, from one period to another, the expected rate of profit is always being realized and confirmed by experience. (See Robinson 1962a: 50–51.) The realized rate of profit is anchored by the rate of accumulation that is going on, and accumulation continues at the same rate because of the expectation that the same rate of profit will continue to exist. The situation is held together by the actions of firms in carrying out investment, their ability to generate profits as a result of that investment, and their confidence that profits will be maintained at the same rate.

Even when these special conditions are fulfilled, there is still no necessary reason why the associated "desired rate" of accumulation should equal the "natural rate" made possible by growth of the labor force and technical progress. This is so because the desired rate of accumulation is determined by the state of "animal spirits." The natural rate, in Harrod's terms, is independently determined by separate factors. It may be noted here that Harrod's conception of an independently determined "natural" rate of growth is rejected by Robinson. She argues, in particular, that "a desired rate that is high relatively to the growth of the labor force may call forth the innovations that it needs" (1962a: 52). Similarly, Kaldor (1961: 210) argues that "one of the two constituents at least of the natural rate of growth, the rate of growth of productivity, is a dependent variable, depending on the rate of growth of capital." He introduces a "technical progress function" to incorporate this relationship.

The point of Robinson's analysis is that, in the capitalist economy, there is some "normal" rate of accumulation rooted in the expectation of a "normal" rate of profit, that rate of profit being itself the result of the act of carrying out investment. From time to time accumulation may rise or fall above this rate. But there is nothing to ensure that it would correspond to the rate required for maintaining full employment. Like Harrod, but for reasons that are quite different, Robinson thus concludes that a golden age of full-employment growth could only be the result of an accident. However, the analysis as it stands is too general. It does not tell us exactly what determines the level at which these "normal" rates become established.

While recognizing the influence of the expected rate of profit on investment decisions, Kaldor (1957, 1961) introduces an additional factor based on the concept of a desired capital-output ratio. Firms are regarded as having some desired ratio of capital to output, and their investment is geared to maintaining that ratio. Thus, if the rate of profit on capital is constant, the rate of accumulation is equal to the expected rate of growth of output, the latter being assumed to be equal to the actual current rate of growth. The rate of accumulation is greater than this if the rate of profit is expected to rise, and less if it is expected to fall.[13]

This type of investment function can be recognized as a modified form of the acceleration principle, according to which the growth of sales "induces" sufficient investment to enable production to grow in line with sales. This principle has been widely used and was the particular specification of investment behavior adopted by Harrod.[14] It is modified by Kaldor so as to allow investment to depend as well on the expected profit rate. In this version the expectation of a rise (fall) in the rate of profit accounts for investment in excess of (below) that required by the acceleration principle. The prospective rate of profit is itself based on the expected profit margin per unit of sales and on the expected capital-output ratio, and is not necessarily equal to the realized rate of profit on existing capital. On the steady-state path, all expectations are fulfilled and the expected rate of profit turns out then to be equal to the realized rate.

Kaldor's formulation is illustrated in Figure 8.2. The curve TT is the technical progress function governing the rate of growth of output

---

[13] This description of the investment function is based upon that given by Kaldor (1961), which meets objections raised to the earlier version (Kaldor 1957). In a subsequent version (Kaldor and Mirrlees 1962), the idea of a "desired" capital stock that is uniquely related to the rate of profit is abandoned.

[14] For a survey of early discussions on the acceleration principle, see Knox 1952.

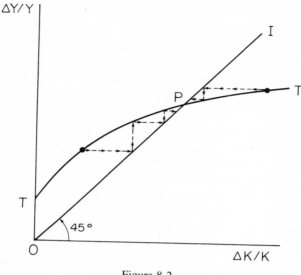

Figure 8.2

($\Delta Y / Y$) resulting from different rates of accumulation ($\Delta K / K$). The 45°
line *OI* represents the rate of accumulation that any given rate of growth
of output would induce if the rate of profit were constant. The rate of
accumulation would be greater than this if a particular rate of growth of
output involves the expectation of a rising rate of profit, and less if it
involves the expectation of a falling rate of profit. The expected rate of
profit is assumed to be based on experience in such a way that, when output
is rising faster than capital (the capital-output ratio is falling), the rate of
profit is expected to rise; it is expected to fall when the capital-output
ratio is rising. Thus, at points on *TT* to the left of *P*, the rate of growth of
output exceeds the current rate of accumulation, the rate of profit is
expected to rise, and firms are planning to raise the rate of accumulation.
At points to the right of *P*, the rate of growth of output is less than the
rate of accumulation, the rate of profit is expected to fall, and firms plan
to reduce the rate of accumulation. The point *P* is consistent with a state
of steady growth such that the capital-output ratio and the rate of profit
are constant.[15]

---

[15] On the assumption that the technical progress function is convex upward and has
positive intercept on the vertical axis, there always exists such a point *P*. Moreover, under
the specified behavioral assumptions and if investment plans are always realized, there

Kaldor assumes that the long-run equilibrium position is one of full employment. In this respect his analysis differs sharply from that of Robinson. The mechanism by which full employment is supposed to be brought about has not been made clear, and this aspect of his analysis has been soundly criticized (see, for instance, Rothschild 1959).

A basic feature of Kaldor's formulation is that there is no unique rate of growth of output, such as Harrod's "natural growth rate," at which alone steady growth can be maintained. The equilibrium rate of growth of output can be at any point on the TT curve, and there are many such points. This is because the growth of output is itself dependent on the rate of accumulation, in accordance with the technical progress function.[16] Each rate of accumulation thus gives rise to its own rate of growth of output, owing to the technical innovations it infuses into the economy. Given the technical progress function, what fixes the growth rate of output is the rate of accumulation, and hence the conditions governing the demand for investment. Underlying the technical progress function is what Kaldor calls "the technical dynamism" of the economy, "meaning by this both inventiveness and readiness to change or experiment" (1961: 208). This governs the height and slope of the TT curve. It is "technical dynamism" in this sense that, in Kaldor's view, "is responsible, in a capitalist economy, for making both the rate of accumulation of capital and the rate of growth of production relatively small or relatively large" (ibid., p. 209).

The preceding conceptions regarding the interdependence of profits and accumulation have much in common with ideas earlier put forward by Kalecki (1954).[17] In particular, Kalecki developed grounds for viewing the current level of profits as dependent on the current level of investment of firms. The argument is summarized in the aphorism *Capitalists get*

---

would be a tendency for an economy to move toward this point, starting from any position. To the left of P, a rise in the rate of accumulation raises the rate of growth of output, but less than proportionately, which leads to a further rise in accumulation, and so on, until P is reached. To the right of P, the same process works in reverse. The logical sequence implied in this process is shown by the arrows in the diagram. The stability properties of the model have been analyzed by McCallum (1969) and Champernowne (1971).

[16] The conception of the process of technical change underlying this function has been criticized by Rothschild (1959), who points out that, for various reasons, there will be no unique technical relation between growth of capital and growth of output.

[17] That the roots of the neo-Keynesian formulation lie as much in the work of Kalecki as in that of Keynes is pointed out by Robinson (1965: 92–99). See also Kaldor 1956: 94, n.3; Kaldor 1961: 211–12; Feiwel 1975.

what they spend and workers spend what they get. He also constructed the case for making investment decisions an increasing function of the expected rate of profit on investment (or the "marginal efficiency of investment"). This was based on the principle that there is "increasing risk" associated with increased investment, depending upon the amount of borrowing by each firm relative to its own capital. (See Kalecki 1937; 1954, chs. 8, 9.) The calculation of risk is either a matter of subjective calculation by the investor or the result of an actual premium charged by the creditor, or both. Given the distribution of own capital among existing firms and the market rate of interest on loans, there is a corresponding relation between the overall amount of planned investment and the sum of marginal risk plus the rate of interest. The total amount of planned investment is determined by the condition that the expected rate of profit equals the sum of marginal risk plus the rate of interest.

An interesting aspect of Kalecki's theory of investment is that, for the individual firm, the size of its investment is determined by the size of its own capital: the greater the own capital, the greater the investment. This would thus explain why different-sized enterprises are started in a given industry at the same time or why there are different sizes of firms. It follows also that the expansion of the firm is closely linked with its internal accumulation of capital out of profits, both because reinvestment of profits reduces its reliance on the capital market and because the attendant increase in own capital extends the limit on investment plans set by the factor of "increasing risk." It is this link that has become part of the chain of causation of the neo-Keynesian theory. The *direction* of that causation, for both Kalecki and the neo-Keynesians, is of course that investment generates the profits (saving) that it needs, and not the other way around.

Limits of Wages, Profits, and Accumulation

On the terms of the argument set out so far, it is possible to have, within the limit of technical feasibility, a state of equilibrium growth at *any* conceivable rate, depending only on the state of "animal spirits" (Robinson) or on the extent of "technical dynamism" (Kaldor). Besides the limit of technical feasibility, what other limits might there be to the operation of these forces? Or, in other words, are there any other controlling factors such as to put a check on the operation of the forces identified so far? The answer is that, within the framework of the neo-

Keynesian formulation, there are such limits, but they are regarded only as *limits* or "boundary conditions" and not as *controlling factors*.

The first of these limits is attributed by Kaldor to the existence of a minimum rate of profit below which firms will not carry out investment.[18] Accumulation of capital cannot go on unless the ruling rate of profit is at least as high as this minimum. The reason given for this is that direct investment in fixed capital, as distinct from other forms of holding wealth, involves "illiquidity risk" due to lack of easy marketability of the physical assets of the firm. If the "pure" long-term rate of interest is taken as the yield of riskless assets, then, in order that an investment project should qualify for adoption, its prospective yield should exceed this rate of interest by a margin necessary to compensate for illiquidity risk. The rate of interest itself, which is determined by monetary factors, has some minimum value greater than zero. The sum of this minimum rate of interest plus the differential due to illiquidity risk sets the level of the minimum rate of profit.

The idea here is related to the familiar Keynesian "liquidity preference theory," but as applied to investment in "real" capital rather than to the market for financial assets. One should note that it applies to the demand for investment and not to the supply of savings. The idea also goes back to Ricardo's conception of a minimum rate of profit necessary to compensate investors "for their trouble, and the risk which they must necessarily encounter in employing their capital productively."[19] In Ricardian economics, however, accumulation comes to a halt in the stationary state when the rate of profit is driven down to this level, and this is seen as a necessary outcome of the process of growth. On the other hand, in Kaldor's analysis, a condition in which the actual rate of profit is equal to the minimum is only one possible outcome for the system, and when that condition holds there is still a positive rate of accumulation depending on the rate of growth of productivity and growth of the labor force (the acceleration principle continues to operate). It is only when the rate of profit is equal to "the supply price of risk capital" (which is the market rate of interest plus the risk factor), whether or not this is at the minimum, that the rate of accumulation in Kaldor's model is limited to the "new" investment opportunities made available by increase of productivity and

[18] See Kaldor 1959b: 287–91; 1961: 189, 217–19.
[19] See Ricardo, *Works* I, 122.

labor force growth. Furthermore, it is argued that the consequence of having a rate of profit below the minimum is the trade cycle and "there is no reason ... to regard the trade cycle as inevitable." Specifically, Kaldor's view is as follows:

> If the rate of profit is insufficient for *steady* growth, this does not mean that the system will relapse into permanent stagnation—if it did, the past history of capitalist economies could not have exhibited the trend rate of growth which it has shown. But what it does mean is that the process of accumulation and growth is periodically interrupted: ... progress proceeds by fits and starts, and not at a steady rate (Kaldor 1959b: 290).

The argument here seems to be more a matter of hindsight than a necessary implication of his theoretical system.

It is also not evident from Kaldor's conception that the minimum rate of profit could ever be effective, since the level of that minimum itself may be quite flexible. Such flexibility comes from taking account of the difference between the *real* rate of interest (i) and the *money* rate of interest (i_m), as determined by the rate of change of prices ($\Delta p/p$). This is expressed in the well-known formula $i = i_m - \Delta p/p$. Thus, even if the money rate of interest is fixed at some minimum level, the real rate of interest could be made lower than this through an appropriate rate of inflation, and the minimum profit rate would vary accordingly.[20] This does beg the question of how such a regime of continuous and steady inflation could be brought about. Since, in the neo-Keynesian framework, movements in the general level of prices are governed by changes in the money-wage rate, the problem is to find the rate of change of money wages that would provide the appropriate rate of inflation. There is no ready answer to this question because the money-wage rate is considered to be an exogenous factor.

Kaldor introduces a second limit associated with the existence of a minimum profit margin determined by "the degree of market imperfection."[21] This limit is based on the notion, taken over from Marshall, that there is a minimum profit margin below which firms refuse to go "for fear of spoiling the market." The level of this margin depends on the

---

[20] Kaldor (1959b: 291) explicitly recognizes this point: "Granted the fact that in the last resort we can always have recourse to a little inflation there is really no reason why an unfavorable constellation between Liquidity Preference and the Marginal Efficiency of Capital should bring capitalism to its ultimate doom."

[21] See Kaldor 1959a: 217; 1961: 201–3.

intensity of competition: the more intense the competition, the lower the margin. This limit could be based, alternatively, on Kalecki's conception of a profit margin determined by "the degree of monopoly." This is related to the long-run process of concentration of capital and displacement of competition by product differentiation and advertising, as well as to the operation of cyclical factors.[22] One may note, however, that Kalecki saw these conditions not only as a limit but also as a controlling factor in the operation of the economy.[23]

Whatever is the minimum level of the profit margin, there is, corresponding to it, a minimum share of profits in total product. If the rate at which firms plan to grow and the saving proportions for profit and wage incomes are such as to require a share of profits below this minimum, steady growth cannot be maintained and the economy lapses into a "stagnation crisis" due to excessive saving relatively to the demand for investment. This situation arises because of downward inflexibility of the profit margin.[24] In Kaldor's analysis the variation of prices in relation to wage costs (or the profit margin) provides the mechanism of adjustment of saving to investment. When this mechanism does not work, some other mechanism takes over. The result is unemployment and stagnation.

Kaldor himself is skeptical of the historical grounds for existence of rigid profit margins. He claims (Lutz and Hague 1961: 379) that "The effects of monopoly on prices and on distribution [have] been tremendously exaggerated. Prices ... come down with falling costs." Thus, in his judgment, this particular minimum, like the previous one, is not likely to be effective. However, the observation that "prices come down with falling costs" is evidently not inconsistent with Kalecki's degree of monopoly principle, according to which prices are *proportional* to prime costs.

The preceding limits operate from the side of profits and the pricing and investment policies of firms so as to determine a minimum profit rate or profit share consistent with an equilibrium of steady growth. There are other such limits. One of these is that the share of profits must

---

[22] See Kalecki 1954, chs. 1, 2. See also the discussion below, pp. 202–10.

[23] The role of the degree of monopoly in this context is examined by Robinson (1970a).

[24] This case is thus to be distinguished from the previous one, where the rate of profit is too low to maintain a continuous inducement to invest. See the discussion of this in Lutz and Hague 1961: 368–69.

be at least as great as that made possible by the technical difference between the average product of labor and the short-period marginal product of labor. This has the implication that the real wage rate cannot exceed the marginal product of labor (see Kaldor 1961: 202). Of these limits only one would apply, namely, that constituting the highest minimum.

We consider next a limit arising from the side of wages. Kaldor conceives of this limit in terms of a minimum level of real wages determined by "subsistence." Robinson conceives of it in terms of an "inflation barrier" that "comes into operation when a fall in real wages is being resisted by raising money wages" (1956: 48–50). In both cases it is argued that some level exists below which real wages cannot be depressed. Under given technical conditions, this determines a maximum rate of profits and, for given saving propensities, sets an upper limit to the possible rate of accumulation.

The concept of an absolute minimum level of subsistence in Kaldor's version of the argument is not well defined. He links it with the Classical notion of a wage rate determined by subsistence requirements for reproduction of the population (Kaldor 1961: 180). However, for the Classics, Ricardo and Malthus in particular,[25] this conception provided a theory of the ruling equilibrium level of the wage rate, whereas for Kaldor a subsistence wage is only a boundary condition. A conception similar to that of the Classics is to be found in the model of Neumann, where the subsistence wage rate is that governing the equilibrium solution of the system.[26] Lewis (1954) develops an alternative conception of a subsistence wage based on the standard of living prevailing in a noncapitalist sector of the economy.

Robinson's conception of an inflation barrier is more meaningful in that it defines the minimum wage rate in behavioral terms as the minimum level to which real wages can fall without leading to "hyperinflation." This definition raises other difficulties, for instance, regarding what rate

---

[25] Kaldor associates this formulation with Marx. But it is highly doubtful that Marx ever adopted such a formulation. Marx firmly rejected the Malthusian conception as "a libel on the human race" and dissociated himself from the notion of an "iron law of wages." For Marx the equilibrium level of the wage rate (or "value of labor power") is governed by historical and social factors quite apart from any demographic or physiological considerations. Marx's analysis can be interpreted either as taking the wage rate as "given" in this sense or as taking the rate of exploitation as given. On this, see the presentation of Marx's analysis in Chapter 10 below and Chapter 3.

[26] See Neumann 1945 and the interpretation of this model by Champernowne (1945).

of inflation constitutes "hyperinflation."[27] On the question of what determines the minimum level of real wages, Robinson's answer is that, where workers are highly conscious of their standard of living and strongly organized in trade unions, the level of real wages experienced in the past sets up a "ratchet effect" behind any decline in real wages, the ratchet being enforced through upward pressure on the money-wage rate. This "barrier" moves over time with the experienced level of real wages. Thus, the minimum level of real wages is determined by historical conditions as reflected in the level established in the past and by social conditions operating through the bargaining power of workers. The rate of unemployment enters here as one of the determining factors. Robinson argues, in particular, that "the bargaining power of workers is not strong enough to check a fall in real wage rates while there is considerable unemployment but is very strong in a situation in which nearly all workers are already employed." This is considered to be the "case which is normal in modern industrial economies" (see Robinson 1956: 49). The argument bears an obvious similarity to Marx's conception of the role of the reserve army of unemployed labor, except that Marx saw the reserve army as being produced by the process of capital accumulation itself.

A Synthesis

The preceding discussion of the neo-Keynesian analysis can be summarized by adapting a diagram used previously (Figure 8.1) to combine various elements of the analysis and provide thereby a synthesis. This is shown in Figure 8.3.

With given technical conditions, there is a maximum rate of profit r_1 corresponding to a given minimum wage rate. The profit realization curve AB therefore reaches a maximum at r_1. The curve $DEFG$ represents the planned rate of accumulation as a function of the expected rate of profit, which, for simplicity, can be regarded as equal to the realized rate. The segment EFG is positively sloped in accordance with Kalecki's "principle of increasing risk" or with Robinson's investment function. The point r_0 is the minimum rate of profit below which firms are unwilling to undertake investment—the planned rate of accumulation falls to zero.

When the investment demand curve cuts the profit realization curve from below, as in this diagram, an equilibrium of steady growth exists at F consistent with the given pattern of saving and state of animal spirits.

---

[27] This point is discussed by Harris (1967).

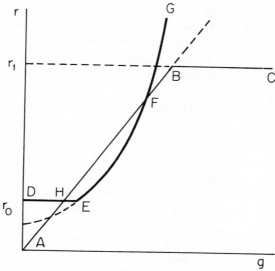

Figure 8.3

There is another position of equilibrium at *H* consistent with the given conditions. But this is such that any departure from it (to the right) would induce firms to seek to raise the rate of accumulation above the current rate, or (to the left) would lead firms to reduce the rate of accumulation to zero, so that this position could not be maintained.

Suppose that the conditions are such that the investment demand curve (above the minimum point) lies entirely to the right of the profit realization curve. In that case, no position of equilibrium could be maintained. At every possible point the firms are seeking to raise the rate of accumulation above the current rate. At the point where the profit rate is at the maximum, the firms are struggling to increase the rate of accumulation and are held in check by the minimum real wage rate. The situation is then associated with hyperinflation—the "inflation barrier" is in operation. When the investment demand curve lies entirely to the left of the profit realization curve, no equilibrium is possible. The economy then faces a chronic "stagnation crisis."

It is evident, on the basis of this simplified analysis, that the assumed conditions may be such that there are many equilibria, just one, or none at all. It follows that, within this particular set of conditions, there is no guarantee of the existence of a unique and "stable" equilibrium of expansion in the capitalist economy.

In addition to these conditions, we need to introduce the conditions of labor supply. Suppose, as in Harrod's formulation, that the effective supply of labor grows at a predetermined rate. Then, even if there is an equilibrium with accumulation taking place at a steady rate, there is no guarantee that the available supply of labor will exactly match the requirements for continued accumulation.

When technical change is introduced, the level of output per man rises over time as new productive capacity incorporating the new techniques of production is installed. For the conditions to be consistent with a steady state, the level of real wages must rise in step with the increase of output per head, so as to enable the same rate of profit to continue to be realized at the existing rate of accumulation. Technical change must be "neutral" so as to keep the capital-income ratio the same and the share of profits constant.

As the analysis is elaborated in this way, by introducing additional conditions and further complications, a detailed picture is built up of the requirements for consistency among the various conditions. It continues to be evident that there is no guarantee of equilibrium. By a similar route Robinson constructs, in her analysis, a number of possible "ages" of growth. These can be interpreted as constituting a taxonomy of possibilities, each of which is identified by a particular set of contradictions underlying the pattern of growth. In this way a framework is constructed for the purpose of explaining the concrete conditions of accumulation in capitalist economies. The framework contains general elements, applicable to a broad range of historical conditions, and particular elements, applicable to a particular set of conditions. There is, however, no indication of the possible connection or transition between one "age" and another, or the possible order these ages might occupy within a conception of the overall process of development of the capitalist economy. In this sense a theory of the development of the capitalist economy is lacking in Robinson's analysis.

In Kaldor's analysis, on the other hand, it seems that a state of steady growth with full employment corresponds somehow to the "stylized facts" of capitalism. The purpose of his analysis is to construct hypotheses to account for these "stylized facts."

Employment, Distribution, and Prices in the Short Run

We turn now to examine the neo-Keynesian theory of the level of employment and its connection with the theory of distribution and prices.[28] A central proposition of neo-Keynesian theory is that, in the short run, the level of investment determines simultaneously the level of employment and the distribution of income between profits and wages. The short run is defined as a period during which the stock of productive equipment (capital goods) of all sorts is fixed and productive capacity is unaffected by the investment going on. In regard to determination of prices, the theory recognizes that markets may not be competitive in the sense that prices are set equal to marginal costs and vary with the level of demand.[29] Instead, it may be assumed that firms pursue a policy of setting prices at a level given by a markup on prime costs. As for what determines this markup, the theory is less definite and a number of alternative formulations have been put forward. In this section we discuss some of the main ideas involved in terms of a simple model, focusing on the implications of alternative assumptions regarding the price policy of firms.[30]

The following relations characterize the model. The first is a function relating total output to employment of labor, or what Joan Robinson (1965: 42) calls the "short-period utilization function" (which should be distinguished from the so-called "production function"). It is assumed that employment consists of a fixed amount of "indirect" or "overhead" labor L_0, which is required for operating equipment as long as output is positive, and an amount of "direct" labor L_1, which varies with the level of output. Output per unit of direct labor is constant for all ranges of output up to full capacity.[31] Thus

$$(8.1) \qquad\qquad\qquad L_1 = bY$$

---

[28] This section is, in part, excerpted from Harris 1973.

[29] Competition in this sense must be distinguished from competition in the sense used in our earlier analysis of accumulation. In the latter case, competition means that capital is free to enter and leave different lines of production. As such, it is therefore an aspect of the process of accumulation of capital. For purposes of short-run analysis, when abstraction is made from the process of accumulation, competition has to be viewed as a matter only of the pricing policy of firms.

[30] The model has certain similarities to those of Asimakopulos (1969, 1970) and Harcourt 1972: 145–52.

[31] It is easiest to assume that a fixed "basket" of commodities is produced. Thus, in what follows, no attention is paid to variations in the composition of output between, say, capital goods and consumption goods. Similarly, the structure of relative prices of commodities is ignored. The analysis presented here can be extended to a situation where the stock of capital goods consists of different "vintages" of equipment resulting from the pattern of accumulation and technical change occurring in the past. Output then varies by bringing into production (or retiring) older vintages with the available labor. For a model of this type, see Kaldor and Mirrlees 1962.

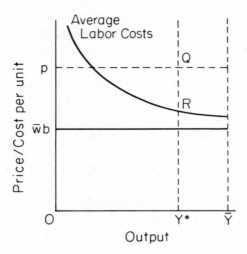

Figure 8.4

(8.2) $$L = L_0 + L_1$$

where Y is aggregate output in real terms, L is total employment of labor, and b is the direct-labor coefficient. Prime costs consist entirely of direct labor costs.[32] The money-wage rate $\bar{w}$ is taken as given in the short period as a result of bargaining between workers and employers. At this wage rate, unit wage costs vary with the level of output in accordance with (8.1) and (8.2). The associated cost curve of the "representative firm" may be drawn as in Figure 8.4, where $\bar{Y}$ is output at fully capacity.

National income in money terms is

(8.3) $$pY = \Pi + \bar{w}(bY + L_0)$$

where Π is the level of money profits and p is the general price index. It is assumed that there are fixed saving propensities for profit and wage income, s_π and s_w respectively, where $s_\pi > s_w$. For saving-investment equilibrium we therefore have

(8.4) $$p\bar{I} = s_\pi\Pi + s_w\bar{w}(bY + L_0)$$

where, in the Keynesian manner, it is assumed that the level of real investment $\bar{I}$ is given exogenously by decisions made in the past.

---

[32] Raw material costs can be ignored on the usual assumption that production is fully integrated.

There are five unknowns to be determined—Y, L_1, L, p, Π—and only four equations. The model is therefore open with respect to one of the variables. It can be closed by introducing a specific hypothesis concerning determination of the price level. Accordingly, we distinguish below a number of possible cases and examine the solution of the model in each case.

Case 1. Suppose that prices are determined by a mark-up on variable costs and that the size of the markup is fixed at a given level, say $\phi = \bar{\phi}$, so that

$$(8.5) \qquad\qquad p = \bar{\phi}\bar{w}b \qquad \bar{\phi} > 1$$

This case corresponds to that of Kalecki's "degree of monopoly" theory.[33] It is illustrated in Figure. 8.4 by taking $p/\bar{w}b = \bar{\phi}$. The size of the markup reflects the degree of monopoly and is taken to be given in the short run. The higher the degree of monopoly, the higher is the markup. In Kalecki's conception, the degree of monopoly is related to long-run factors associated with the process of concentration of capital and displacement of competition by product differentiation and advertising.

Apart from the influence of such long-run factors, Kalecki saw the degree of monopoly as also subject to change in the course of the business cycle.[34]

By substituting (8.5) into (8.3) and (8.4) and solving, we get

$$(8.6) \qquad\qquad Y = \frac{\bar{\phi}\bar{I} + (s_\pi - s_w)L_0/b}{s_\pi(\bar{\phi} - 1) + s_w}$$

$$(8.7) \qquad\qquad \frac{\Pi/p}{Y} = \frac{\bar{\phi} - 1 - L_0/bY}{\bar{\phi}}$$

Thus, the equilibrium level of output (and real income) is determined by the level of real investment $\bar{I}$ and by the level of employment of indirect labor L_0.[35] These factors operate through a multiplier effect that is related to the saving propensities (s_π, s_w) and to the degree of monopoly as

---

[33] See Kalecki 1954. A similar formula has been proposed by Weintraub [1959] arguing on the basis of empirical constancy of the markup.

[34] See, for instance, Kalecki 1954: 17–18. That Kalecki does specify such independent factors determining movements in the degree of monopoly is clear from his work. There is therefore no basis for the claim that the concept of degree of monopoly is tautological. For a useful discussion of this point, see Riach 1971.

[35] Strictly speaking, the term L_0/b in (8.6) is the level of output produced by indirect labor if it were to be employed as direct labor.

reflected in the markup $\bar{\phi}$. The share of profits depends on the degree of monopoly and varies directly with the overall level of output (or, strictly, with the ratio of direct to indirect labor bY/L_0). It can be seen from (8.6) that a higher level of investment raises the level of output and real income. At the higher level of output the share of profits is higher according to (8.7). This is because the profit margin is greater at the higher level of output, owing to lower unit labor costs at constant prices.

Kalecki assumed that prime costs are constant over the entire range of output levels up to full capacity.[36] This assumption can be accommodated in the present model by setting $L_0 = 0$. The results are modified accordingly. In particular, the share of profits is now uniquely determined by the degree of monopoly. The *share* of profits no longer depends on the level of output, and hence on the level of investment, but the *level* of profits does. Assuming in addition that $s_w = 0$, we find that the level of profits is uniquely related to the level of real investment and to the saving propensity for profit income $\Pi/p = \bar{I}/s_\pi$, which is a familiar and simple result in this framework.

Case 2. A possible basis for determining the markup has been suggested by Robinson (1969: 260) in the following terms: "Profit margins, in each market, settle at the level that yields the expected rate of profit (the best attainable in the given conditions) at an average degree of utilization of plant (permitting super-normal profits in a seller's market and sub-normal profits in a buyer's market to be realized through changes in output at constant prices ...)." Accordingly, let output corresponding to the "normal" level of utilization in the given short period be Y^*. The price equation now becomes

$$(8.8) \qquad p = \phi^* \bar{w} \left(b + \frac{L_0}{Y^*} \right), \qquad \phi^* > 1$$

where ϕ^* is a parameter indicating the size of the markup on wage costs. This case involves a specific conception of the markup as being tied to the expected rate of profit at the normal degree of utilization of capacity. Although formally not very different from the previous case of the degree of monopoly, it may involve a different determination insofar as the rate

---

[36] He argued, "In fact unit prime costs fall somewhat in many instances as output increases. We abstract from this complication which is of no major importance" (Kalecki 1954: 12, n.2).

of profit and normal degree of utilization remain to be determined.[37] It is illustrated in Figure 8.4 by taking $QR/RY* = \phi* - 1$.

For the equilibrium solutions in this case we get

$$(8.9) \qquad \frac{Y}{Y*} = \frac{(1 + L_0/bY*)\phi*\bar{I}/Y* + (s_\pi - s_w)L_0/bY*}{(1 + L_0/bY*)\phi*s_\pi - (s_\pi - s_w)}$$

$$(8.10) \qquad \frac{\Pi/p}{Y} = 1 - \frac{1 + (L_0/bY*)Y*/Y}{(1 + L_0/bY*)\phi*}$$

The equilibrium level of output relative to the normal level is determined by the ratio of investment to the normal level of output ($\bar{I}/Y*$), by the saving propensities (s_π, s_w), by the level of the markup $\phi*$, and by the ratio of indirect to direct labor at the normal level of utilization ($L_0/bY*$). The equilibrium share of profits in income depends on the size of the markup, on the ratio of indirect to direct labor, and on the equilibrium level of output relative to the normal level. The profit share is below normal when output is below the normal level ($Y < Y*$) and above normal in the opposite case.

Case 3. Suppose finally that the size of the markup is left as an unknown. We now write

$$(8.11) \qquad p = \phi\bar{w}b, \qquad \phi > 1$$

where ϕ is a variable to be determined by the model. This gives us an extra equation and an extra variable so that there is still one degree of freedom. The model can be closed by setting the level of output at the level appropriate either to the capacity of existing plant and equipment or to full employment of the available labor force, whichever is less. By solving the system of equations on the assumption that $Y = \bar{Y}$, we get

$$(8.12) \qquad \frac{\Pi/p}{\bar{Y}} = \frac{\bar{I}/\bar{Y} - s_w}{s_\pi - s_w}$$

$$(8.13) \qquad \phi = \frac{1 + L_0/b\bar{Y}}{1 - \Pi/p\bar{Y}} = \frac{(s_\pi - s_w)(1 + L_0/b\bar{Y})}{s_\pi - \bar{I}/\bar{Y}}$$

The equilibrium share of profits and level of the markup are determined by the saving propensities and the investment-income ratio. The markup

---

[37] A similar specification of the markup under long-run conditions is suggested by Riach (1971). See also Asimakopulos 1975.

is determined also by the ratio of direct and indirect labor employed. It can be seen that both the share of profits and the markup vary directly with the share of investment in income. For the profit share and markup to be positive, it is required that $s_\pi > \bar{I}/\bar{Y} > s_w$.

This case corresponds to the situation in Kaldor's (1959a) model, where the economy is assumed to operate at full employment and the rate of investment is exogenously determined. The distribution of income is determined by the rate of investment (strictly, by the ratio of investment to full employment output) and the saving propensities. But there is no explanation of why full employment is a necessary feature of equilibrium. This is the aspect of Kaldor's model that has been a puzzle.[38] One may note also that, insofar as the size of the markup is a variable to be determined by the conditions of the model, it is required that firms pursue a very special kind of price policy; namely, that they set prices in accordance with the requirement of full employment equilibrium.[39] Alternatively, this could be viewed as an accidental or knife-edge case, where the level of (exogenous) investment plans of firms and the size of the markup, determined as in any of the other two cases or even by the interaction of demand and supply in competitive markets, happened to be such that the total demand forthcoming at the associated distribution of income is just sufficient to absorb full employment output. In the short period, this would be a rare and fortuitous occurrence such that any variation in investment from the level consistent with full employment would be associated with unemployment or inflation.[40]

Actually, the sort of price policy involved in Case 3 would seem more relevant to a planned economy than to a capitalist economy. Indeed, the role of this principle of pricing in a socialist economy was pointed out much earlier by Dobb (1937: 326–27; 1939: 716).

The preceding analysis brings out the crucial role of the price policy of firms in a theory of employment and distribution. We have examined various alternative ways of conceiving of that policy and their implications

[38] See Harcourt 1972: 210. On this, see also Robinson 1969 and Kaldor 1970.

[39] This aspect of Kaldor's model is examined by Harcourt (1963).

[40] Kaldor (1956: 99–100; 1957: 622) explicitly recognizes that his model may not work in an arbitrarily given short period. He argues that it is applicable to a state of steady full-employment growth ("periods in which the rate of growth of capital and income is normal" [1957: 594]). In Joan Robinson's terminology, this would be the "mythical" condition of "a golden age."

within the framework of the neo-Keynesian theory.[41] The other side of the coin is the behavior of workers as it affects the money-wage rate and other relations in the economy. Relatively little attention has been paid to this in the context of the neo-Keynesian theory.[42] In this respect, one consideration that is missing here, as Rothschild (1965: 655) observes, is "the influence and effects of group action (Marx's class struggle) on the distributional problem."

A number of ideas on this are introduced by Rothschild into Kaldor's model: (a) the role of trade union action geared to maintaining a "traditional" wage share or wage level, (b) the effect of trade union pressure on entrepreneurs' saving and consumption standards, and (c) the dependence of workers' savings on the consumption standards of profit earners. Dobb (1928: 103) expressed ideas similar to (a) and (b). Related to (c) is the idea of Duesenberry (1949) that the saving propensity of individuals depends on their relative position in the income distribution. Kalecki (1971) considers the effects of trade union power on distribution and employment operating through the size of the markup.

Other limitations of the analysis as presented here might also be noted, such as, for instance, its assumptions of fixed propensities to save independent of price changes and fixed *real* investment irrespective of price changes (cf. Sen 1963). Most severe are the limitations imposed by confining the analysis to the conditions of a single "short period."

In concluding this section, we may note that the contribution of Keynes's analysis was to show that unemployment and excess capacity were the rule rather than the exception in the capitalist economy, where the total amount of investment is the aggregated outcome of individual plans.[43] But Keynes clung to "the fundamental postulate" of the "Classical" theory of employment, that perfectly competitive pricing

---

[41] The recent study of Eichner (1976) carries further the analysis of the conditions of price formation in the large modern corporation.

[42] Robinson (1956: 48–50) introduces this factor through the concept of an "inflation barrier," which is a situation where a wage-price spiral sets in, owing to the reaction of workers to a fall in real wages. Kaldor (1959a,b) discusses some of the forces governing money wage increases. Harris (1967) examines in a growth model the implications of an assumption that money-wage rates are determined so as to satisfy a "dynamic wage- adjustment function."

[43] For a more comprehensive assessment of Keynesian theory, see the essays in Lekachman 1964. See also "The Place of Keynes in the History of Economic Thought," in Meek 1967. Robinson (1965: 56–69) and Leijonhufvud (1968) point to a resurgence of "pre-Keynesian" theory in a "Keynesian" garb after Keynes.

prevailed such as to establish equality of the real wage rate and the marginal product of labor.[44] It was Kalecki who pointed out not only that unemployment and excess capacity are the normal case under contemporary capitalism but also that prices and profit margins are governed by the monopoly position of firms. His "degree of monopoly" theory was developed to explain this situation. The neo-Keynesian theory combines Keynes's contribution with that of Kalecki. The case corresponding to what we have called "Kaldor's model" stands in between as a special sort of hybrid in which all the possibilities of competitive pricing, monopoly pricing, autonomous investment decisions, and full employment could be present at the same time because all of these happened by accident to be consistent.

Conclusion

The neo-Keynesian theory brings to the forefront of analysis the expansionary drive of firms and their "technical dynamism" as basic forces governing the operation of the capitalist economy. The theory focuses upon the interconnections between profits and accumulation as the structural links through which these forces operate. The realized rate of profit emerges from this analysis as determined within the conditions of saving and consumption on the part of different income groups so as to be consistent with the overall rate of accumulation that is going on. No systematic theoretical account is provided of the conditions of determination of the profit rate from the side of production and the relations of production.

Within this overall conception, emphasis is given to the existence of unemployment and excess capacity as chronic features of the operation of the capitalist economy, which are in turn connected with the volume of investment activity being undertaken from one period to the next. It is argued that there is no automatic self-adjusting mechanism such as to bring about continuous expansion at full employment. In these respects, Kaldor's analysis is an exception.

Determination of the rate of accumulation itself is problematical for this theory. Related to this is a problem of characterizing the nature of the firm, its pricing and profit-retention policies, and the conditions of its expansion within a world of firms. The work of Kalecki has suggested a

---

[44] See Keynes (1936: 17). He did go on from this to introduce the notion of "user cost" to account for profit margins under competition, as well as a concept of "normal cost" pricing.

way of resolving some of these problems within a conception of the economy as a whole, characterized in terms of its competitive structure or the "degree of monopoly." This conception has been carried further by Steindl, who builds upon these ideas and others developed from the Marxian tradition. In a much neglected work, Steindl (1952) offers a theoretical account of the process of expansion of the capitalist economy as a whole, focusing upon the central role of the "monopolistic type of industry" and the long-term structural changes associated with its emergence as a central feature of modern capitalism.

A significant line of development of Keynesian theory after Keynes was in the area of business cycle analysis. This involved a concerted attempt to explain, within the framework of this theory, the cyclical dynamics of the capitalist economy. This effort seems to have been diverted by a concern for analyzing the properties of steady states and for explaining a limited set of "stylized facts."

Chapter Nine

The Neoclassical Approach

Introduction

In the controversies arising from the discussion of Harrod's problem, the neoclassical approach has come to occupy the center of the stage. It is held by its exponents to offer an alternative answer to Harrod's problem and to provide the basis for a theory of growth and distribution.[1] The object of our investigation in this chapter is to examine the substance of the neoclassical approach and the theoretical foundations upon which it is constructed.

We examine first the internal structure and meaning of a neoclassical "parable" based on the concept of a "surrogate production function." We go on from this to show how the parable fits into the framework of a specifically neoclassical theory of growth and distribution. Then, an elaboration of the neoclassical theory in the context of a two-sector model of production is considered. Finally, the main elements of a theoretical critique of this approach are presented, and some broad conclusions are drawn from the discussion.

The form of the neoclassical conception as presented here has provided the analytical basis for study of a wide range of economic problems at both a theoretical and an empirical level. Specifically, in this form, the neoclassical theory has been applied to problems of the labor market, the demand for capital and investment, the "optimal" rate of saving, the "sources of economic growth," and the economic effects and requirements of government policy, as well as to international comparisons of income distribution, economic stagnation in underdeveloped economies, and the economic history of capitalist economies. Many such applications exist

[1] See Solow 1956, 1970a; Swan 1956; Meade 1961.

that are too numerous to mention. We do not go into the question of their meaning and validity. Rather, the discussion is limited to an evaluation of the theoretical content of the neoclassical conception itself. It should be clear, however, that this evaluation must have direct implications for assessing the validity of all such applications.

The Production Function and Distribution

The neoclassical parable is set out in terms of an economy which produces a single commodity, say, corn, using labor and stocks of corn as capital good (seed corn). At the center of the parable is the production function for corn, or the "surrogate production function."[2] Write this as

(9.1)
$$Y = F(K,L)$$

which relates output of corn Y to inputs of corn-as-capital-good K and labor L.[3] The stock of corn depreciates at a fixed rate δ per period. Production is assumed to be subject to constant returns to scale (F is linear-homogeneous). Because of this we can rewrite (9.1) per unit of labor as

(9.2)
$$y = f(k) \qquad y = \frac{Y}{L}, \quad k = \frac{K}{L}$$

The function $f(\cdot)$ is continuously differentiable with positive and diminishing marginal products of the factors. In particular, a "well-behaved" production function which satisfies the Inada conditions[4] is characterized by

(9.3)
$$f(0) = 0, \qquad f(\infty) = \infty$$
$$f'(k) > 0, \qquad f''(k) < 0$$
$$\lim_{k \to 0} f'(k) = \infty, \qquad \lim_{k \to \infty} f'(k) = 0$$

The full significance of these conditions will appear subsequently. For the moment their meaning should be clear: it is always possible to find techniques for producing more (or less) output of corn per man by adding to (or reducing) the stock of corn relative to labor (the corn-labor ratio) no matter what the size of that stock is, short of infinity.

---

[2] The concept of a "surrogate production function" is due to Samuelson (1962). Hicks (1965, ch. 24) has proposed as an alternative a "sophisticated production function." The arguments considered here apply also to this construction.

[3] All that is said here applies with equal force to the neoclassical notion of a production function that shifts over time in accordance with technical change.

[4] See Inada 1965.

The preceding describes the available technology. Given this technology and facing competitive markets with given price of output, wage rate of labor w, and gross rental rate of the capital good $\delta + r$ (which, in this context, is the same as the rate of gross profit),[5] firms choose that technique of production (a corn-labor ratio corresponding to a point on the production function) which maximizes profits for the firm (minimizes costs). This requires that in equilibrium that technique is chosen at which the marginal product of each input equals its price. We therefore have the equilibrium conditions

$$(9.4) \qquad \delta + r = \frac{\partial Y}{\partial K} = f'(k)$$

$$(9.5) \qquad w = \frac{\partial Y}{\partial L} = f(k) - f'(k)k$$

By combining (9.2), (9.4), and (9.5), we get $y = f(k) = w + (\delta + r)k$. Thus, payment of the factors according to their marginal products automatically exhausts the total product, which is in keeping with Euler's theorem.[6]

The same conditions could be derived in terms of our earlier analysis of the choice of technique as follows. By assumption, the technology consists of an infinity of pairs of production coefficients (y,k) corresponding to the locus described by the function $f(\cdot)$. Since there is a single homogeneous commodity, units of output exchange one to one against each other (their relative price is unity). In equilibrium, this price covers costs of production consisting of wages plus gross profits. Thus we have for each technique

$$(9.6) \qquad 1 = w\left(\frac{1}{y}\right) + (\delta + r)\left(\frac{k}{y}\right)$$

Hence

$$(9.7) \qquad r = \frac{f(k) - w}{k} - \delta$$

---

[5] Throughout the subsequent discussion we isolate for consideration the rate of *net* profit, which is r, and the corresponding share of net profits in income. The rate of profit is also regarded as synonymous with the rate of interest in accordance with neoclassical usage; but see pp. 44–48.

[6] On the role of Euler's theorem in the marginal productivity theory of distribution, see Robinson 1934 and Stigler 1941, ch. 12.

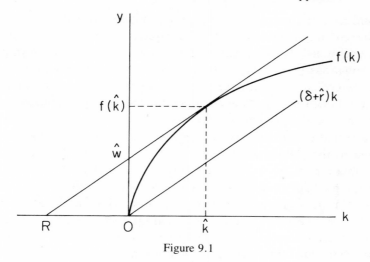

Figure 9.1

Now, let the wage rate be given, say $w = \bar{w}$. Then, maximize r with respect to k. The conditions (9.4) and (9.5) follow from the condition for a maximum. In particular, for a maximum we have from (9.7) the first-order condition

$$\frac{dr}{dk} = \frac{kf'(k) - f(k) + w}{k^2} = 0$$

which evidently requires $w = f(k) - f(k)k$, as in (9.5). Substituting this solution into (9.7) gives $\delta + r = f'(k)$, as in (9.4). The assumed properties of the production function ensure that a maximum always exists and that it is unique.

An illustration of the choice of technique is presented in Figure 9.1 for a given production function $f(k)$. Let the wage-rental ratio be OR. From OR a line is drawn tangent to the production function. This point of tangency determines a unique profit-maximizing technique $\hat{k}$. The corresponding values of w and r follow from the marginal-product conditions. Alternatively, $\hat{k}$ is the profit-maximizing technique corresponding to a given wage rate $\hat{w}$ or to a given profit rate $\hat{r}$.

The marginal product conditions (9.4) and (9.5) thus express in this context the profit-maximizing (or cost-minimizing) criterion for choice of technique that would be observed by each and every producer operating in competitive markets. Of course, under competitive conditions, the quantities w and r are *given* to the producers. But, from the point of view of the economy as a whole, there is still a question of how these magnitudes are determined. We may express this point another way by saying that the equations (9.4) and (9.5) by themselves are sufficient to determine only two of the three variables w, r, k. One of these variables (or a ratio of two of them, say, the "wage-rental ratio") must be given independently in terms of additional equation(s).

Note that certain analytical complications are being suppressed here, owing to the assumption that there is only one capital good which is the same commodity as the single output. In a model of production with many capital goods, if we continue to maintain the neoclassical assumption of a well-behaved production function with the different capital goods as inputs, then there is a marginal product for each of the capital goods taken separately in each line of production. The competitive equilibrium condition expressing the profit-maximizing choice of technique is that the money value of the marginal product (which is the marginal product times the price of output) of each type of capital good is equal to the money rental of the capital good (which is the price of the capital good times the rate of profit) and is the same in all lines. Thus the connection between the marginal product of the individual capital goods and the rate of profit is indirect: it goes by way of the prices which themselves depend on the rate of profit. When there is only one produced commodity which serves as capital good, the situation becomes quite different. For then the relative price of this commodity is unity (it exchanges one to one against itself). Prices therefore drop out of the marginal product condition, and, there being only one capital good, there is correspondingly only one such condition. A direct relation is thereby established between the marginal product of the capital good, which is a purely technological datum, and the rate of profit. The marginal product of the capital good is in turn uniquely related to the stock of the capital good per man, owing to the assumptions concerning the production function. An analogy may be found here with Ricardo's case of a corn-producing economy in which the overall rate of profit is uniquely determined by technical conditions in the production of corn and a wage rate that is fixed in terms of corn (see Chapter 1, p. 8 (n. 7). There is, nevertheless, a basic difference insofar as the neoclassical parable requires not only that a commodity such as corn exists but that it is the only produced commodity, and that the techniques of production are infinitely variable.

Consider now a difference in equilibrium positions associated with a difference in the rate of profit. At a given rate of profit, one technique is chosen. At a different rate of profit, corresponding to a different equilibrium position for the economy as a whole, the technique chosen, and hence the corn-labor ratio, would be different. We can derive from the production function and the marginal-product conditions the exact relations that would prevail among the wage rate, profit rate, and quantity of the capital good per man in different equilibria. Specifically, by differentiating (9.4) and (9.5) we get

(9.8) $$\frac{dr}{dk} = f''(k) < 0$$

(9.9) $$\frac{dw}{dk} = -f''(k)k > 0$$

which give the slopes of the equilibrium relations, the signs of which reflect the assumptions governing the production function. These relations are graphed in Figure 9.2. Associated with any corn-labor ratio is a unique set of factor prices, and vice versa. An increase (decrease) in the quantity of one factor relative to the other is associated with a lower (higher) relative price of that factor.

We can combine the two relations (9.4) and (9.5) to get a relation between the wage and profit rates that would prevail in different equilibria. By virtue of the conditions (9.3), $r = f'(k) - \delta$ is a single-valued function and therefore has an inverse such that

(9.10) $$k = k(r), \qquad k' < 0$$

Substituting (9.10) and (9.4) into (9.5) gives

(9.11) $$w = f[k(r)] - (\delta + r)k(r)$$

This is the wage-profit frontier corresponding to the given technical conditions. A frontier such as this, giving the wage and profit rates consistent with a given technology under competitive conditions, could be computed from any technology in which any number of commodities (not just one) are produced by themselves and labor.[7] Because of the

---

[7] This relation was named the "factor-price frontier" by Samuelson (1962). Names are, of course, important. The importance of this particular name is that it expresses the neoclassical conception of profits as the price or reward of a "factor." But this is to attach a particular view of the nature and origin of profits arising out of a particular theory of profits to a relation that is equally consistent with any relevant theory of profits.

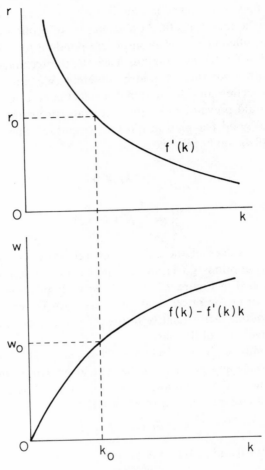

Figure 9.2

special conditions underlying this particular frontier, however, certain special results follow. Specifically, from differentiation of (9.11)—or from dividing (9.9) by (9.8)—it follows that

(9.12)
$$-\frac{dw}{dr} = k$$

so that the absolute value of the slope of the frontier at any point on that frontier is equal to the quantity of the capital good per man. Furthermore, after multiplying (9.12) by r/w we get

$$-\frac{r}{w} \cdot \frac{dw}{dr} = \frac{rk}{w} = \pi$$

which says that the elasticity of the frontier at any point is equal to the ratio of total profits per man and wages per man, or the relative share π of profits and wages in the net product.[8]

Thus the parable tells us that, knowing only the quantity of the capital good per man and the technology, we can find from the frontier the corresponding wage and profit rates that would rule under competitive conditions. The elasticity of the frontier at that point gives the relative share of profits and wages. The distribution of income is therefore completely determined by technology and relative "factor endowments." An increase (decrease) in the quantity of one factor relative to the other lowers (raises) its price. The distribution of income varies accordingly, depending on the particular form of the technology, that is, depending on the "elasticity of substitution."[9] In this way, the analysis incorporates the argument that relative factor prices reflect relative "scarcity" of the different factors, and the amount which each factor gets from the national product is determined by technology and relative factor endowments. As J. B. Clark (1891: 313) earlier expressed it: "What a social class gets is, under natural law, what it contributes to the general output of industry."

All of this story is "true," meaning logically consistent, for a "one-commodity" world, that is, a world in which only one commodity is produced.[10] Beyond this, it is claimed that this story can be used as a "parable," or a stand-in, for a more complex world in which many commodities are produced and there are many different capital goods. The production function, it is argued, can serve as a "surrogate" for the relations which prevail in this sort of world. To quote Samuelson (1962: 194): "We can sometimes predict exactly how certain quite complicated

[8] Were it not for the special conditions underlying it, this might be thought to be a remarkable result. Samuelson, who was the first to derive it, evidently thought so. He remarked in this connection: "the Frontier can ... give us more information than merely what the wage and profit rates will be at any point. Improbable as it may first seem to be, it is a fact that the behavior of stationary equilibria *in the neighborhood* of a particular equilibrium point will completely determine the possible level(s) of relative factor shares in total output *at* that point itself. It is as if going from New York to its suburbs were necessary and sufficient to tell us the unseen properties of New York City itself." (*Ibid.*, p. 199.)

[9] For a discussion of the concept of elasticity of substitution, see Hicks 1936 and Allen 1967, ch. 3. When the elasticity of substitution is unity, as in the case of the well-known Cobb-Douglas production function, the distribution of income is independent of the capital-labor ratio and depends only on the technology.

[10] The characteristics of this particular case were derived in the context of our earlier analysis (see pp. 150–54).

heterogeneous capital models will behave by treating them *as if* they had come from a simple generating production function (even when we know they did not really come from such a function)." And again (p. 201): "Simple neoclassical models in a rigorous and specifiable sense can be regarded as the stylized version of a certain quasi-realistic . . . model of diverse heterogeneous capital goods processes."

On the face of it, given the very special assumptions on which the parable is constructed—the one-commodity assumption is especially severe—one might be tempted to dismiss the parable as simply uninteresting, if not irrelevant. As Joan Robinson has suggested in this connection, it is rather like putting the rabbit into the hat in full view of the audience and then pulling it out again. Suppose, however, that we agree to treat it seriously as a theoretical construct. We might then go on to examine to what extent, if at all, the relations which hold in the parable world can be said to represent the relations in a more complex world. One need not thereby accept the conception of theory as "parable" or "fairy tale."[11] Instead, it is possible to view the preceding formulation as a first approximation based on simplifying assumptions.[12] Further *theoretical* analysis then needs to be carried out through introducing the relevant complications and checking to see whether the essential propositions of the parable continue to hold.

The implications of introducing some of these complications, as related specifically to the heterogeneity of capital goods viewed in terms of their technical methods of production, can already be grasped from the analysis presented in previous chapters. They constitute the basis for a critique of the internal logic of the neoclassical conception. We shall return to this below (pp. 237–43). Before going on to that, we consider in the next section how the parable fits into the broader context of the neoclassical theory of growth.

The Neoclassical Theory of Employment and Growth

Is it possible to have steady growth with full employment in the capitalist economy? This is the question, as posed by Harrod, to which the

[11] These terms are due to Samuelson (1962). Neoclassical writers in the recent tradition have been noticeably reluctant to state explicitly their own methodology. It is therefore difficult to grasp what exactly is intended to be the scientific status of the notion of "parable" or "fairy tale." This is especially so in view of the innumerable attempts that have been made to obtain direct estimates of the production function, recognized as a relation located in a "parable" world, from empirical data generated in the "real" world.

[12] Samuelson (1957: 891) observed: "Modern science and economics abound with simplifying first approximations, but one readily admits their inferiority to second ap-

neoclassical theory of growth was designed to provide an answer. Harrod's answer to this question, it will be recalled, was that there existed only one "warranted" rate of growth at which the economy could expand consistent with equilibrium of saving and investment. Therefore, only by accident could this rate equal the "natural" rate made possible by growth of the labor force and technical change. If the actual rate happened to differ from the warranted rate, the system was unlikely ever to achieve equilibrium. Instead it might proceed by a series of investment booms interrupted by slumps or relapse into a state of complete stagnation.

In the neoclassical theory, by contrast, the warranted growth rate can always be made equal to the natural rate, whatever the latter might be. Furthermore, the system tends to approach an equilibrium of steady growth, starting from any position different from that required for steady growth. The essential core of this argument, starting with the contributions of Solow (1956) and Swan (1956), was set out utilizing the concept of an aggregate production function as described in the previous section. The argument can be sketched as follows.

Let there be given quantities of corn-as-capital-good K_0 and of labor L_0 available for employment. At any moment the available supply of factors is thrown inelastically upon the market. Factor markets can clear if factor prices settle at a level such that firms are willing to choose, in accordance with the profit-maximizing criterion expressed in equations (9.4) and (9.5), the particular combination of factors consistent with the available supply (K_0, L_0). In this sense there can always be full employment of available labor and "capital," provided that wage and rental rates in real terms (that is, in terms of corn as numeraire) are free to settle at the appropriate level. Unemployment can occur only if, for some unexplained reason, the wage rate (or rental rate) is too high. In formal terms, what this means is that the procedure described in the previous section for obtaining the profit-maximizing choice of technique is now reversed. Instead of finding the corn-labor ratio appropriate to a given wage or profit rate, we now find the wage and profit rates appropriate to given quantities of the factors. The assumed properties of the production function ensure the existence of a unique solution at positive levels of w and r for any arbitrary quantities K_0, L_0.

---

proximations and drops them when challenged." He was then concerned with dismissing the simplifying first approximation of a labor theory of value based on the assumption of a production system with a uniform organic composition of capital. It is interesting to note that this same assumption is crucial for the neoclassical parable to hold.

What ensures that the output produced by employing all the available labor is sold? In the parable world, whatever is not consumed (saved) from the total output of corn must be invested. This is because corn is the only form in which wealth can be accumulated, and its investment in production always yields the going rate of profit. Thus there can never be any discrepancy between saving and investment decisions. The Keynesian problem of unemployment due to shortage of effective demand and the Marxian problem of realization of surplus value are thereby ruled out. With full employment thus assured, the equilibrium level of income is obtained from the production function.

Assume now that net saving is a fixed proportion s of total income. For saving-investment equilibrium we have, after deducting depreciation, $I = sY$, and the warranted rate of growth of "capital" is then

$$(9.13) \qquad g = \frac{I}{K} = \frac{sf(k)}{k}$$

Suppose that available labor grows over time at a constant rate n, which is exogenously determined; then $L = L_0 e^{nt}$. For steady full-employment growth at a constant corn-labor ratio, it is required that the stock of corn grow at the same rate as labor, or

$$(9.14) \qquad g = n$$

From (9.13) and (9.14) it follows that $f(k)/k = n/s$. The assumptions concerning the production function ensure that a unique value of the

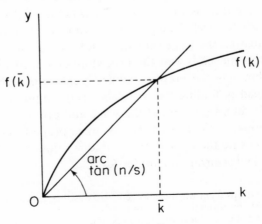

Figure 9.3

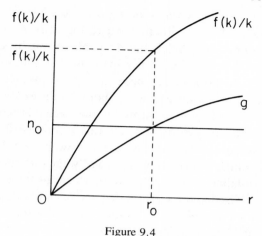

Figure 9.4

corn-labor ratio always exists that provides a solution to this equation.

The solution is illustrated in Figure 9.3. Given the labor-force growth rate n, the saving proportion s, and the technology represented by $f(k)$, we find a value of $k = k^*$ such that $n/s = f(k^*)/k^*$, and it is unique.

The solution in the case of saving behavior represented by $0 < s_w < s_r$ is shown in Figure 9.4. Here we draw a relation between the rate of profit r and the output-capital ratio $f(k)/k$ consistent with the given technology. From the investment/saving equilibrium condition we get the corresponding warranted growth rate as

$$(9.15) \qquad g = (s_r - s_w)r + s_w \frac{f(k)}{k}$$

This relation is represented by the g-curve in the diagram. Intersection of this curve and the horizontal line corresponding to the growth rate n_0 determines the profit rate r_0 and the output-capital ratio $\overline{f(k)/k}$. In this case, the profit rate and output-capital ratio are simultaneously determined.

It is easy to go on to show in this framework that, starting from any position which is different from that required for steady growth (implying that $k_0 \neq k^*$), the economy will undergo an adjustment process leading eventually to attainment of steady growth. Suppose that, by historical accident as it were, the economy starts out in a position where saving out of full-employment income exceeds the investment required at the existing corn-labor ratio to provide employment for the increment in the labor force. The existing corn-labor ratio is, so to speak, too low. In Harrod's terms we have a situation where the warranted growth rate exceeds the natural rate. Since the available saving is automatically invested, the total stock of corn per man rises by the amount of this saving. Once the investment has been made, it turns out that there is too much corn to employ the available labor with the existing production technique. Competition among firms for the available labor drives up the wage rate, and, correspondingly, the rate of profit falls. At a higher wage rate (lower profit rate), firms find it now profitable to adopt a technique with a higher corn-labor ratio. The wage rate rises to the point where that corn-labor ratio is selected at which all the available stock of corn is fully utilized and the excess demand for labor disappears.

If the warranted growth rate continues to exceed the natural rate in subsequent periods, these adjustments are repeated. As the process continues, the total stock of corn per man is rising all the time, the rate of profit is falling, and the technique of production is being continually adjusted—*a higher corn-labor ratio for a lower profit rate*—so as to maintain full utilization of "capital" and labor. But, as the corn-labor ratio rises in this way, the same amount of saving provides less and less employment. Eventually, a point is reached where the corn-labor ratio is such that the available saving is just sufficient to employ the increment in the labor force. The gap between warranted and natural growth rates is then eliminated and the situation becomes consistent with a steady state.

When the warranted rate is less than the natural rate, a similar process operates in the opposite direction. In this case, the amount of saving is not enough to employ the increment in the labor force. The wage rate falls (the profit rate rises) and correspondingly the corn-labor ratio falls until a steady state is reached.

All of this shows that the system is *stable* in the sense that any departure from the steady state will bring into operation an adjustment process such as to induce a return to it. The argument is illustrated in Figure 9.5 for the case of a uniform saving proportion. The curve $sf(k)$ represents the amount of saving at full employment for each level of the corn-labor ratio k. The ray nk represents the investment required to maintain full employment at each corn-labor ratio when the labor force grows at the rate n. If $sf(k)$ is above nk, then k is rising; if below, then k is falling. The arrows indicate the direction of movement in each case. The appropriate steady-state value of k is k^*.

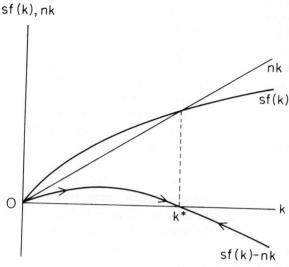

Figure 9.5

It may be noted that the argument is conducted throughout in terms of a process of movement "up" (or "down") the production function. Specifically, the economy is assumed to undergo a process of accumulation involving a continuous increase (decrease) in the stock of corn per man while the rate of profit falls (rises) and the technique of production is continually adjusted to each successive level of the profit rate. Here we see the significance of the assumptions concerning technology and production. In particular, accumulation consists of adding part of the output of corn to the stock of corn already in existence. A change in production technique for the entire stock of preexisting and "new" corn can be implemented instantaneously and without cost in response to a change in "factor prices" simply by varying the quantity of corn per man employed. In this sense, there is direct substitution of "capital" for labor. Because of the assumptions concerning the production function, such substitution can be carried out indefinitely while continuing to yield positive wage and profit rates. Therefore, full employment of available labor and "capital" is always possible, whatever the size of the labor force and stock of "capital." Furthermore, such substitution can always go on until the steady state is reached.

A striking feature of this analysis is thus that there is no need to distinguish between the comparison of different steady states and a process of change through which an economy moves. Every point on the production function corresponds to a particular steady state, each with a given set of conditions, as well as to a point on the path of movement of an economy toward a steady state. All of this is made possible by the assumption of a one-commodity economy. In such an economy, there is no such thing as a given stock of means of production specific to particular uses. The stock of "capital" is assumed to be instantaneously adaptable to employ any quantity of labor and to produce any quantity of output. Accordingly, there is no problem of the degree of utilization of a given stock of capital equipment varying with the level of demand in the short run. Indeed, there can be no problem of demand at all, since whatever is produced is either consumed or invested. Say's Law holds without exception. It is assumed, moreover, that "factor prices" are free to respond appropriately in any given situation. In particular, the real wage rate moves up or down to the appropriate extent in response to any excess demand or supply of labor. The profit rate falls or rises as soon as there is any oversaving or undersaving.

There is an obvious question in all this about whether—and, if so, how—the process of adjustment would work itself out in an economy in which stocks of equipment are specific to different uses and there is a (changing) structure of relative prices of the different commodities, in which firms make investment decisions in the light of expectations of future profits, wealth is held in the form of money, and the wage rate (in terms of money) is set by bargaining between workers and employers. The preceding analysis is incapable of dealing with these matters by virtue of the assumptions on which it is based.[13] In this connection, it may be noted that the process by which an economy is supposed to adjust from an arbitrary initial position to the steady state raises a number of serious problems for the neoclassical theory, once allowance is made for the existence of more than one type of means of production (see, for instance, Hahn [1968]). These problems are effectively suppressed within the framework of assumptions of a "one-commodity model." What is in-

---

[13] Neoclassical models have been constructed in which a concept of money is introduced. See, for instance, Tobin 1955, 1965. But the nature of money in this conception is such as to be a purely external condition with no real basis in the ongoing economic process itself. This must of necessity be so as long as the assumption of a one-commodity economy is retained. For, with one good produced, which can be exchanged directly with labor, the necessity of a distinct mechanism for the expression of general purchasing power is eliminated. In general, this class of models fails to provide a meaningful account of the monetary relation itself and is therefore unable to deal adequately with the essential properties of a monetary economy.

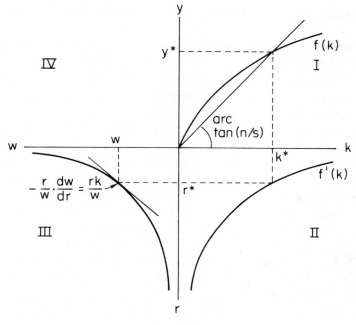

Figure 9.6

volved here, quite apart from the other matters discussed in this chapter, is the failure of the neoclassical theory to provide an account of the *process of change* in a capitalist economy, except through the artificial device of a "sequence of momentary equilibria."[14]

Growth and Distribution

We can now bring together the various elements of the neoclassical formulation so as to exhibit the nature of the interdependencies and causal links that are involved. These relations are depicted in Figure 9.6. The production function is drawn in quadrant I. Quadrant II gives the equilibrium profit rate consistent with each corn-labor ratio. Quadrant

---

[14] Robinson (1971a: 14–15) refers to the neoclassical conception of a process of accumulation with changing technique and falling rate of profit as a "Wicksell process," noting that "Wicksell himself gave it up in despair." She points out that "The difficulty of the problem arises . . . from attempting to rig up assumptions to make it seem plausible that a private-enterprise economy would continuously accumulate, under long-period equilibrium conditions, with continuous full employment . . . , without any cyclical disturbances, in face of a continuously falling rate of profit." (Robinson 1959: 433.)

III describes the wage-profit frontier corresponding to the given technology.

From the point of view of the problem of distribution, it can be seen that the basic idea here is that of a one-to-one correspondence between the relative size of factor endowments (the corn-labor ratio) and the price of those factors and hence the distribution of income. Once we know the factor endowment k and the technology corresponding to the production function $f(k)$, we can find from the frontier the corresponding distribution of income. When this notion is embedded in a theory of growth, a further explanation is provided concerning the determination of relative factor endowments. Corresponding to a given saving proportion and growth rate of labor, there is a unique corn-labor ratio consistent with steady growth, as in quadrant I. A higher saving rate is associated with a higher corn-labor ratio, and a higher growth rate of labor with a lower corn-labor ratio. From quadrants II and III we see that the distribution of income varies according to the level of the corn-labor ratio. We conclude from this that the distribution of income depends on relative factor endowments and on technology. The factor endowments themselves reflect the habits of thrift of the population represented by the uniform saving proportion s and the forces underlying expansion of the labor force at the rate n.[15]

Strictly interpreted, the conception of distribution involved here makes no specific statement regarding the distribution of income either between classes or between individuals. There is no reference to the distribution of income between capital and labor as social classes or between owners of means of production and owners of labor power. Rather, the conception is one that relates to determination of the prices of factors of production consistent with their relative scarcity and with the given technical conditions. These factor prices, or rates of return to factors, would be associated with a specific distribution of income among individuals depending on the specific amounts of the factors that each individual owns. To provide

---

[15] Note, however, that this interpretation hinges critically upon the assumption of a uniform saving proportion for all categories of income and all classes. When the overall rate of saving depends upon the distribution of income between profits and wages, the profit rate and corn-labor ratio are simultaneously determined. There is then no room for a one-way relationship between factor endowments, technology, and income distribution. Furthermore, if it is assumed that saving out of wages is zero, the profit rate is determined by the growth rate and the saving proportion for profits, and is *independent of technology and factor endowments*. Similarly, under the conditions of Pasinetti's (1962) theorem, the profit rate is completely determined by the growth rate and saving propensity of a class of "pure capitalists" (see Chapter 7).

a determination of the distribution of income among individuals, it would therefore be necessary to provide a specification of the ownership distribution of factors among them and to account for the specific pattern of that ownership distribution. There is no basis for such a determination within the neoclassical conception, except by arbitrarily taking the ownership distribution as given.

Thus the neoclassical approach resolves the problem of income distribution first by altering radically the terms in which the problem is posed in such a way as to shift attention away from different classes of income recipients, or classes with a specific location within the economic process as a whole, and toward the pricing of factors of production. In this sense, there is no theory of distribution at all, since the pricing of factors does not itself account for the distribution of ownership of factors. The distribution of income between individuals is the result of the quantity of their initial factor endowment, and this latter is regarded as outside the scope of the analysis.

It is evident that what sustains the growth of the economy in this scheme is the expansion of the labor force, the rate of such expansion being presupposed as an unexplained datum. Given this growth rate and the saving habits represented by s, the rate of expansion of capital adjusts so as to provide the capital required to maintain full employment of the available labor force at the corn-labor ratio appropriate to a steady state. Steady growth at full employment is guaranteed by the assumptions that (1) firms are willing to carry out investment corresponding to whatever saving is going on, (2) techniques of production are sufficiently variable so as to allow for choice of the appropriate technique, and (3) markets for labor and "capital" operate to ensure the wage and profit rates consistent with that technique.

The entire underlying rationale for growth must be seen to lie here in the maintenance of the equilibrium corn-labor ratio so as to provide employment for an autonomously growing labor supply. Growth is simply the manner in which the economy adjusts to the increasing supply of labor. Being subordinated in this way, both to the labor supply and to autonomous saving decisions, accumulation of capital can have no independent force such as is found, for instance, in the neo-Keynesian analysis presented in the previous chapter. Thus, what is specific to the neoclassical approach to the theory of economic growth is the conception of growth as a form of adjustment to savings decisions and to factor supplies. It is presumed, furthermore, that there always exists a unique state of steady growth with full employment to which the economy will adjust, given enough time.

Insofar as the saving proportion s and the labor force growth rate n are merely taken as *given* (that is, their status is that of parameters), then this formulation is consistent with any theory of saving and any theory of labor-force growth that determines the quantities s and n in terms of exogenous conditions. Of course, the assumption that these quantities can be considered to be exogenously determined is already quite special. However, for the particular purposes of the neoclassical conception, an appeal is usually made to the presumed "intertemporal preferences" of individuals as the determinant of savings and the presumed "work-leisure preferences" of individuals as the determinant of the labor supply. This appeal is made on the basis of a "full-blown" theory, the neoclassical theory of general equilibrium. It is then apparent that what is even more specific to the neoclassical approach is the conception of growth as an adjustment to independently given preferences of individuals.

A number of theoretical elaborations of this scheme are possible, all hinging on the specified properties of the production function. For instance, it can be shown that lower profit rates are associated with higher corn-labor ratios, and these with higher levels of output and consumption per man up to a maximum. This association is thought to be consistent with the neoclassical idea that lower profit rates give rise to investment in "more mechanized" techniques of production, which yield greater output and consumption per man as a return to the "sacrifice" of current consumption involved in investing in the more mechanized technique.[16] The "golden rule of accumulation" can be shown to hold so that consumption per man is maximized when the rate of profit is set equal to the rate of growth (see Phelps 1966, Koopmans 1965).[17] By a slight reconstruction the analysis has also been made to apply to the problem of economic stagnation in underdeveloped economies (see Solow 1956: 90; Nelson 1956; Buttrick 1958, 1960).

The Neoclassical Formulation in a Two-Sector Model

So far as the formal structure of the neoclassical conception presented here is concerned, it might appear, on the surface of it, to be a charming edifice. For, in one stroke, two sets of problems appear to be solved. First, the analysis shows that steady growth with full employment is

---

[16] This element of the neoclassical conception is discussed on pp. 241–43.
[17] This result was examined in the context of our earlier analysis (see pp. 167–72).

always possible in the capitalist economy and will tend to be established starting from any position. Second, the distribution of income (or, strictly, the pricing of factors of production) on the steady-state path is explained as a function of technology and prevailing factor endowments, those endowments being related to saving behavior and population growth. But it is necessary to examine further the logic of this conception and the propositions derived from it. Accordingly, in this section we examine another form in which the neoclassical conception has been elaborated. In particular, this conception has been elaborated in the context of a system which produces two commodities, a capital good and a consumption good.[18] We consider here whether certain basic elements of this conception hold up in this context, specifically concerning the determination of the rate of profit and distribution of income between wages and profits.

In the neoclassical two-sector model the capital good is assumed to be physically homogeneous for all techniques of production. All complications associated with heterogeneity of capital goods between one technique and another are thereby avoided. The consumption good is also assumed to be the same for all techniques, but this is a less drastic assumption for present purposes. The production functions for both commodities (or sectors) display constant returns to scale, continuous and infinite substitutability between capital and labor, and diminishing returns to each factor. They may be written as

$$(9.16) \qquad y_1 = f_1(k_1) \qquad y_1 = Y_1/L_1, \quad k_1 = K_1/L_1$$

$$(9.17) \qquad y_2 = f_2(k_2) \qquad y_2 = Y_2/L_2, \quad k_2 = K_2/L_2$$

where the subscripts 1 and 2 signify, repectively, capital good and consumption good sectors and the functions $f_1(\cdot)$ and $f_2(\cdot)$ satisfy the usual conditions. The stock of capital depreciates at a fixed rate δ per period in both sectors.

Firms facing competitive markets choose the technique of production that maximizes profits. This requires that in equilibrium the following marginal product conditions hold in each sector:

$$(9.18) \qquad\qquad \delta + r = f_1'(k_1)$$

---

[18] On this, see Uzawa 1961, 1963; Solow 1961; Drandakis 1963; Inada 1964. For a direct comparison of the neoclassical two-sector model with the two-sector model of production used in our earlier analysis (in Chapters 4, 5, and 6 above), see Gram 1976.

(9.19) $$w = p_1[f_1(k_1) - f_1'(k_1)k_1]$$

(9.20) $$\delta + r = \frac{f_2'(k_2)}{p_1}$$

(9.21) $$w = f_2(k_2) - f_2'(k_2)k_2$$

where r is the rate of net profit, w the real wage rate, p_1 the price of the capital good, and the consumption good is taken as the numeraire. These four equations are sufficient to determine four of the five variables w, r, p_1, k_1, and k_2 for a given value of one of them. This is as we should expect: what we have here is the problem of choice of technique for which the rate of profit r (or the real wage rate w or w/p_1) must be given. The relative price of the commodities is in turn determined by technology and distribution.[19]

The manner of solution of the equations (9.18–21) can be conceived as follows. Let the rate of profit be given. For the capital-good sector we then find from (9.18) and (9.19) the profit-maximizing technique and wage rate in terms of the capital good. The rate of profit must be equal between the two sectors; so also must the wage rate. Thus, by equating (9.18) and (9.20) or (9.19) and (9.21), we get the relative price as

(9.22) $$p_1 = \frac{f_2'(k_2)}{f_1'(k_1)} = \frac{f_2(k_2) - f_2'(k_2)k_2}{f_1(k_1) - f_1'(k_1)k_1}$$

The price equation, together with equations (9.20) and (9.21), determines the profit-maximizing technique for the consumption-good sector and the wage rate in terms of the consumption good. It is easily checked that, corresponding to any arbitrarily given profit rate, there is a unique technique of production for each sector (or sectoral capital-labor ratio) and that the equilibrium capital-labor ratio is inversely related to the profit rate. This follows from the assumption that the production functions are well behaved.

---

[19] There is a direct correspondence between these equations and the price equations (4.1) and (4.2). To see this, we substitute (9.18) into (9.19) and (9.20) into (9.21). We then get

$$p_1 = w\frac{1}{f_1(k_1)} + (\delta + r)p_1\frac{k_1}{f_1(k_1)}, \qquad 1 = w\frac{1}{f_2(k_2)} + (\delta + r)p_1\frac{k_2}{f_2(k_2)}$$

which are the price equations for this model. As in the model of Chapter 4, we know that, given the wage rate (or profit rate) and the profit-maximizing technique corresponding to that level of w or r, there is a relative price p_1 that covers cost and is independent of the composition of demand.

Alternatively, let the wage rate be given in terms of the capital good. We then find from (9.18) and (9.19) the profit-maximizing technique in the capital-good sector and the rate of profit. This is the equilibrium level of the rate of profit for the entire production system. Thus, in this case, the overall rate of profit is determined by the given wage rate and by the technical conditions of production in the capital-good sector alone. Specifically, at the given wage rate, the rate of profit is uniquely related to the marginal product of the capital good in its own production. A formal similarity (but *only* a formal one) may be found here with Ricardo's example where the technical conditions in the corn-producing sector uniquely determine the rate of profit for the entire economy once the wage rate in terms of corn is given.[20] The same result would hold in any production system, regardless of the number of production sectors, if in that system there is one commodity which uses only its own output as capital good and the wage rate is given in terms of that commodity. A fortiori it holds also in an economy with only one sector. This is exactly what we found in the "one-commodity model," and in this light, that result now seems perfectly straightforward.

So far as the consumption-good sector is concerned, matters are quite different. The marginal product condition (9.20) involves the relative price of the two commodities. Hence, even if the wage rate is to be regarded as given in terms of the consumption good, the rate of profit cannot be known before this price is known, and the price is itself dependent on the rate of profit. No room exists, therefore, for interpreting the rate of profit in terms of a purely technical datum.

Whatever the case, it is evident that solution of the equations of this system requires that the rate of profit or the wage rate is given in advance, that is to say, *from outside the technical conditions of production.* Given, say, the profit rate, the marginal product conditions serve only to deter-

---

[20] There is a basic distinction between this case and that of Ricardo. The special feature of this case is that the possibility arises of interpreting the rate of profit as corresponding to the marginal product of "capital" viewed as a technical input into production. This feature is contingent upon the underlying assumption that "capital" and labor are technical substitutes in production. Moreover, it must be assumed that it makes sense to take the wage rate as given in terms of the capital good. (This could hardly be so from the point of view of the workers when the capital good, by definition, cannot be consumed.) In Ricardo's case, on the other hand, there is no fixed capital, or else it is employed in *fixed* proportions with labor, and so there can be no marginal product of such a technical input. Capital as property consists (entirely) of the wage fund (corn to be consumed by the workers) and of seed corn. The rate of profit paid to the owners of property represents a pure surplus of the product above wages after payment of rent.

mine the profit-maximizing technique and the wage rate in terms of own product for each sector. Similarly, given the wage rate, the rate of profit is determined. The latter corresponds to the marginal productivity of "capital" as a technical datum only when it is assumed that one commodity —which may or may not be the only produced commodity—serves both as the sole capital good (substitutable with labor) in its own production and as the sole wage good.

Consider now the wage-profit frontier for this system. For this purpose, take the wage rate measured in terms of the capital good. Since the capital good is assumed to be the same for all techniques, we can represent the wage-profit frontier in terms of this measure of the wage. By virtue of the conditions (9.3), we have

$$(9.23) \qquad k_i = k_i(r), \quad k_i' < 0 \qquad i = 1, 2$$

Accordingly, the frontier is derived from (9.18) and (9.19) as

$$(9.24) \qquad \frac{w}{p_1} = f_1[k_1(r)] - (\delta + r)k_1(r) = \varphi_1(r)$$

and by differentiation we get

$$(9.25) \qquad \frac{d(w/p_1)}{dr} = -k_1(r) < 0$$

If follows that the slope of the wage-profit frontier measured in terms of the capital good is exactly equal to the capital-labor ratio of the capital-good sector. Therefore the share of profits relative to wages in this sector is equal to the elasticity of the frontier (multiply both sides of (9.25) by rp_1/w). Thus, when the wage is specified in terms of the capital good, the *share* of profits in the capital-good sector is uniquely related to the technical conditions of production in that sector. This conforms to our finding above regarding the *rate* of profit under the same conditions relating to the wage. But there is, of course, no necessary reason why the share of profits in this particular sector should correspond to that prevailing in the system as a whole.

Now, take the wage rate measured in terms of the consumption good. From (9.20) and (9.21) we get the wage-profit frontier as

$$(9.26) \qquad w = f_2[k_2(r)] - (\delta + r)p_1(r)k_2(r) = \varphi_2(r)$$

where $p_1(r)$ is given by the price equation (9.22). By differentiation

$$(9.27) \qquad \frac{dw}{dr} = -k_2 p_1 \left(1 + \frac{\delta + r}{p_1} \cdot \frac{dp_1}{dr}\right) = -k_2 k_2' f_2'' < 0$$

In this case, the slope of the frontier is equal to the *value* of capital in the consumption-good sector, measured at the numeraire price of the capital good, plus a *price effect* due to a difference in price associated with the difference in the profit rate. It follows that, in this case, no direct connection can be drawn between the share of profits and the technical conditions of production such as that found in the previous case.

We can see from the result in (9.27) that, if the price of the capital good were invariant to the profit rate ($dp_1/dr = 0$), the share of profits relative to wages in the consumption-good sector would exactly equal the elasticity of the frontier. The price equation (9.22) shows that one condition guaranteeing invariance of the price of the capital good is that the production functions of the two sectors are the same. For, then, the capital-labor ratios of the two sectors are the same at every profit rate and the relative price is unity. We are then effectively back to the conditions of the one-commodity model, where, as we saw before, the overall distribution of income is uniquely related to the technology. Outside of these special conditions, however, no such relation can be found.[21] Once this point is recognized, it is not evident what role, if any, is left for the technical productivity of factors per se as a distinctive determinant of the rate of profit and distribution of income between wages and profits.

Consider, finally, the relation between the overall quantity of capital per man and the rate of profit. For this purpose, we need to add the relations for the allocation of total labor and capital stock to each sector and for the composition of output. These are

$$(9.28) \qquad K = K_1 + K_2 = \frac{k_1}{f_1(k_1)} Y_1 + \frac{k_2}{f_2(k_2)} Y_2$$

$$(9.29) \qquad L = L_1 + L_2 = \frac{1}{f_1(k_1)} Y_1 + \frac{1}{f_2(k_2)} Y_2$$

$$(9.30) \qquad Y_1 = (g + \delta)K$$

The saving/investment equilibrium condition (after subtracting depreciation) is

[21] This was shown by Solow (1968: 451–53) in the context of a two-sector model like the present one.

$$(9.31) \qquad g = s_r r + s_w \frac{w}{p_1} \cdot \frac{L}{K}$$

and for steady-state growth it is required that $g = n$.

Solving this system we find that

$$(9.32) \qquad \frac{Y_2}{K} = \frac{f_2(k_2)}{k_2} \left(1 - (g + \delta) \frac{k_1}{f_1(k_1)} \right)$$

$$(9.33) \qquad k = \frac{K}{L} = \frac{f_1(k_1)k_2}{(k_2 - k_1)(g + \delta) + f_1(k_1)}$$

$$(9.34) \qquad g = \frac{s_r f_1(k_1)k_2 + s_w \varphi_1(r) f_1(k_1)}{f_1(k_1)k_2 - s_w \varphi_1(r)(k_2 - k_1)}$$

It can be seen that, for a given rate of accumulation equal to the growth rate of labor, the rate of profit is determined from the growth-profit relation (9.34) so as to be consistent with the given growth rate, with the saving rates, and with the technology. At that profit rate, the sectoral capital-labor ratios are determined by the profit-maximizing choice of technique. The overall quantity of capital per man is determined from (9.33) so as to correspond to the sectoral capital-labor ratios and to the steady-state growth rate of capital.

We conclude from this that there is no basis in this system for conceiving of the steady-state solution in terms of a one-way relation going from relative factor endowments (as represented by k) to the profit rate. In general, the overall quantity of capital per man is dependent on the profit rate through the choice of technique, which determines the sectoral capital-labor ratios.[22] If $s_w = 0$, then (9.34) reduces to $g = s_r r$, and by setting this equal to the given growth rate of labor, the rate of profit is determined independently of technical conditions and of factor endowments.

So far as equilibrium comparisons are concerned, the pattern of variation of the quantity of capital per man in relation to the profit rate can be identified by differentiation of (9.33). Since the capital good is the same for all techniques, comparison can be made directly in terms of

---

[22] Note that this conclusion holds regardless of what the pattern of saving behavior is assumed to be. By contrast, we saw in the one-commodity model that, when there is a uniform saving proportion, it is possible to obtain the quantity of capital per man directly from the steady-state condition and the production function. The equilibrium quantity of capital per man k^* is then independent of the profit rate. The rate of profit is determined so as to be consistent with the given k^*. In the two-sector model this possibility no longer exists.

physical units of the capital good. Differences in the quantity of capital per man (thus defined) between equilibria can be separated into what we have previously called composition and substitution effects. It turns out that, even under the assumed conditions of this case, there is in general no inverse relation between the quantity of capital per man and the rate of profit. For this relation to hold, additional conditions must be satisfied.

One condition that would do is clearly $k_1 = k_2$ for all r. This takes us back to the one-commodity model. Another condition is that $k_2 > k_1$ for all r (the consumption-good sector is always relatively more "capital-intensive").[23] Other such conditions can be found (see, for instance, Drandakis 1963). They all imply specific restrictions on the price, composition, and substitution effects. These are obviously very special conditions, chosen on an ad hoc basis, without adequate theoretical justification. Outside of these very special conditions, no such relation as that required by the neoclassical parable can be found. Accordingly, no validity can then be given to an interpretation of the rate of profit as reflecting the relative scarcity of "capital" viewed as a factor of production. There is, furthermore, no room for the neoclassical conception of a "stable" adjustment process leading to the steady state through a rise in the quantity of capital per man (that is, a process of "substitution" of capital for labor) as the rate of profit falls, and vice versa.

Capital, Technique, and the Rate of Profit

We may now consider some reasons for the failure of the neoclassical parable as a theoretical construct. One may note in this connection that a central element of the parable is the idea of an inverse monotonic relation between the quantity of "capital" per man and the rate of profit. On this relation rests the conception that profits are the return to a factor of production, the rate of profits varying according to the scarcity of that factor relative to labor. On this relation rests also the notion that technical substitution between "capital" and labor as factor prices change can be relied upon to bring about a state of steady growth with full employment. For this relation to hold in a world of heterogeneous capital goods, the parable strictly requires that some independent measure of the quantity of "capital" exist, representing all of the different capital goods, which, when put into a production function of the form $y = f(k)$, where $f'(k) > 0$,

---

[23] The "capital-intensity condition," $k_2 > k_1$, together with the assumption that $s_w = 0$ (which guarantees that $dg/dr > 0$), was used by Uzawa (1961).

$f''(k) < 0$, would satisfy the marginal product condition $r = f'(k)$ and also the product-exhaustion condition $y = w + rk$.

The relation $r = f'(k)$ provides the linchpin of this whole approach. More generally, it posits a single-valued relation between the quantity of "capital" per man and the rate of profit such that $r = \psi(k)$ with $\psi' < 0$ and $k = k(r) = \psi^{-1}(k)$. If such a relation existed, it is argued, the parable would provide a "good" representation of the world of heterogeneous capital goods. With the production function, we could "predict" the unique value of r corresponding to any given value of k. In this sense we could say that technical conditions and relative factor endowments "explain" the rate of profit.

Outside of the conditions under which the parable itself is constructed, however, there is no *theoretical* justification for assuming in general that the overall quantity of "capital" per man should be inversely related to the profit rate, let alone that it should go from zero to infinity (with output per man increasing accordingly) through technical substitution of "capital" for labor and that the relation should be continuously differentiable. In general, the capital goods that enter into production consist of heterogeneous commodities. They can be expressed as a single quantity by valuing them at their respective prices, or exchange values, in terms of a chosen numeraire. There is a different set of prices for each level of the profit rate, the exact pattern of differences depending on the technical conditions of production of the different commodities.[24] The physical quantity of the capital goods and the methods by which they are produced may also be different from one equilibrium profit rate to another. The variation of the overall exchange-value of capital per man between different steady states can be viewed in terms of a price effect, a composition effect, and a substitution effect.[25] But, conceived in this way, the ratio of capital to labor cannot be regarded as necessarily an inverse function of the profit rate.

The quantity of capital in this sense, that is, as a sum of exchange value

---

[24] The reason for this is clear. In competitive equilibrium, prices equal money costs of production, consisting of wages plus profits calculated at the ruling rate on the exchange value of the stock of capital goods employed. At a higher (lower) rate of profit, the wage rate is lower (higher). The difference in total costs and price depends on the exact pattern of employment of labor and means of production throughout the whole interdependent production system.

[25] For an analysis of this relation in these terms, see above, Chapters 4 and 6, and Harris 1973.

obtained by valuing the different capital goods at the ruling prices, depends on the rate of profit. Therefore, one cannot argue that the quantity of this capital (or its "marginal product," whatever that might be supposed to mean in this context) determines the rate of profit without reasoning in a circle. For there is in general no one-way connection going from the quantity of capital in this sense to the rate of profit.[26] To express the different capital goods in terms of a single number, one could have recourse instead to a number such as their physical weight. But then there would be, in general, no unique relation between that number and the rate of profit. And, whether unique or not, it would be of no special interest from the point of view of the economic problems under consideration. By contrast, the number representing the exchange value of the stock of means of production does have economic interest, though from a different point of view. Namely, it represents the market value of the property the capitalists own and in terms of which they each receive a share in the total of profits generated in the economy. It is therefore essential both to the conception of competition between different capitals and to the treatment of the expansion of capital as a whole.

Heterogeneous capital goods, as the products of labor, can of course be reduced to the quantity of labor directly and indirectly embodied in them, that is to say, to their labor value. This particular quantity provides as good a measure as any other of the quantity of "capital" in homogeneous units. It would not, however, be an appropriate measure from the point of view of the neoclassical conception. This is for the reason that, measured in this way, capital is then simply a quantity of labor, embodied or "stored up" in means of production. Therefore the quantity of capital in this sense could be assigned no independent existence *as a factor of production*, separate and distinct from labor, which receives a share in the product in accordance with its technical productivity. By contrast, from the point of view of Marxian theory, this measure, the labor value measure, would be the theoretically correct one for analysis of distribution, and carries a special qualitative significance within the framework of that theory. Specifically, its significance is that, among other things, it expresses the

---

[26] So far as the prices are concerned, it can be shown that, under fairly general conditions, these are uniquely determined in terms of technical conditions and the rate of profit and are independent of the composition of demand (see Chapter 3). This is the full significance of the well-known "nonsubstitution theorem." For this result to hold, the rate of profit has to be, so to speak, given in advance.

social-historical character of capital as the productive power of labor materialized and transformed into objects that become instruments for domination of the laborer through his employment to the capitalist.[27]

In moving from the parable world of one commodity to a more complex world of production with heterogeneous capital goods, we find also that the neoclassical argument runs up against another difficulty, which is related to, but analytically distinct from, the previous one. This takes the form of the reswitching of techniques of production, that is, the recurrence of the same technique at different levels of the profit rate even though that technique is dominated by others at intermediate levels of the profit rate. It follows from this result that, in general, techniques cannot be uniquely ordered according to the rate of profit. The neoclassical production function is based on the assumption that such a unique ordering exists. It is on this basis, as we have seen, that an attempt is made to draw a direct and unique connection between technology and distribution. But this assumption is contradicted as soon as allowance is made for such a small complication as that the method of production of the capital good differs from one technique to another. The presumed connection between technology and distribution is thereby effectively destroyed.

As a formal matter, the essential point in all this is that the neoclassical parable assumes that "capital" is a homogeneous substance measurable independently of distribution, the quantity of which can therefore be made to "explain" distribution. In this form, "capital" is a direct input into the production process and can thus be put on the same footing as labor (considered as a homogeneous unit). But "capital" can be so regarded on one assumption only, that is, that there is a given price system for measuring the various commodity inputs and that this price system is invariant with respect to the rate of profit. This in turn presupposes that only one commodity is produced or that different commodities are perfect technical substitutes in production so that the price ratio between them is fixed. This is the special construction on which the neoclassical parable is initially based. When the scaffolding is removed, various assumptions have to be introduced if the initial structure is to be maintained. These assumptions are essentially of an ad hoc character.[28] They therefore provide weak foundations on which to base a theory of distribution and growth.

---

[27] On this see Marx, *Theories*, part 1 (1963), pp. 389–92. Marx points out here that "his [the capitalist's] domination is only that of materialised labour over living labour, of the labourer's product over the labourer himself."

[28] Hahn (1965) grants that they are all "terrible" assumptions.

Champernowne (1953) has constructed a "chain index of capital," which, under some quite restrictive conditions, permits a unique ordering of techniques in relation to the profit rate and seemingly satisfies the marginal product condition for any two consecutive techniques in that ordering. For such a "chain" to be constructed, however, the rate of profit must be treated as an independent variable, which cannot therefore be explained by the quantity of "capital" in this sense. More recently, in seeking to get away from the problem of an aggregate measure of "capital" that would be consistent with the neoclassical parable, Solow (1967) has defined a new concept, the "social rate of return," and shown that it is equal to the rate of profits. Pasinetti (1969) shows that this concept is a purely definitional relation and cannot in any meaningful sense be said to determine the level of the rate of profits.

Consumption and the Rate of Profit

Another element of the neoclassical conception is the notion that capital is "productive" in the sense that investment in "more capital-intensive," "more mechanized," or "more roundabout" methods of production yields greater consumption per man (up to a maximum). As Samuelson (1973: 598) expresses it: "It is taken to be a technological fact of life that you can get more future consumption product by using indirect or roundabout methods." The increment in consumption is regarded as the return to the "sacrifice" of current consumption involved in investing in the more mechanized technique. The profit (interest) rate is supposed to reflect, on the one hand, the trade-off between the return of future consumption and the sacrifice of current consumption consistent with the prevailing preferences of "society." On the other hand, it is supposed to reflect the "net productivity of capital" viewed as a technical characteristic of the roundabout methods.

It is not evident, at this level of analysis, what meaning is to be given to the concept of "society" conceived independently of the social classes that compose it and the distribution of income and property among those classes and to the concept of "sacrifice" related to saving, which the argument presupposes. Whatever might be thought of these concepts (see above, Chapter 1), it can be seen that the logic of the argument requires, first, that the profit rate falls as the degree of capital intensity or round-aboutness increases in consequence of the sacrifice of consumption. Here we have reliance being placed again on the presumption of an inverse relation between the rate of profit and the capital intensity of production as measured, for instance, by the quantity of capital per man. Now, however, it is required in addition that consumption per man rises as the profit rate falls and capital per man increases. On this basis, we should therefore expect to find in any production system that an inverse relation exists between consumption per man and the profit rate (up to a maximum of consumption) within the range of available techniques. This is a relation that is required to hold *at the level of the production process* conceived as a purely technical process.

It turns out, however, when we examine a given production system, that the very opposite relation may be found. In particular, between different steady states, a lower rate of profit may be associated with either the same or a lower level of consumption per man.[29] This possibility is clearly demonstrated by the existence of reswitching of techniques of production. Specifically, reswitching means that the same technique is adopted at both a high and a low rate of profit though not at profit rates in between. With the same growth rate prevailing in the two situations, consumption per man would be the same. Thus it is possible for the profit rate to be lower without alteration in technical conditions and in the associated stocks of capital goods and without difference in consumption per man. It would thus seem, in this case, that the profit rate is divorced from any connection with the "net productivity of capital" and from anything to do with the "sacrifice" of consumption for future return. The situation described could, of course, be explained within the framework of a theory of exploitation by noting that, at the lower profit rate, the wage rate is higher. Therefore the rate of exploitation is correspondingly lower.

The possibility of reswitching of techniques of production cannot be ruled out in general. Moreover, even in production systems where reswitching does not occur, it could happen that consumption per man is lower when the profit rate is lower.[30] All of this makes for the untenability of the neoclassical conception insofar as this particular element of it is concerned. Samuelson (1966), in his "summing up" of the reswitching debate, acknowledges this. He seems also to suggest (p. 582) the possibility of discovering that situations incompatible with the neoclassical requirement are "empirically rare." But it is not at all clear what sort of empirical evidence, if any, could be brought to bear on the matter at this level of analysis. The

---

[29] This possibility was pointed out by Morishima (1964: 126). A demonstration of this was developed on pp. 132–37 and 167–72.

[30] On this, see the analysis on pp. 132–37, above. See also Bruno et al. 1966.

central issue is clearly a conceptual one and must therefore be considered prior to any appeal to empirical data. The conclusion one can draw is that there is no reason, at the level of abstractness and generality at which this analysis is situated, to assume the validity of the neoclassical conception except by arbitrarily ruling out the situations in which it is invalid.

The other side of the neoclassical conception is the notion that profits are explained by the presumed preference of individuals for present over future consumption, variously referred to as "time preference" (Fisher), "abstinence" (Jevons), or "waiting" (Marshall). For this purpose, an appeal must be made to the subjective preferences of the rentiers who lend finance to capitalist firms to carry out accumulation. But why there should necessarily be a *positive* rate of time preference in this sense for society as a whole has never been satisfactorily explained.[31]

Neoclassical Theory in General

Going beyond the failure of the neoclassical parable, however, we need to recognize that the parable, as a theoretical construct, does not stand by itself in complete isolation. Rather, it stands in a very definite relation to the whole corpus of neoclassical theory. Samuelson (1962: 193) grants as much when he indicates that "such simple models or parables do, I think, have considerable heuristic value in giving insights into the fundamentals of interest theory in all its complexities." We come here to the real meaning and significance of the neoclassical parable. What the neoclassical parable reveals is the *basic conceptual structure*, the "fundamentals," of a theory that, in all its complexities, was designed to explain distribution (and growth) in the capitalist economy. The parable serves to give an identifiable shape to that structure, to reveal its essential links, to expose its "internal logic." It follows that, if some of the links in that structure have now become unhinged at the level of the parable, this can only reflect back upon the base from which it derives its theoretical validity and in relation to which it has its heuristic value.[32] What is called into question also is the application of that structure, whether in the form of the parable or otherwise, to the study and analysis of any "real" capitalist economy.[33]

[31] Ultimately, the presumption is based on Bohm-Bawerk's "Reasons" for the existence of interest (1959). For a useful critique of this conception in the context of the subjective theory of value, see Bukharin 1972 and Dobb 1940, ch. 5.

[32] Some aspects of this line of reasoning are developed by Garegnani (1970).

[33] See, in this connection, Abramovitz and David 1973; Williamson and Kelley 1973.

In general terms, the conceptual structure here referred to is one that conceives of the distribution of income in the capitalist economy as emerging from the pricing of goods and factors of production in a general equilibrium of competitive markets, the outcome being determined by the quantity of available factor endowments, the technology of production, and the preferences of individuals.[34] Using Euler's theorem it can be shown, under well-known conditions, that the value of the output produced with those factors and estimated at the prevailing market prices is exhausted by distribution back to the factors in accordance with their marginal productivities. The owners of the factors receive an amount of income corresponding to the specified amounts of the factors that each owns times their productivities. These conditions apply only to the market for factors. The formal statement of the theory is completed by addition of markets, in the "present" and in the "future," for the flow of goods produced with those factors, some or all of which goods may themselves constitute the stock of factors viewed as produced capital goods.

This set of relations emerges in a particularly simple and straightforward way, as shown in this chapter in the "one-commodity" model with two factors. Upon this set of formal relations, however simple or complex, neoclassical economists have sought to build a conception of factors of production other than labor, or specific capital goods, as independently productive of value. Consistent with this conception, they have gone on to conceive of accumulation as a matter of the addition of new capital goods from the flow of current output to the preexisting stock of capital goods, and hence as a matter of the time path of evolution of the stock of factors.[35] The capitalist firm is seen merely as an intermediary between the individuals as suppliers of factors from their predetermined "endowments" of those factors and the individuals as rentiers engaged in arranging the pattern of their consumption over time by exchanging consumption "today" for consumption "tomorrow." The interest rate (or profit rate)[36] is supposed to emerge from all this as a reflection on the one

[34] As Solow (1963: 14) puts it, "the theory of capital is after all just a part of the fundamentally microeconomic theory of the allocation of resources, necessary to allow for the fact that commodities can be transformed into other commodities over time." For a restatement of this view in the light of the reswitching debate, see Bliss 1972. Relevant expositions of various elements of the neoclassical theory of capital can be found in Ferguson 1969 and Hirshleifer 1970.

[35] This particular way of treating the problem of accumulation is exhibited with unusual clarity in the neoclassical textbook by Burmeister and Dobell 1970.

[36] For present purposes the rate of profit and rate of interest are regarded as synonymous.

hand of the productivity of the capital goods and on the other of the presumed intertemporal preferences of the rentiers involved in refraining from consuming the current output of goods (or the existing stock).

A conception which is central here and which the parable brings directly to the fore is that of the productivity and scarcity of capital goods as independently determining the value which capitalists receive. This conception constitutes one blade of the scissors with which it had been thought possible to cut the connection which Marx had drawn between the existence of profits (surplus value) and the exploitation of labor and between these and the accumulation of capital as exchange value.[37] It is this neoclassical conception which has now been shown to be without meaning and which must therefore be abandoned. Lying behind this failure is a failure to conceive of the existence of *social classes* with a specific location in the production system. In neoclassical theory, society is conceived rather as an aggregation of particular individuals, each with a particular vector of factor endowments and particular preferences.

There is in general no analytical connection which can be drawn between the technical productivity or scarcity of factors (capital goods) and the income which capitalists receive from the total product so as to be consistent with the specific requirements of the neoclassical theory. That particular point having been made, attention can now be turned once again to those forces in capitalist society, operating at the level of the *social* relations of production, which account for the exploitation of labor and determine the share of income which capitalists receive. Consistent with this, the problem of accumulation and the role of capitalist firms can also be reformulated. It should then be possible to dispense with the other blade

---

In this connection, it is important to emphasize that the category of *interest*, whatever else it might be supposed to mean, is first and foremost a category relating to the distribution of income in capitalist economy. It is the income that accrues to the owners of capital and can be used in this generic sense interchangeably with the term profits. For other purposes it may be relevant to distinguish, say, between the profits that accrue to a given enterprise and the interest that that enterprise pays out on borrowed finance. In the context of investment decisions, the rate of profit (or "rate of discount") is also a measure of *expected* capitalist income. Considerable confusion is created by reference to these rates indifferently as the "rate of time preference," a term that has meaning and acquires an independent conceptual status *only* in the context of neoclassical theory.

[37] Cf. J. M. Clark 1931: 64–65: "The marginal theories of distribution were developed after Marx; their bearing on the doctrines of Marxian socialism is so striking as to suggest that the challenge of Marxism acted as a stimulus to the search for more satisfactory explanations. They undermine the basis of Marxian surplus value doctrine by basing value on utility instead of on labour cost and furnish a substitute for all forms of exploitation doctrine, Marxian or other, in the theory that all factors of production not only are productive but receive rewards based on their assignable contribution to the joint product."

of the scissors represented by the conception of rentiers' intertemporal preferences as a determinant of the rate of profits.

Of course, in the formal statement of the equilibrium conditions of the neoclassical system, there still remains a condition of equality of the relative rentals of different factors and their relative marginal productivities or "marginal rates of transformation." These marginal equalities hold rigorously as a condition for minimizing money costs of production in competitive factor markets.[38] It can be debated whether this condition contains an accurate description of the rules actually observed by capitalist firms faced with the problem of choice of technical methods of production. But that is a different matter.[39] The point is that this condition expresses, within the framework of this theory, only the criterion for cost-minimizing choice of technique subject to *given* prices of goods, *given* rentals of the factors, and *given* technology. It cannot by itself provide any explanation of the determination of those rentals and prices.

What remains of the neoclassical theory of economic growth? The basic idea, which is starkly portrayed in the parable, is that the capitalist economy is inherently capable of undergoing a sustained equilibrium of steady growth with divergences that are "fairly small, casual, and hardly self-accentuating" (Solow 1970a: 11). This idea is supposed to remain essentially the same after all the complications, excluded from the simple parable, are introduced. It turns out, however, upon further analysis, that this presumption is unfounded, once allowance is made for the heterogeneity of means of production which characterizes an advanced division of labor. Under these general conditions, not only is the neoclassical growth equilibrium not necessarily unique, but also the stability of the approach to any such equilibrium cannot in general be guaranteed (see Hahn 1966, 1968). Efforts to resolve these problems have so far involved a

---

[38] Differentiability of the production functions describing the relation between inputs (factors) and outputs is not a necessary requirement for this condition to hold. With discreteness in the technology, it can be reformulated in terms of marginal inequalities. All that is necessary is that the technology set be linear and convex in the neighborhood of an equilibrium point. The condition can be shown to hold, in particular, either in a model of production with discrete production processes (the "linear model of production") or in a model with smooth substitutability.

[39] Another matter for debate concerns the assumption of linearity in the technology (or constant returns to scale) *under conditions of technical change*. Little attention has been paid to this assumption in the recent debates. But in the context of a larger critique of the basic structure of neoclassical theory, it is another damaging issue that was raised quite early by Sraffa (1926) and Young (1928). For a recent return to this, see Kaldor 1972.

resort to ad hoc assumptions that are unsupported by any systematic theoretical justification.

Admittedly, these analytical problems that the neoclassical theory faces are quite serious at a formal level. Nevertheless, when viewed on the plane of the system of neoclassical theory as a whole, these problems are of a relatively minor nature. On this plane, the crucial question is, rather, whether that system of theory, *qua* theory, has anything at all to say about the process of accumulation in the capitalist economy. In its original and basic conception, neoclassical theory constitutes the process of accumulation as a process of "deepening the structure of capital," in which the saving decisions of atomistic individuals drive the economy to a stationary state. Continued expansion occurs in the neoclassical system only if it is assumed that there is an autonomous increase in "factor supplies," consisting of the labor force, and autonomous changes in technology, both of which are unexplained *data*. In this respect, if continued expansion occurs, it is for reasons that cannot be found within the theory and hence there is no *theory* of growth at all. Furthermore, the process of expansion is not so much a process as it is a "sequence of momentary equilibria." To the extent that accumulation occurs at all, it is conceived essentially as a matter of piling up stocks of means of production (either in the form of "putty" or "corn" or as a heterogeneous collection of physical objects) under the reign of Say's Law in an economy of simple commodity production (see Burmeister and Dobell 1970). In such a world, crises of overproduction and unemployment, booms and depressions, which are recurrent features of the entire history of development of industrial capitalism, do not arise except as temporary aberrations of the system. In such a world, there is no identifiable class of workers, displaced from property in the means of production, who must depend on employment in capitalist production, with its ups and downs, for their economic survival. It is therefore difficult to see what real historical phenomena, if any, this system of thought is intended to explain. The central analytical question that is treated throughout all variants of the theory remains, not one of the historical laws of motion of capitalism, but rather one of the efficient allocation of resources in accordance with consumers' preferences.[40] This is evidently the whole basis of the singular concern of neoclassical theory with the problem of "optimal growth."

---

[40] The classic statement of this analytical position is Malinvaud 1961.

It appears, therefore, that the problems faced by the neoclassical theory in providing an account of the accumulation process in the capitalist economy are not merely formal ones. Moreover, they cannot be escaped by abandoning the simple parable as a bastard child and retreating into the supposedly more legitimate realm of neoclassical general equilibrium theory. For, if there is such a thing as a neoclassical theory of economic growth, the substance of it must be capable of some form of coherent expression. Otherwise it remains the hollow shell of a system of differential equations.

Chapter Ten

Reproduction, Accumulation, and Crises

Introduction

The aim of this chapter is to develop an analytic reconstruction of some of the substantive questions and issues which underlie the modern theory of growth as presented in previous chapters. For this purpose we draw upon certain elements of Marxian theory. In so doing, we deal selectively with the Marxian framework of analysis, ignoring much that would be necessary for a more comprehensive treatment of its theoretical structure and its derivation of the "economic laws of motion" of the capitalist economy. We focus, in particular, on Marx's scheme of reproduction, seeking to develop with the aid of this scheme an analysis of the process of accumulation in the capitalist economy.[1]

The scheme of reproduction occupies a significant place in Marx's analysis.[2] With it he sought to show the structural interconnections that exist in the economy as a whole, focusing on the components of the total value produced in each sector of production and on the associated pattern of reciprocal exchanges between the different sectors. Interdependence and exchange are seen to arise from the material requirements of production in each sector and from the pattern of utilization of the product as related to the division of the total value produced among the classes of society. It is seen, furthermore, that these exchanges and the associated pattern of production must satisfy certain crucial balancing conditions if the overall process of reproduction is to continue without interruption.

[1] The analysis draws, in part, upon Harris 1972c, 1975.
[2] See *Capital* I, ch. 23; II, chs. 17–21. For various uses and interpretations of Marx's scheme, see Evenitsky 1963; Lange 1959, 1969; Luxemburg 1951; Morishima 1956; Naqvi 1960; Sweezy 1956; Tsuru 1956.

In identifying the specific conditions that are required for continued reproduction, the scheme has an analytic content which is of a *dual* character. On the one hand, the scheme indicates precisely how it is possible for reproduction to take place, or, in other words, what the necessary conditions are for reproduction. It is evident that these are conditions that the system *as a whole* must satisfy. These conditions are, in this sense, *social* requirements—requirements for reproduction of capital as a whole or of the "aggregate social capital." On the other hand, and at the same time, the scheme locates in these conditions specific points at which inconsistency may arise in the course of reproduction in the capitalist economy. This is because of specific peculiarities of the capitalist process of reproduction and, in general, because that process is carried on by a multiplicity of individual capitals with the overriding objective of individual profits and without conscious social coordination and control. In this connection, Marx observed (*Capital* II, 495):

The fact that the production of commodities is the general form of capitalist production . . . engenders certain conditions of normal exchange peculiar to this mode of production and therefore of the normal course of reproduction, whether it be on a simple or on an extended scale—conditions which change into so many conditions of abnormal movement, into so many possibilities of crises, since a balance is itself an accident owing to the spontaneous nature of this production.

At the heart of the matter, in Marx's conception, is the dialectic of the relationship between aggregate capital and individual capitals arising from the fact that coordination of the circuits of individual capitals takes place only through the "anarchy" of the market. The problem is also rooted in a contradiction between production as a social process of producing *use values* for human consumption and the specific characteristic of capitalist production that its objective is the expansion of *exchange values* for the profit of individual capitals.

The scheme of reproduction is thus a powerful analytical device. Care must be taken, however, not to appear to attribute too much significance to the scheme itself in its purely formal aspect. As Lenin (1964: 62) noted in this connection, "Schemes alone cannot prove anything: they can only *illustrate* a process, *if its separate elements have been theoretically explained*" (emphasis his).

In seeking to develop the analytical implications of the scheme, it seems useful to work within the particular assumptions and analytical categories that Marx used. The scheme presented here is accordingly constructed on this basis. We then proceed to recast the analysis in a form that has the advantage of exposing more clearly certain technical and price relations not explicitly dealt with in Marx's original presentation. We go on from this to apply the scheme to analysis of the problem of accumulation and crises in capitalist economy. Marx himself did not leave a finished theory of crises, though he frequently discussed the problem and certain broad theoretical conceptions of it can be found in his major works. The problem has also been taken up in subsequent work in the Marxian tradition.[3]

The basic presumption underlying the analysis presented here is that the purpose of the scheme is to constitute on an abstract and simple level the process of "reproduction and circulation of the aggregate social capital" in an expanding capitalist economy (see *Capital* II, part 3). In this context crises can be seen to be associated with failure of the system to satisfy completely the requirements of continued reproduction and, hence, with "disturbances" or interruptions of the process of reproduction.[4] This failure is shown here to derive from one or another of several *proximate* causes that are internal to the accumulation process itself. In this way a specific analytic content is given to the concept of internal contradictions in the reproduction process of capital deriving from the "anarchy" of capitalist production.

The analysis abstracts from the role of money and credit as component elements of the whole circuit of capital and from the process of technical change. This may be considered severe, though not intolerable as a first step.

Capital as a Whole and Its Circuits

At the outset it is necessary to take account of Marx's conceptualization of the capitalist process as a whole as a process that is based on the circuits of individual capitals (see *Capital* I, chs. 4–6; II, chs. 1–4). It is in this form that some of the essential features of the capitalist process are revealed and expressed. It is in this form also that the general possibility of crises and general causes of their recurrence are made transparent. In general, the capitalist process is revealed as a *totality*, where the constituent

---

[3] Marx's broad conceptions as well as the post-Marxian literature on the subject are comprehensively surveyed by Sweezy (1956, part 3).

[4] Sweezy (1956: 77–78) notes that "the reproduction scheme lays the groundwork for an analysis of *discrepancies* between aggregate supply and aggregate demand which . . . manifest themselves in general disturbances of the productive process."

elements of that totality are seen to come together as an organic unity. It is revealed also as a *process*, which involves a dynamic movement, and is therefore antithetical to the conception of "a thing at rest." Moreover, it is revealed as a *contradictory* process, where the forms of its contradictions derive from the inner logic of the process itself.

In specific terms, Marx conceived of the circuit of a single unit of industrial capital (this being the dominant form of capital in general) as involving a constantly increasing renewal, going from money capital, through production and circulation of commodities, and again into money capital expanded in each round by the profit that the circuit yields. This is represented by the sequence

$$ M - C\left(\begin{matrix} L \\ MP \end{matrix}\right)\dots P\dots C' - M' $$

where $M' > M$. The first phase of the circuit consists of the exchange of money for commodities through the advance of an amount of money capital M for the purchase of commodities C consisting of labor L and means of production MP. The second phase involves combination of the labor and means of production thus acquired so as to undergo production P, which results in an output of new commodities C'. In the third phase this output of commodities is brought to market and its sale results in realization of an amount of money M'. The circuit thereby comes to completion but only to begin again through another advance, and again through subsequent advances, continuing in this manner as an interminable process. Expansion of exchange value in the form of an increased total of money is the objective and motive of the process. The success of the circuit is measured by the amount of that increase which may be represented as the rate of profit $r = (M' - M)/M$. In this sense, the rate of profit is the pivot upon which turns the whole circuit of capital. Insofar as the rate of profit is positive, the circuit is one of self-expansion of capital, the source of that expansion being the surplus value that the circuit yields. Insofar as the increase is capitalized and advanced as additional money capital, the process as a whole is an expansionary one and grows in a never-ending spiral.

There are analytically distinct phases or moments of the circuit. These consist of an initial movement in the sphere of exchange or circulation of commodities, followed by a movement in the sphere of production and, in the third phase, a return to the sphere of exchange. But they are not separate or disconnected phases; they come together as a unity of production and circulation. The reasons for this are clear. In particular, exchange presupposes production because it is through production that the commodities to be exchanged are made available. At the same time, production presupposes exchange because, with production based on individual capitals and a highly developed division of labor, the means of production can be acquired only through exchange. Furthermore, insofar as the objective of production is (expanded) exchange value and not the use value of the articles produced, the commodities that are produced must be sold in order to realize their value in money form and this presupposes exchange of commodities.

However, the sphere of exchange in general extends beyond the circuit of capital as such to encompass spheres of "simple commodity exchange." These include, for instance, workers' consumption. Specifically, workers purchase commodities from the circuit for their own consumption, thereby constituting a market for commodities. But since the commodities that circulate in this way do not themselves become means of production to produce commodities with the objective of realizing surplus value, they do not form a complete circuit of capital. The same is true of capitalists' consumption. The same would also be true of trade with noncapitalist producers. All such exchanges, while being linked to the circuit of capital, involve a movement outside of that circuit. In these respects, it is evident that the circuit of capital cannot be conceived as a completely closed circuit.

But there is another and ultimately more fundamental reason why the circuit of capital is not a closed circuit. This is evident even if we abstract from exchanges related to capitalists' consumption and to trade with noncapitalist producers. It arises from the nature of labor power as a commodity. In particular, labor power is a commodity that is not itself produced within a circuit of capital. It is nevertheless a commodity that is requisite and uniquely indispensable to the circuit of capital. Therein lies a condition that is of crucial significance for the operation of the capitalist process as a whole and that constitutes a possible source of hitches or crises in that process.

Since the circuit is conceived to be circular and continuous, each phase in it may be considered the starting point of the circuit or its end point. It follows that there are analytically distinct *forms* of the circuit of capital, each such form corresponding to a different phase as the starting point in

Sraffa

the circuit. There is, first, a circuit of money capital which takes the form of the sequence described above. A second form of the circuit is the circuit of productive capital, represented as the sequence $P \ldots C' - M' - C' \ldots P$. It starts with production, goes through exchange of commodities, and ends in further production. The third form of the circuit starts with exchange of the output of commodities for money and purchase of other commodities, goes through production, and ends with a new output of commodities. This is the circuit of commodity capital and is represented by the sequence $C' - M' - C' \ldots P \ldots C''$. These three forms of the circuit refer to different aspects of the movement of capital and thereby reveal the complexity of that movement. They may also be thought of as different functions of capital, the first as money, the second as means of production, and the third as commodities bearing exchange value. However, though different, these forms of the circuit are nevertheless inseparable from the unity of all three forms within the whole circuit of capital. Moreover, it follows from this unity that a failure to carry out one or another function of capital may be the cause of an interruption in the whole circuit.

Finally, we may note that a circuit of capital is the movement of an individual capital or single unit of capital. There are many such circuits of individual capitals, each linked together through competition of capitals and on the basis of interdependence in both production and exchange of commodities. The circuit of each and every unit of capital therefore presupposes the existence of other circuits. These individual circuits come together to form the movement of capital as a whole or the system of capitals. As Marx expressed it (*Capital* II, pp. 353–54): "The circuits of the individual capitals intertwine, presuppose and necessitate one another, and form, precisely in this interlacing, the movement of the total social capital . . . ; the metamorphosis of the individual capital appears as a link in the series of metamorphoses of the social capital." Thus, the system of capitals or the aggregate social capital is an entity formed on the basis of circuits of individual capitals. It is also an entity that requires for its reproduction certain definite conditions to be fulfilled by the system as a whole. But those conditions must be realized through the privately motivated and directed activity of the individual capitals, as coordinated by the mechanisms of the market and operating through competition of capitals. Herein lies an immanent source and general possibility of crisis that must continue to recur insofar as social reproduction continues to take place on this basis.

However, to identify the general possibility of crisis is not to locate its particular causes. For the latter, it is necessary to carry out further and more detailed analysis of the specific requirements and conditions of the process of reproduction as a whole. This is our concern in the following sections.

Value and Price

To proceed, a well-known problem in Marx's analysis must first be got out of the way. This has to do with the relation between prices of production and labor values. Many of the riddles connected with this have already been cleared up.[5] We know that, under competitive conditions when there is a uniform rate of profit, the relative price of each commodity (in terms of any numeraire) is such as to cover wage costs plus profit at the going rate on the prices of the capital employed. These are the "prices of production" at which commodities and means of production are exchanged. With a constant technology, labor time (measured in homogeneous units) employed per unit of output of each commodity is constant. Output can be valued in labor time, that is, in terms of the amount of labor directly and indirectly required to produce it. Then the labor value in this sense of a unit of output is given.   *Pasinetti.*

Relative prices of commodities correspond to labor values if the technology is such that the value of means of production employed per worker and the time pattern of production are uniform in all lines of production, or if prices are calculated using a notional profit rate equal to zero. Otherwise, prices depart from labor values. Under certain assumptions, all of them well founded in the Marxian theory of value, a unique relation may be shown to exist between them. There is, however, no *general* rule by which the latter can be transformed into the former. The problem is compounded in the presence of joint production due to fixed capital and when technology is changing.[6]

The position taken here is that the concept of values and that of prices

[5] See above, Chapter 3. See also Seton 1957, Sraffa 1960, Morishima 1973, Medio 1972, Bortkiewicz 1952, Baumol 1974.

[6] All of this concerns only the logic of the problem. There remains a question of the significance of transformation of values into prices as an actual *historical* process. Meek (1967: 154–57) favors a historical interpretation. But this could be taken to be a superfluous adjunct to what is an otherwise valid logical construction. The case against a historical interpretation of the transformation problem is cogently argued by Morishima & Catephores (1975).

are both equally relevant, each in its own sphere. Values offer an objective basis for assessing the amount of the social product above the value of labor power which is appropriated by the owners of the means of production, and hence for analyzing the outcome of class relations in the society. Surplus value in this sense represents an amount which the workers put into the production process but which they do not get back. It is "unpaid labor." Contrary to a vulgar interpretation, this makes no normative judgment about which class deserves or should get that amount. Prices, on the other hand, enter into the actual relations of exchange, where they perform the role of distributing the surplus among the capitalists at an equal rate (under competition) on the amount of capital which each owns (cf. Baumol 1974). Going from the value system to the price system makes it possible to see exactly what this role is. In this way, the analysis in terms of values provides the foundation for the theory of distribution and prices. As we shall see subsequently, it also provides the foundation for a theory of accumulation and crises.

The Scheme of Reproduction

The scheme of reproduction dichotomizes the economy into two departments or sectors: Department I, producing means of production (machines and raw materials), and Department II, producing consumption goods. Production takes one period, the same in each department, and the means of production are assumed to be used up in a single period. These are obvious simplifications which get away from complications due to different time periods of production for different commodities and the existence of fixed capital.

Gross output of each department covers replacement of means of production ("constant capital," or c), wages advanced to the workers at the beginning of the period ("variable capital," or v), and surplus value, s, which goes to the capitalists. In this and the next two sections we follow Marx in measuring all magnitudes in terms of labor values. Thus:

$$(10.1) \qquad \begin{aligned} c_1 + v_1 + s_1 \qquad &\text{(Dept. I value)} \\ c_2 + v_2 + s_2 \qquad &\text{(Dept. II value)} \\ \hline c \ + v \ + s \qquad &\text{(total value)} \end{aligned}$$

The organic composition of capital, regarded as a given constant, is

(10.2) $$k_i = \frac{c_i}{v_i} \qquad i = 1, 2$$

Marx expected that this ratio would tend to rise over time, owing to technical change. Such considerations are ruled out here by the assumption of constant technology. Changes in the organic composition of capital may nevertheless occur, owing to changes in the value of labor power. The rate of exploitation is the ratio of surplus value to variable capital, such that

(10.3) $$\epsilon_i = \frac{s_i}{v_i}$$

Marx tended to assume that

(10.4) $$\epsilon_1 = \epsilon_2 = \hat{\epsilon}$$

that is, the rate of exploitation in both departments is uniform and equal to a given constant. Uniformity of the rate of exploitation is an implication of competition and mobility of labor. By definition, the rate of net profit is the ratio of surplus value to the value of capital, the latter consisting of the value of means of production plus the wages advanced. Thus,

(10.5) $$r_i = \frac{s_i}{c_i + v_i} = \frac{\epsilon_i}{1 + k_i}$$

If the rate of exploitation is to be the same across departments, the rate of profit, defined in this way, must differ in accordance with a difference in the organic composition of capital. For the rate of profit to be uniform, the rate of exploitation must differ, and this would contradict (10.4). The two rates can be uniform only in the special case that the organic composition of capital is uniform.

Actually, the difficulty here is only apparent.[7] What is needed is to recognize that a uniform rate of profit has no meaning in the system of labor values, only in the system of prices. Under competitive capitalism, the formation of a general rate of profit takes place in the market (that is, within the sphere of circulation) through the effort on the part of each capitalist to expand his "money" profits. Thus, it is the rate of money profits that tends to uniformity among different industries. Prices adjust to accommodate the difference in profits, calculated at this uniform rate, corresponding to a difference in the quantity of capital. In the price system,

---

[7] The issue was raised by Robinson (1947: 15; 1951a: 17).

the ratio of profits to wages then differs between departments in accordance with the difference in the ratio of capital to labor. A restatement of the problem along these lines will be considered below. Meanwhile, as will become clear, the dynamics of the system can be set out by continuing to deal in terms of labor values. In so doing, there is no necessary presumption that commodities are sold at their values.

How does this system move through time, and what are the economic relations which then prevail within it? The answer is that certain special conditions must be satisfied if the system is to be capable of reproducing itself without interruption from one period to the next. Abstracting from technical change, we find that these conditions depend, in part, on what is done with the surplus. Workers do not save, because there is no margin between the wages they get and the necessaries of consumption. Only capitalists save, and their saving out of the surplus appropriated in one period provides additional capital in the next period. Marx considers two cases: simple reproduction and expanded reproduction. We consider each in turn.

Simple Reproduction

In simple reproduction, by assumption, all surplus value (as well as wages) is consumed, net accumulation is zero, and the economy reproduces itself on the same scale from one period to another. For the flows between departments to balance, purchases by one from the other must match sales. Demand for output of Department I comes from its own purchases for replacement of constant capital plus those of Department II. Thus,

$$(10.6) \qquad c_1 + c_2 = c_1 + v_1 + s_1$$

where the right-hand side is production and the left-hand side is demand. Demand for output of Department II comes from expenditure on consumption by capitalists and workers in both departments. Thus,

$$(10.7) \qquad v_1 + s_1 + v_2 + s_2 = c_2 + v_2 + s_2$$

By canceling common terms in (10.6) and (10.7), we get the balancing condition

$$(10.8) \qquad c_2 = v_1 + s_1$$

This can be seen to imply, after dividing by v_2 and substituting from (10.2), (10.3), and (10.4),

(10.9)
$$\frac{v_1}{v_2} = \frac{k_2}{1 + \epsilon_1}$$

This case, chosen for its simplicity, thus isolates a critical property of the system. According to (10.9), the amounts of variable capital used to hire labor in each department must bear a definite relation to each other depending on the value of k_2 and ϵ_1. This is the only relation ensuring that production in each department is consistent with the pattern of demand while the economy simply maintains the same scale of operation from period to period. It is, so to say, the equilibrium condition of the system and determines a unique allocation of labor between the two departments. Employment being thus determined, output produced in each department is also determined. The distribution of the product between capitalists and workers conforms to the independently given rate of exploitation.[8]

But in a capitalist economy, where production is organized by individual capitalists without conscious coordination, there is no automatic mechanism to guarantee that the capitalists, taken together, would advance just the right amount of wages and in the right proportions. There is therefore no guarantee that the system could achieve equilibrium.

Expanded Reproduction

In expanded reproduction, net accumulation is positive. The capitalists invest in each period a certain proportion, say α_i, of their surplus carried over from the previous period. This amount goes to provide additional means of production in each department (Δc_i), plus the additional variable capital (Δv_i) needed to hire the extra labor to work with the extra means of production at the same organic composition of capital.

A problem concerns the allocation of investment between departments. Marx treated this by assuming that capitalists in each department reinvest their surplus in the same department. This is not a very satisfactory assumption, and it will be relaxed in the next section.[9] Meanwhile its implications can be easily worked out.

---

[8] At this point the limitations of Marx's system of classification become apparent. All of the relevant magnitudes are expressed in terms of *value* aggregates and as such can provide only the conditions for aggregate equilibrium. To translate them into physical terms such as output, we need to know the technical coefficients of production, but these are not specified. All we know about the technology is the overall organic composition of capital. For the same reason the system as it stands is incapable of showing the *quantitative* relation between the accumulation of means of production and the growth of output.

[9] The assumption that investment of surplus is restricted to the department (or business)

Investment in each department is

(10.10) $$I_i = \alpha_i s_i$$

and its allocation between variable and constant capital is

(10.11) $$I_i = \Delta c_i + \Delta v_i$$

$$\Delta v_i = \beta_{vi} I_i$$

$$\Delta c_i = (1 - \beta_{vi}) I_i$$

It follows from (10.10), (10.11), and (10.3) that

(10.12) $$g_{vi} = \frac{\Delta v_i}{v_i} = \beta_{vi} \alpha_i \epsilon_i$$

(10.13) $$g_{ci} = \frac{\Delta c_i}{c_i} = (1 - \beta_{vi}) \frac{\alpha_i \epsilon_i}{k_i}$$

The growth rates of constant and variable capital (g_{ci}, g_{vi}) are thus dependent on the proportion of investment allocated to each type of capital, on the proportions of surplus value invested, and on the rate of exploitation. Constancy of the organic composition of capital requires $g_{vi} = g_{ci}$. From (10.12) and (10.13), this can be seen to imply

(10.14) $$\beta_{vi} = \frac{1}{1 + k_i}$$

Since k_i are given constants, the proportions β_{vi} are therefore fixed and so are the growth rates in each department.

In each period, the increment in means of production and variable capital represents additional demand for the output of both departments over that prevailing in simple reproduction. For the flows between departments to balance in this case requires

(10.15) $$v_1 + s_1 = c_2 + \Delta c_2 + \Delta c_1$$

which, after a little manipulation, leads to

---

in which the surplus is appropriated seems contrary to the assumption of competition, which requires free mobility of capital between departments. Moreover, as Robinson (1951a: 17) pointed out: "This is a severe assumption to make even about the era before limited liability was introduced, and becomes absurd afterwards." For a recent attempt to work with a similar assumption concerning investment behavior in a two-sector model, see Inada 1966.

(10.16)
$$\frac{v_1}{v_2} = \frac{k_2(1 + g_{v2})}{1 + \epsilon_1 - k_1 g_{v1}}$$

Thus, as in simple reproduction, equilibrium for the system as a whole requires that the amounts of variable capital used to hire labor in each department be proportional. The proportionality relationship depends in this case on ϵ_1, k_1, k_2, and the growth rates of capital in the two departments. For the equation (10.16) to be economically meaningful, it is required that $1 + \epsilon_1 - k_1 g_{v1} > 0$, which says simply that net output of Department I must exceed its own requirements for net investment in means of production.

Suppose, now, that growth takes place at the same rate in both departments such as to maintain a constant proportional allocation of labor between departments consistent with (10.16). This is a special case of balanced growth. It implies that $g_{v1} = g_{v2}$ and requires, according to (10.12), that

(10.17)
$$\frac{\beta_{v1}}{\beta_{v2}} = \frac{\alpha_2}{\alpha_1}$$

But from (10.14) we have

(10.18)
$$\frac{\beta_{v1}}{\beta_{v2}} = \frac{1 + k_2}{1 + k_1}$$

Therefore, an equilibrium with balanced growth of both departments exists only if[10]

(10.19)
$$\frac{\alpha_2}{\alpha_1} = \frac{1 + k_2}{1 + k_1}$$

The meaning of this result is clear. The capitalists in each department allocate their total investment to the increase of constant and variable capital so as to maintain the given organic composition of capital. Balanced growth requires an amount of investment such that total capital in each department grows at the same uniform rate. By assumption, total investment in each department comes entirely out of the surplus

---

[10] This particular coincidence is the basis of the numerical solutions that have been obtained for Marx's scheme. Cf. Robinson 1951a: 19; and Naqvi 1960. In Marx's example (*Capital* II, pp. 509–13), the rate of exploitation is the same and the organic composition of capital different; so, to obtain a solution, he has to choose

$$\frac{\alpha_2}{\alpha_1} = \frac{1 + k_2}{1 + k_1} = \frac{3}{5}$$

value produced in the same department. Since the same rate of surplus value is produced in each department, growth can be balanced only if the proportion of surplus value invested relative to the value of total capital is the same in each department. This is what (10.19) says.[11] But, since α_i and k_i are independently given, there is nothing to ensure that this condition would hold. Therefore, an equilibrium with balanced growth might not exist.

There is, of course, no necessary reason why growth should be balanced in the above sense. This is simply a special assumed case, and many other cases of nonproportional growth are conceivable. Whatever the case that is assumed, whether it is balanced growth or not, there is still no guarantee that the system could achieve equilibrium.

It is evident that the problem here is of a twofold nature. It is, first, as in the case of simple reproduction, a problem of ensuring the correct allocation of labor between departments consistent with balance of production and demand. Second, and this is peculiar to expanded reproduction, there is an additional problem of ensuring that the correct amounts of investment are allocated to maintaining the given organic composition of capital and, in the particular case of balanced growth, to maintaining a uniform rate of expansion of the total capitals in each department. It is presumed that the structure of a capitalist economy is such that there is no automatic tendency for these conditions to be satisfied.

We note, finally, that even if an equilibrium were to exist, there is no reason why the growth rate of employment corresponding to it should necessarily equal that of the available labor force. Continued accumulation may therefore run up against a shortage of labor. To resolve this problem, the process of change in the organic composition of capital has to be brought into the analysis and, with that, the role of the reserve army of the unemployed. As Marx showed, these play a crucial role in the dynamics of the capitalist economy (see *Capital* I, ch. 25).

A Restatement of the Scheme

We proceed now, in the spirit of Marx's analysis, to provide a restatement of the scheme. A similar two-department structure is assumed, but stated in a form which exposes more clearly the underlying technological relations, value relations, and price relations. We build on this an analysis

---

[11] This condition could be derived more directly by noting that, as a matter of definition, the growth rate of total capital in each department is $g_i = \alpha_i r_i (i = 1, 2)$. Equating these rates and using (10.4) and (10.5) gives (10.19).

of the problem of crises in capitalist economy. This analysis does not deal with the mechanism of the business cycle, which represents the practical working out of the crisis, but with the broad conjunctures which may at one time or another underlie the existence of a crisis.

The starting point of the analysis is the process of production of value and surplus value under conditions of capitalism. Production consists of the production of commodities through employment of labor and means of production which are themselves the product of labor. The problem of fixed nonproduced resources (such as land) arises at a lower level of abstraction and, for purposes of a theory of accumulation, has to be dealt with in the context of an analysis of technical change which is being left out of account in this discussion.

From the value produced in a day's labor, a proportion, say ω, goes to sustain and reproduce the labor power of the worker. The rest constitutes surplus value or unpaid labor. This ω is a socially determined magnitude. It is the labor value of the necessaries required to maintain the worker at a given standard of life, as determined by historical and social conditions, including in those conditions the organized struggle of the workers vis-à-vis the capitalists, i.e. the conditions of the class struggle.[12] The rate of surplus value (or rate of exploitation), ϵ, is related to the value of labor power as

(10.20)
$$\epsilon = \frac{1 - \omega}{\omega}$$

and it is the same in all sectors as long as ω is uniform.[13]

Capitalists appropriate surplus value at the rate ϵ, and competition dictates that the total amount of surplus value is distributed among them at a uniform rate in proportion to the total price of their respective capitals. The rate of (net) profit r is determined as the outcome of a market process of free exchange in which competition reigns because capital is freely mobile and prices of commodities are equated to their costs of production, consisting of wages, plus profits, plus depreciation.

[12] This is a very broad and general statement that is on the whole consistent with Marx's broad treatment of the determinants of the value of labor power. However, there still remains a question about the precise quantitative determination of this value and its relation to the wage (or price of labor power). This is being left open at this point. The problematical character of the Marxian treatment of this issue must be emphasized (see Chapter 1). We shall return to it below (see pp. 280–82).

[13] For the derivation of this relationship, see Chapter 3, pp. 82–85. We are here ignoring variations in the length of the working day as a factor in the determination of the rate of exploitation.

A well-defined relationship exists between the level of the rate of profit and the value of labor power, corresponding to the given technique of production (see Chapter 3).

All of these propositions hold in the general case of production of *many* commodities. They hold also with or without joint production in the form of fixed capital and with one or many alternative techniques of production.[14] For the sake of simplicity we now assume, like Marx, a system in which only *two* commodities are produced, each in a different sector (or department). Sector 1 produces a capital good and sector 2 produces a consumption good. There is a single, uniform period of production, and stocks are used up in the period. For their maintenance and reproduction, workers consume a given quantity, b, of the consumption good per unit of labor. Then, labor values embodied in the two produced commodities are

$$(10.21) \qquad \lambda_1 = a_{01} + a_{11}\lambda_1 = a_{01} + A_{01}$$
$$\lambda_2 = a_{02} + a_{12}\lambda_1 = a_{02} + A_{02}$$

where a_{0i} are direct labor coefficients, a_{1i} are stocks, and A_{0i} are quantities of indirect labor. The value of labor power is

$$(10.22) \qquad \omega = b\lambda_2$$

Total value produced in each department is divided as

$$(10.23) \qquad \lambda_1 = A_{01} + a_{01}\omega + \epsilon a_{01}\omega$$
$$\lambda_2 = A_{02} + a_{02}\omega + \epsilon a_{02}\omega$$

where ϵ is the rate of surplus value. It follows that

$$(10.24) \qquad \epsilon = \frac{\lambda_i - a_{0i}\omega - A_{0i}}{a_{0i}\omega} = \frac{1 - \omega}{\omega}$$

In the price system, prices cover costs of production. Define the prices p_i as prices per unit of labor value. Then, under competitive conditions we have

$$(10.25) \qquad p_1\lambda_1 = (p_1 A_{01} + p_2 a_{01}\omega)(1 + r)$$
$$p_2\lambda_2 = (p_1 A_{02} + p_2 a_{02}\omega)(1 + r)$$

[14] See Sraffa 1960, Morishima 1973.

where wages are paid out of capital. It is assumed here that the wage is just sufficient to enable workers to buy the quantity of necessaries, no more and no less, at the prevailing price of the consumption good. In this sense, the price of labor power is equal to its value. We are thus ignoring conditions that would cause any systematic departure of price from value in the case of labor power. Setting $p_2 = 1$ and solving this system for r gives a quadratic from which, taking $r > 0$, we get

$$(10.26) \qquad r = \rho(\eta_1, \eta_2, \omega), \qquad \eta_i = \frac{A_{0i}}{a_{0i}}$$

Thus, given the value of labor power ω and the ratios of indirect to direct labor (η_1, η_2) corresponding to the given technique of production, the rate of profit is uniquely determined. If it is assumed that $\eta_1 = \eta_2 = \eta$, then it follows that

$$r = \frac{\epsilon}{1 + \eta/\omega}$$

which is analogous to (10.5). Relative prices are determined from (10.25) so as to satisfy

$$P = \frac{p_1}{p_2} = \frac{\lambda_2 a_{01}(P\eta_1 + \omega)}{\lambda_1 a_{02}(P\eta_2 + \omega)}$$

It is evident that relative prices differ from labor values in accordance with differences in η_i.

Consider now the conditions for balance of production and demand in this system under conditions of expanded reproduction. From the total pool of surplus value produced in each period, an amount goes to provide additional means of production (constant capital) in each sector, plus additional variable capital to hire extra labor. The rest is used for capitalists' individual consumption. Let the rate of accumulation in each sector be g_i. Then, at output levels x_i, net investment in value terms is

$$I = (A_{01} + a_{01}\omega)x_1 g_1 + (A_{02} + a_{02}\omega)x_2 g_2$$

and capitalists' consumption is the difference

$$\epsilon\omega(a_{01}x_1 + a_{02}x_2) - I.$$

Demand for output of sector 1 comes from replacement of worn-out means of production in both sectors plus net investment in additional means of production. Accordingly, balance of production and demand in sector 1 requires

(10.27) $$\lambda_1 x_1 = A_{01} x_1 (1 + g_1) + A_{02} x_2 (1 + g_2)$$

Demand for output of sector 2 comes from consumption requirements of workers at the current level of employment, plus additional workers' consumption due to accumulation at the rate g_i, plus capitalists' consumption. Balance of production and demand in sector 2 requires

(10.28) $$\lambda_2 x_2 = a_{01} \omega x_1 (1 + g_1) + a_{02} \omega x_2 (1 + g_2) \\ + \epsilon \omega (a_{01} x_1 + a_{02} x_2) - I$$

The pattern of demand is seen here to arise out of technical and social conditions as related to (1) the wearing out of means of production, (2) the reproduction of labor power at the socially determined standard of workers' consumption, and (3) capitalists' requirements for consumption and accumulation. Equations (10.27) and (10.28) express in value terms the conditions that have to be met in order that the levels of production undertaken in the different sectors may be consistent with the pattern of demand. Expression of these conditions in value terms, that is, in terms of quantities of labor, explicitly recognizes that, as requirements of production, they have direct implications for the allocation of the total labor of society to the different departments of social production. Specifically, both of the balancing conditions (10.27) and (10.28) can be seen to imply, after substituting from (10.23),

(10.29) $$z = \frac{a_{01} x_1}{a_{02} x_2} = \frac{\eta_2 (1 + g_2)}{(1 + \epsilon)\omega - \eta_1 g_1}$$

Thus, given the rates of accumulation (g_1, g_2), there is a unique allocation of labor between sectors which is required for balance of production and demand. That allocation of labor is governed by the social and technical parameters ϵ, ω, η_1, η_2 and by the rates of accumulation g_1, g_2.

However, it is on the basis of prices, and not values, that investment decisions and exchange activities are carried out in the capitalist economy. This requires introduction of the relevant relations in the sphere of exchange, or sphere of circulation of commodities. In particular, capitalists receive income in the form of profits from sale of the product and not directly in the form of a quantity of labor (surplus value). Their investment expenditure is also financed out of such profits. What remains to be specified are the conditions of *realization* of profits.

Assume that, from the total net profits which they receive, capitalists save in the aggregate a proportion s for investment. The rest is spent on consumption. Workers receive wages, and their net saving as a class is zero. Investment (in price terms) consists of expenditure on capital accumulation in each sector. With accumulation taking place at the rate g_i in each sector, the overall rate of accumulation is the weighted sum

$$(10.30) \qquad\qquad g = t_1 g_1 + t_2 g_2$$

where the weights t_i are given by

$$t_i = \frac{a_{0i} x_i (P\eta_i + \omega)}{\Sigma_i a_{0i} x_i (P\eta_i + \omega)}$$

For overall balance in the flow of income and expenditure, it is required that aggregate savings equal aggregate investment. Thus we have, as the equilibrium condition in the sphere of exchange,

$$(10.31) \qquad\qquad sr = g = t_1 g_1 + t_2 g_2$$

It is assumed here that profits may be invested in any sector, not only in the sector in which they are appropriated. The saving condition is consistent with a more concrete formulation in terms of corporations that are owned and controlled by capitalists, which retain a proportion α of total profits and distribute the rest to a rentier class who save at the rate s_r out of distributed profits. The saving rate of the whole capitalist class is, then, $s = \alpha + s_r(1 - \alpha)$. It must be emphasised, however, that, in contrast to a standard "Keynesian" construction, the distinction between saving and investment as posited here does not presuppose a separation between individuals who save and individuals who invest (that is, between "rentiers" and "entrepreneurs"). From the standpoint of Marxian theory, what is crucial is that the activities of saving and investment take place through the agency of individual capitals and without conscious co-ordination or control, with the result that in the aggregate (for capital as a whole) there is no necessary equality of saving and investment *ex ante*. Associated with this, and indeed a necessary requirement for that result to hold, is the existence of money.

Now, let us introduce explicitly the investment plans of the capitalist class as a whole. We ignore differences in accumulation rates between different sectors and groups of capitalists. Alternatively, as a special case we could assume equal rates of expansion, or balanced growth, as in the analysis of the section above (pp. 259–62).[15] The overall rate of accumulation may be represented as an increasing function of the expected rate of profit, r^e, and it is assumed for simplicity that the expected rate of profit is equal to the realized rate. Assume also that there is a minimum rate of profit, r_0, below which capitalists do not invest. Thus,

$$(10.32) \qquad g = g(r^e), \qquad r^e = r, \qquad g(r_0) = 0$$

This formulation is readily recognized to be a shorthand though fully adequate expression for a complex process. It leaves aside the specific concrete conditions which may at one time or another govern the state of investment activity. For present purposes these may be regarded as causing shifts in the function $g(.)$. On a social and historical plane, these conditions would include not only the inducement mechanisms of the market operating through obsolescence and change in methods of production, as well as the accelerator-multiplier effect of investment itself and the effect of wars, but also the social mechanisms determining entry and mobility within the capitalist class, various methods of "primitive" accumulation, and the role of the state. While all of this is not capable of being captured in the simple formula of an investment function, it does require further articulation and analysis in theoretical terms.[16] Nevertheless, these more specific considerations are not strictly necessary at this stage of the analysis. This is because of the particular level of abstraction at which the analysis is situated, that is, at the level of the reproduction and circulation of capital as a whole. At this level it is fully adequate to recognize that the drive for profits is the basic motive force underlying the expansion of capital. In this respect investment activity springs from the most fundamental characteristic of capitalist production and not from any arbitrary subjective or psychological motives (e.g. time preference) on the part of individuals.

Total employment of labor at any level of output is $a_{01}x_1 + a_{02}x_2$. Beyond this, accumulation at any positive rate sets up an increasing demand for labor. Specifically, with the given technique of production

---

[15] There is, of course, no empirical basis for such an assumption. It requires justification on other and quite different grounds. The rationale is strictly a theoretical one and is to be found in the specific focus of the analysis at this stage. In particular, the analysis is concerned with the reproduction and expansion of capital as a whole. For this purpose, the assumption of balanced growth is convenient and adequate. It leaves aside the problem of relative expansion of different sectors of capital.

[16] There is already an initial basis for such an analysis in the works of Kalecki (1971b), Steindl (1952), Sylos-Labini (1969), and Baran and Sweezy (1966), among others.

and with sectoral accumulation occurring at the rates g_1, g_2, demand for labor grows at the rate

$$(10.33) \qquad l_d = \frac{1}{1 + z}(zg_1 + g_2) = l_d(g)$$

The requirement of an increasing labor force to match this demand is an independent condition of the problem. Expansion of the available labor force may take place in a variety of ways which are *internal* to the system of capitalist production, as, for instance, through changes in the techniques of production involving increased mechanization, through increase in the number of hours worked per worker, or through absorption of an existing reserve army of labor viewed on a world scale (by means of immigration and capital export). It may take place also *on the margins* of the system of production, as, for instance, through erosion of household work and other noncapitalist forms of production. In these and other ways accumulation creates the labor supply required for its own continuation. However the connection between supply of and demand for labor is neither fully automatic nor perfectly synchronized. For simplicity, we may express the conditions of determination of labor supply in formal terms by taking the rate of growth of labor supply as a function of the overall rate of accumulation

$$(10.34) \qquad l_s = l_s(g)$$

These formal relationships, (10.21)–(10.34), constitute the basic structural and behavioral conditions governing the expanded reproduction and circulation of capital. Consistency among them, taken together, is required for the process of reproduction and circulation to be smoothly carried out. Inconsistency among them accounts for a rupture or a crisis in the process. It can be seen that there are different possible types of crises and underlying causes, depending on the particular pattern of such inconsistency. In the next section, we consider some of the possible types of inconsistency which may arise.

Accumulation and Crises

Equations (10.29) and (10.31) give us two conditions involving the sectoral rates of accumulation and the sectoral allocation of labor. Condition (10.29) says that, corresponding to any given set of rates of accumulation (g_1, g_2), there exists a unique allocation of labor between sectors which is consistent with sectoral balance of production and demand. Condition (10.31) says that, given the allocation of labor between sectors, the pattern of accumulation in each sector must be such as to give rise to an overall rate of accumulation which exactly matches the total quantity of available savings at the existing profit rate. However, at any moment, the actual allocation of labor between sectors is governed by production decisions taken by individual capitalists. There is therefore no guarantee that the allocation would be such as to satisfy condition (10.29). Even if condition (10.29) were satisfied, there is no guarantee that aggregate investment, as the outcome of investment decisions of individual capitalists, would turn out to be exactly what is required to satisfy condition (10.31). It follows that there are two possible types of imbalance which can be located within this particular set of conditions.

The first, which arises when condition (10.29) is not satisfied, is an imbalance due to disparity between production and demand at the level of individual sectors. This means, specifically, that the capitalists in one sector undertake to purchase means of production and labor power in order to carry out production at a certain level but find that there is either an excess or a deficiency of demand forthcoming for their product. If this is so for one sector, it must be so for both, since the balancing condition (10.29) is the same for both sectors. The situation is therefore one of a general all-round imbalance between demand and supply for all products. What essentially characterizes it is that there is a disproportional allocation of labor between the different sectors relative to what is called for by the existing pattern of demand for products. Since it is a matter of disproportionality in this sense, we may call it *a disproportionality crisis.*

To correct the imbalance associated with such a crisis requires adjustment of the pattern of accumulation in the different sectors so as to match the composition of demand to the structure of production. Otherwise, it can be corrected only by alteration of the social and technical conditions governing the parameters ϵ, ω, η_1, η_2.

A second type of imbalance arises when condition (10.31) is not satisfied. Specifically, there is an imbalance due to inconsistency between the overall rate of accumulation coming out of the aggregated investment plans of individual capitalists and the overall rate of savings from the profits that are being appropriated.

For further consideration of this type of situation, let us examine the relationships underlying condition (10.31). These are exhibited in Figure

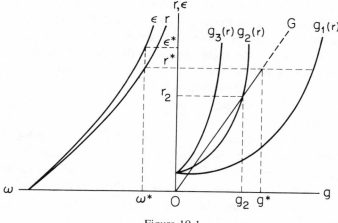

Figure 10.1

10.1. The left-hand quadrant of Figure 10.1 describes both the exploitation curve and the relationship between the rate of profit and value of labor power consistent with the given technical conditions. At a given value of labor power, ω^*, and associated rate of exploitation, ϵ^*, the equilibrium rate of profit which allows competitive distribution of surplus value among capitalists is r^*. In the right-hand quadrant the ray OG defines the relationship between the growth rate and profit rate consistent with overall balance of income and expenditure when capitalists save at the rate s. Call this the *profit realization curve*. It represents the profit rate that would be realized from sales of the product at any given rate of accumulation. It has a maximum at (r^*, g^*) corresponding to the existing rate of exploitation. The curves $g_i(r)$ represent the planned rate of accumulation as a function of the (expected) rate of profit. Three such curves are drawn, each representing a different state of investment plans corresponding to a particular set of historical conditions. Consider the meaning of each case.

Case 1. When investment plans are at the level corresponding to $g_1(r)$, accumulation at any positive rate above some minimum enables the capitalists to realize a rate of profit which induces them to expand at a higher rate. The capitalists are seeking then to increase the rate of accumulation. With a higher rate of accumulation, a higher rate of profit would be realized and the capitalists would plan to grow at a still higher rate. There is, however, an upper limit to the rate of profit and rate of accumulation given by (r^*, g^*). At this limit the capitalists are, so to speak, straining at the bit to expand the size of their capital, $g_1(r^*) > g^*$. They are held in check by the rate of exploitation corresponding to the existing conditions. Under these conditions the planned rate of accumulation cannot be sustained. We may say that a crisis exists. It is due in this case to excessive accumulation in relation to the pool of available surplus value. It may be manifested, for instance, in the form of an inflationary spiral.[17]

The actual rate of accumulation could be higher if the value of labor power were lower, thereby permitting a higher rate of profit. This would require a readjustment of existing class relations as related to the costs of reproduction of labor power. Alteration of the technique of production, such as to lower the embodied-labor ratios and the labor embodied in wage goods, would have the same effect.[18] The actual rate of accumulation could also be higher if capitalists were to save at a higher rate. Otherwise, the only possible basis for resolving the crisis is through an adjustment in the planned rate of accumulation itself.

Case 2. This is the case of investment plans corresponding to $g_2(r)$. Under such conditions, there exists a point (r_2, g_2) such that, when capitalists accumulate at the rate g_2, the realized rate of profit is just sufficient to induce them to continue to accumulate at the same rate. An equilibrium exists, in this sense, with respect to the overall balance between production and demand. At the same time, however, the realized rate of profit is less than that allowed to them at the existing rate of exploitation, but the latter cannot be realized. Thus there exists a crisis. Call this *a realization crisis.* It may manifest itself, for instance, in a deflationary tendency (under competition) as prices fall below values and the rate of utilization of productive capacity declines below normal.

The realized rate of profit could be higher if the level of investment plans were higher than $g_2(r)$, or if the capitalists were to consume at a higher rate. In this sense, a realization crisis is due either to underinvestment or underconsumption on the part of capitalists or to both. It is a matter of interpretation to which the analysis at this level is indifferent. Whatever the case, it is evident that there is no connection between the realized rate of profit and consumption on the part of workers.

[17] Compare the concept of an "inflation barrier" in Robinson 1956: 48–50.

[18] It is the possibility of such an adjustment in production coefficients, viewed singularly as a matter of substitution along a given production function, that constitutes the central idea of the neoclassical parable (see Chapter 9).

In particular, with capitalists' investment and consumption unchanged, a higher level of workers' consumption would leave the *realized* rate of profit unchanged but reduce the *potential* rate at which capitalists as a whole can appropriate surplus value. A lower level of workers' consumption would raise the potential rate of profit without altering the realized rate. In any event, a change in the wage cannot come about without an adjustment in the prevailing class relations.

Case 3. With investment plans at the level corresponding to $g_3(r)$, the system is in a process of decelerating to a condition of zero growth with the realized rate of profit at its minimum level. There exists what we may call a *stagnation crisis.* It may be viewed as a degenerate case of a realization crisis.

Case 4. What if the state of investment plans were such as to correspond to a curve which passed through the point (r^*, g^*) from below? Then, at g^*, the realized rate of profit equals that appropriate to the existing rate of exploitation and is exactly what is required to maintain accumulation at the rate g^*. The situation need not, however, be fully consistent with equilibrium. This is because the requirement of a labor force to match the expanding demand for labor may not be fulfilled. If $l_d(g^*) > l_s(g^*)$, the system is in the course of exhausting the available reserve army of labor, being unable to replenish it sufficiently through internal or external means. Alternatively, if $l_d(g^*) < l_s(g^*)$, the reserve army is expanding because the growth of demand for labor is too low to absorb the labor that is becoming available. Whatever the case, it is to be expected that each of these possibilities would in turn have effects on the rest of the system. These effects are likely to operate through variations in the bargaining power of workers and therefore on the wage rate, rate of exploitation, and rate of profit, with consequent feedback effects on the rate of accumulation. In this way the mechanism of the reserve army turns out to be crucial for the system as a whole (cf. Sweezy 1956: 150). This would suggest also that we have to give up the assumption that the real wage is fixed at some predetermined level.

In the next section we examine the implications of introducing the mechanism of the reserve army with the wage rate as a variable.

Wages and Accumulation

Throughout the preceding analysis it is assumed that the wage is exactly equal to the purchase price of necessaries. In this sense the price of labor power is equal to its value. It is evident that the effect of this condition is to impose an upper limit on the rate of accumulation. In this respect, the accumulation process is subject to an external barrier in the form of a rigidly fixed real wage.

We now have to take account of the possibility that the wage rate itself may vary and that the manner of its variation is dependent on the accumulation process. Marx expressed this by saying: "The rate of accumulation is the independent, not the dependent, variable; the rate of wages, the dependent, not the independent, variable" (*Capital* I, 620).

Assume, in particular, that the conditions of determination of the wage are such as to be sensitive to variations in the size of the reserve army resulting from differences between the demand for and supply of labor associated with the accumulation process. Let the wage equation in this case be

$$(10.35) \qquad w = b'P + w_0$$

where $b'P$ is necessary consumption and w_0 is a "bonus" in excess of necessary consumption. The conditions of determination of the bonus are such that

$$(10.36) \qquad \dot{w}_0 = \phi[l_d(g) - l_s(g)]; \phi(0) = 0, \phi' > 0$$

which expresses the effect of accumulation on the wage through the mechanism of the reserve army. We need not continue to assume that necessary consumption is fixed. For instance, it may vary over time in accordance with the experienced level of real wages. Altogether, the wage may then be seen to have a determination that is *internal* to the accumulation process as a whole.

Let us examine the implications of this specification for the analysis of the accumulation process. The relevant relations may be represented as in Figure 10.2. The upper quadrant represents the relations between the growth rate and the profit rate for two different states of investment plans, $g_1(r)$, $g_2(r)$, corresponding to different historical conditions. OG is the profit realization curve associated with a given saving rate of capitalists. The lower quadrant describes the labor demand and supply curves relating the rate of growth of labor demand and supply to the rate of accumulation. At g^* the conditions of labor demand and supply are in balance so that the mechanism of the reserve army operates to keep the real wage constant. At any point to the right of g^* this mechanism operates to push up the wage; at any point to the left it tends to depress the wage.

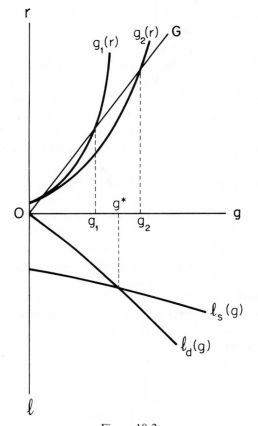

Figure 10.2

Now, consider the situation with investment plans corresponding to $g_1(r)$. The conditions of accumulation are such that, at g_1, the capitalists are realizing profits at a rate that is just sufficient to induce them to continue to accumulate at the existing rate. But at that rate of accumulation the mechanism of the reserve army is operating to push down the wage, and hence to raise the rate of profit. At any higher rate of profit, however, the conditions of accumulation are such as not to allow that rate of profit to be realized. Therefore, the system would then be in a realization crisis. We may say that the situation at g_1 is tending toward a realization crisis. The crisis is being precipitated by the falling tendency of the wage due to the mechanism of the reserve army.

Consider, next, the case of investment plans corresponding to $g_2(r)$.

At g_2 the capitalists are realizing profits at the rate appropriate to the existing rate of accumulation. But in this case the mechanism of the reserve army is operating to drive up the wage, and hence to lower the rate of profit. At any lower rate of profit, the conditions of accumulation are such that the capitalists would be seeking to expand at a greater rate than is consistent with that rate of profit. The situation would then involve a tendency to overaccumulation in relation to the available pool of surplus value. That crisis is being forced upon the system by the downward pressure on the rate of profit due to the mechanism of the reserve army.

It is only when the conditions of accumulation are such that $g_1 = g_2 = g^*$ that smooth, uninterrupted, crisis-free reproduction could take place. But since the process of reproduction is carried out through the agency of individual capitals without conscious coordination, there is nothing to guarantee that this situation could be achieved. If it were to be achieved, any variation in the conditions of accumulation would entail a crisis of one sort or another.

In order to obtain a result that the wage rate is driven down to the level of necessary consumption, it is necessary to posit a situation such as that represented at g_1. It is also evident that such a situation is associated with a chronic realization crisis.

Features of a Marxian Analysis

Robinson (1951a:19) remarked with reference to her numerical solution of Marx's scheme: "This model bears a strong family resemblance to Mr. Harrod's warranted rate of growth." Both the similarity and the difference between Marx and Harrod should now be apparent.

For both, abstract equilibrium relations are significant not in themselves but for what they have to say about possible sources of disequilibrium (Harrod) or crises (Marx) in concrete situations. Harrod's conditions identify two such sources: (1) a discrepancy between the amount of investment required for steady growth (the warranted rate of growth) and the amount the capitalists plan to invest (the planned rate of growth); (2) a discrepancy between the warranted rate and that made possible by growth of the labor force and technical progress (the "natural rate") (see Chapter 2). As is apparent from the preceding analysis, similar but much wider and deeper inferences can be derived from Marx's scheme. The similarity is that, for both Marx and Harrod, the discrepancy is seen as arising systematically within the accumulation process. It is also presumed that there is no automatic self-adjusting mechanism within the capitalist economy to remove the discrepancy.

Despite the similarities, however, the structure of the Marxian analysis and the underlying theoretical system are in fact quite different from Harrod's. In particular, there is no presumption in the Marxian analysis of a "natural rate of growth" given by an autonomous movement of technology and exogenous growth of the labor force. In Harrod's analysis the conception of a class structure of capitalist society disappears altogether. There is correspondingly nothing to determine the distribution of income either between capital and labor or between wages and profits. In Harrod's analysis also the saving rate is assumed to be uniform for all classes and categories of income. The equilibrium rate of accumulation or "warranted rate of growth" is fixed by this uniform rate of saving and a given overall ratio of capital to income. By contrast, in the Marxian analysis, given the saving rate of capitalists and the organic composition of capital in the different departments, the rate of accumulation may take any level up to the limit determined by the existing rate of exploitation.

The Marxian analysis also pinpoints a problem arising from the possibility of an imbalance between demand and supply at the level of individual sectors. This follows immediately when the *ex post* magnitudes in the balancing conditions (10.8) and (10.15) are viewed in *ex ante* terms. That *partial* overproduction in this sense could give rise to a state of *general* overproduction was an explicit element in Marx's attack on Say's Law (cf. Shoul 1957). Viewed from the standpoint of the production system as a whole, the problem of balance between demand and supply in individual sectors is shown here to be a matter of the allocation of labor between the different sectors of production. A disproportionality crisis occurs when the actual allocation of labor fails to satisfy the exact proportions required for balance of production and demand. The analysis thus points to the fundamental source of the problem as arising within the mechanisms of *private* production and appropriation, which govern the *social* allocation of labor in the capitalist economy.

What is there to ensure that accumulation takes place at the appropriate rate? This is the problem of investment demand. Marx himself does not appear to have given much weight to the problem of investment demand as such. He tended to assume that competition would force the capitalists to reinvest their surplus in order to survive in the competitive struggle. An answer was found by later writers, such as Lenin (1939), Hilferding (1923), and Luxemburg (1951), to lie in the growth of capital export and imperialism. The problem was to become a central, but unresolved, element in Keynes's analysis of "effective demand."[19] It is taken up again in the neo-Keynesian analysis, where it is made to depend on the "animal spirits" of capitalists and their "technical dynamism" (see Chapter 8 above).

From the preceding analysis, one of the central concepts of the neo-Keynesian analysis can be seen to fall into place as an aspect of the problem of realization of surplus value. This is the meaning that can be given to the idea that the rate of profit is dependent on the saving rate of capitalists and on the rate of accumulation. Specifically, this idea says that the rate of profit which can be realized from sales of the product depends on the consumption and investment expenditures of capitalists. This is evidently consistent with the Marxian conception of the realization problem.[20] The difference is that, in the Marxian analysis, the realization problem is treated as one side of the dual problem of production and appropriation of surplus value, or as one moment in the general circuit of capital as a whole.

The preceding analysis shows also that there is no support for any presumption that a change in wages would provide a way of resolving a realization crisis, quite apart from the question of how such a change could come about. In particular, if the wage is assumed equal to necessary consumption, then a lower level of workers' consumption is associated with a higher potential rate of profit, but the realized rate of profit is unchanged as long as capitalists' consumption and investment expenditures are unchanged. Similarly, a higher level of workers' consumption lowers the potential rate of profit and leaves the realized rate of profit unchanged. If, alternatively, the wage is a variable subject to determination by the mechanism of the reserve army, then it may be that a falling wage is itself what accounts for the realization crisis. But under those circumstances, a higher wage could be sustained only if it were possible to alter the conditions of operation of the reserve army.

[19] For a discussion of the inadequacy of Keynes's treatment of investment demand, see Sweezy 1972.
[20] Capitalists' consumption must be conceived here to refer not only to their "individual consumption" but also to the whole range of expenditures which do not contribute to the increased production of surplus value, such as on advertising, armaments, and rockets to the moon. For a discussion of concrete elements of this problem, see Baran and Sweezy 1966.

We may note here that the neoclassical approach introduces the idea of substitution among different methods of production, focusing thereby on the problem of choice of techniques of production within a purely static and technical conception of the nature of production alternatives. By this means, and with the presumed operation of Say's Law (or an omniscient state authority), an attempt is made to show that the capitalist economy is inherently driven toward a state of steady growth with full employment. In this way, the realization problem is made to disappear. By this means also an attempt is made to find a theory of distribution through marginal productivity pricing of factors of production. We have seen that there are serious logical difficulties in sustaining these ideas (Chapter 9). Even so, while it would be foolish to deny the feasibility of adjustments in the conditions of production, it is quite another matter to raise this to the level of a sufficient or even necessary condition for the resolution of a crisis. Because means of production are technically specific and particular patterns of organization of work and hierarchical relations of production are built around them in the factory, changes in production conditions are neither costless nor instantaneous. Neither are such changes a purely technical matter; they run up against the organized resistance of the workers.

As to which of the various causal factors are primarily important in explaining crises, the formal relations set out here are completely neutral. One cannot deduce from them support for either "underconsumption" or "disproportionality" as the primary cause of crises (cf. Sweezy 1956: ch. 10). The problem of crises requires further theoretical analysis, taking account of the whole circuit of capital going from money capital through production and circulation of commodities into expanded money capital. The problem also has to be situated in the context of a proper theoretical analysis of the process of structural change and development of capitalism. In that context, the particular forms and mechanisms of crises may be seen to have a determination specific to each particular stage in the process of capitalist development. To choose between various causes of crises requires systematic investigation of concrete historical conditions (cf. Luxemburg 1951).

Similarly, nothing can be deduced from the preceding analysis about which department has priority in determining the equilibrium position of the system. Luxemburg (1951: 125) seemed to assign such priority to Department I, as does much of subsequent Marxist literature. Priority of

Department I in determining the long-run growth rate of the economy can, however, be deduced from a condition of specificity of means of production in the different departments.[21]

As for the theory of distribution involved here, it is evident that the crucial concept is the rate of exploitation. This, in turn, is rooted in Marx's theory of surplus value. In this theory, the rate of exploitation is the result of a complex determination involving, among other things, the formation of the value of labor power, the determination of the pace, intensity, and duration of work, and the evolution of methods of production. The whole process is presumed to be conditioned by the state of the class struggle.[22] The present analysis, in the first instance, takes the rate of exploitation simply as a given magnitude. Thus, as a theory of distribution, this formulation is essentially incomplete. It is incomplete because it takes as given what is itself to be explained. This is a legitimate procedure as a first step. To say that the rate of exploitation is "given" is, in this sense, not a mere definition but an expression of certain historical and social conditions which remain to be taken into account. In formal terms, once the real wage rate is taken as equal to a given basket of necessaries, then there is a rate of exploitation corresponding to it under given technical conditions. The question then is deflected from what determines the rate of exploitation to what determines the real wage.

Now, unlike Malthus and Ricardo, Marx did not have a subsistence theory of the wage. The point is that labor power, being a commodity, has a value that is equal to its cost of reproduction. This cost is equivalent to "the value of the necessaries required to produce, develop, maintain and perpetuate the labour-power" (Marx and Engels, *Selected Works*, 1968, p. 211). These necessaries include also a "historical and moral element" (*Capital* I, 171) and therefore vary in accordance with changing

---

[21] See the model of G. A. Feldman elaborated by Domar (1957); also Harris (1972a,b).

[22] In particular, Marx wrote: "We can ... say that, the limits of the working day being given, the *maximum* of profit corresponds to the *physical minimum of wages*; and that wages being given, the maximum of profit corresponds to such a prolongation of the working day as is compatible with the physical forces of the labourer. The maximum of profit is, therefore, limited by the physical minimum of wages and the physical maximum of the working day. It is evident that between the two limits of this *maximum rate of profit* an immense scale of variations is possible. The fixation of its actual degree is only settled by the continuous struggle between capital and labour, the capitalist constantly tending to reduce wages to their physical minimum, and to extend the working day to its physical maximum, while the working man constantly presses in the opposite direction. The matter resolves itself into a question of the respective power of the combatants." (Marx and Engels, *Selected Works*, 1968, p. 226.)

historical conditions that are brought about by the process of capitalist development itself. There is a presumption that the wage rate tends to be driven down to the level given by the quantity of necessaries. This is the result of competition in the labor market and operation of the reserve army of unemployed labor, not of a Malthusian law of population growth. Competition between unemployed workers and the employed labor force serves to hold wages down. The reserve army itself is continually reinforced by the process of capital accumulation through the introduction of new techniques of production which raise the organic composition of capital, through the increasing concentration and centralization of capital, the uneven development of capital as a whole, and the erosion of non-capitalist methods of production, as well as through the mechanism of "the industrial cycle." In this way a connection is established in Marxian analysis between the conditions of determination of the wage and the process of accumulation and technical change.

The analysis presented here introduces a simple specification of the mechanism of the reserve army so as to account for variations in the wage. In this way, the analysis gives a particular expression to the effect of accumulation on determination of the wage. It must be recognized, however, that the quantitative determination of the wage and its relation to the value of labor power is a complex problem which requires further analysis and investigation.[23] This requires giving an account of cyclical variations in the real wage as well as its overall movement with the development of capitalism. There are forces which, as Marx himself indicated, would operate to produce a systematic (as distinct from merely random or accidental) deviation between the value of labor power and the wage. These would include, for instance, the effects of monopoly and the role of the state, as well as other indirect effects of the general "transformation" of values into prices of production. Furthermore, it must be recognized at a more concrete level that it is the *money wage* which the wage bargain determines, at least in the first instance. The real wage emerges out of

[23] That there exists an unresolved problem in Marxian analysis with regard to application of the general law of value to determination of wages was early pointed out by Bortkiewicz (1952: 57). It was subsequently considered by Lange (1935), and taken up again by Robinson (1947: 29–34), Sweezy (1956: 84–92), and Meek (1973: 185–86, and 1967: 113–28), among others. The problem has recently reemerged in the context of discussions of "domestic labor" (Gardiner, et al. 1975), development of "peripheral capitalism" (Amin 1976), and "unequal exchange" (Emmanuel 1972). Some of the issues are reviewed in the recent study of Harvey (1976). Although various ways of resolving the problem are indicated in these discussions, a systematic analytical solution still remains to be worked out.

the relation between the money wage and prices of workers' means of consumption. This relation is in turn dependent on other economy-wide forces, such as the prevailing "degree of monopoly," the overall rate of accumulation, pattern of change in labor productivity, policies of the state, and the organized action of workers.

For the rest, what is required to give a full account of the rate of exploitation is an analysis of the labor process itself and its historical development through the process of evolution of technology broadly conceived. The broad outlines of an approach to this analysis were developed by Marx in terms of the concept of *production of relative surplus value* (*Capital* I, chs. 12–15). This line of inquiry has been neglected so far in the development of Marxian analysis. It has been reopened recently with the work of Braverman (1974).

Within the framework of Marx's conception of the reproduction process of capital as a whole, the question of relative prices of commodities is a decidedly subsidiary one, and is completely neglected in his formal statement of the reproduction scheme. But, as we have seen, prices can be introduced without altering the underlying conception. The "transformation problem" nevertheless points to the need to have a correct formulation of the relation between prices, distribution, and production conditions.[24] Further elaboration of the analysis of distribution also needs to be carried out so as to give an account of the formation of rent and interest as component shares in the total pool of surplus value.[25]

There is a presumption in Marx's own analysis that the accumulation process is associated with a falling tendency of the overall (average) rate of profit (*Capital* III, chs. 13–15). This presumed tendency is contingent upon prior assumptions regarding the process of evolution of methods of production as it affects in particular the organic composition of capital and the rate of exploitation. The presumption is subject to an ongoing debate about its exact status within the Marxian theory of accumulation as well as its empirical validity (see, for instance, Sweezy 1973). We are not in a position to evaluate this presumption here, owing to the fact that the analysis itself abstracts from the process of evolution of methods of production. This is an important direction in which the analysis might

[24] That Marx himself was aware of the problem from the start and subsequently returned to it is made clear by Meek (1967: 143–57).

[25] On this, see *Capital* III, which continues to represent the level of development of the Marxian analysis of these questions.

be taken, but it awaits the articulation of an adequate theory of the process of technical change.

Finally, we may note that, within the larger context of Marxian theory as a whole, the growth of the capitalist economy is conceived as a process which involves not only quantitative expansion but also qualitative changes in economic and social relations. The theory seeks to account for these structural changes within the growth process itself because of the internal contradictions it entails.[26] This is an important distinguishing feature of the Marxian approach which points to an essential limitation of the analysis presented here.

Conclusion

In this chapter, we have presented an analytic reconstruction of the problem of growth of the capitalist economy drawing upon various elements of Marxian theory. The analysis is presented in terms of a simple scheme which represents a restatement of Marx's scheme of reproduction.

Apart from the foregoing, there is more that can be said with this simple scheme, though one soon runs up against the limits of its simplicity. To complicate the analysis, we have to introduce the conditions of technical change, the role of money, and so on. Further analysis would also require explicit recognition of the fact that the wage bargain is conducted in terms of money wages. The analysis has to be constituted at the level of individual capitals so as to deal with the relations among firms and the essential problem of monopoly. The conditions and processes of accumulation on a world scale, involving relations between different national capitals, need to be worked out. The analytical difficulties are compounded when the problem of the state is introduced.

The objective of the analysis throughout is to provide historically based explanations of why one or another set of crisis conditions comes to dominate the process of expansion of capital, to account for the mechanisms through which the crisis is resolved, and to explain the associated structural changes which occur in the system as it moves from one crisis to another. Enough has been said here to indicate some broad features of the analytical approach. But evidently much remains to be done in

---

[26] See Levine 1975 for a useful attempt to sketch, in broad outline, the form that such a conception might take and to provide thereby a theoretical identification of distinct periods in the historical development of capitalism.

developing the structure of the analysis as a whole and constituting it upon a solid theoretical basis which is consistent with the conditions of modern capitalism. That work is currently proceeding on many fronts.

All of the foregoing discussion is not to be taken to deny that expanded reproduction is possible and does occur in fact in capitalist economies. Rather, it means that recognition must be given here to Marx's argument that the process of reproduction under capitalist conditions is a *contradictory* process. It is effected only through the regular recurrence of crises of one sort or another. While constituting an *interruption* in the reproduction process, crises simultaneously recreate the very conditions upon which renewed expansion can take place, but only for a time: "The crises are always but momentary and forcible solutions of the existing contradictions. They are violent eruptions which for a time restore the disturbed equilibrium." (*Capital* III, 249.) Marx saw the fundamental contradiction giving rise to such crises as a contradiction between the social character of production and the private or individual character of appropriation. It is, furthermore, because of the existence of such contradictions that the system develops and changes: "Capitalism cannot develop except in a whole series of contradictions, and the indication of these contradictions merely explains to us the historically transitory nature of capitalism, explains the conditions and causes of its tendency to go forward to a higher form." (Lenin 1964: 60.)

Chapter Eleven

General Conclusion and Prospect

We break off, in mid-passage as it were, after an extended excursion into the present state of the theory of growth of the capitalist economy, with attention focused on the interrelations of capital accumulation and income distribution. We acquire from this exercise a sense of the limitations, inadequacies, and achievements of the main contemporary lines of approach to a theory. We leave behind a trail of questions that remain to be answered. No attempt is made to offer definitive solutions of all the problems. Rather, an effort has been made to clarify and structure the terms of the required theoretical solution, drawing upon the conceptual foundations that were laid by the Classical economists and by Marx. Some partial elements for such a solution are to be found in recent work, especially that of Robinson, Kalecki, and Steindl, among others. But these elements have to be situated within a broader, more fundamental, and integrated system of analysis. Such a general framework is provided by the theory of capitalist production first put forward by Marx and subsequently elaborated by others, where that theory itself is seen to be in a state of ongoing internal development.

A program of continuing efforts directed at resolving the remaining theoretical questions is evidently called for. Many of these questions emerge sharply from the analysis and discussion conducted in the preceding pages. Others are apparent from the gaps remaining. It is worth taking stock of the broad issues at this point and indicating the general directions in which they lead.

To begin with, the overall magnitude and scope of the theoretical project itself need to be recognized. In broad terms, a theory of economic

growth is to be conceived as an explanation of the causes of the contradictory development of the capitalist mode of production, based on the
observable historical reality of an immense expansion of productive
forces and revolution in methods of production under capitalism combined with the persistence of unevenly developed sectors over large
areas of the capitalist world-economy and with periodically recurring
crises affecting all or most of the major branches of industry. What is
to be explained is this specific form of capitalist development: the nature
of the forces which propel the system forward in this way and which
account for the particular contradictory form of its forward movement.
A theory of growth is, in this conception, *a theory of the expanded reproduction of the capitalist mode of production on a world scale.*

Within this overall conception the basic questions have to do, in the
first place, with the expansionary momentum of capital as a whole and
the determinants of the rate of expansion. Expansion of capital entails,
on the one side, expansion of markets. The ways in which the market
problem, as an aspect of the general problem of realization of surplus
value, is solved requires explanation. This is connected with a question
of the process of formation of demand for products, where production
and consumption are viewed as mutually dependent moments of a *social*
process.

On the other side, expansion of capital entails expansion of production.
When it is conceived as a process of production of commodities by
means of commodities and labor, production as a whole is a self-
determined process, at least so far as the supply of material means of
production and consumption is concerned, if not the supply of labor.
In this respect, production also provides its own internal markets. But
there is still a problem of the theoretical significance of exhaustible
resources and raw materials. This is, in part, a problem of ownership
rights and to that extent is associated with the distribution of income
and the formation of prices. In addition, when it is viewed from the
perspective of capital as a whole and its long-run expansion, this problem
becomes an aspect of the process of technical change through which
capital creates the conditions for its continued expansion by development
of new resources, new products, and new methods of production. At the
same time, this problem has a link with the problem of markets and with
the problem of the overall rate of accumulation insofar as the opening
up of new resources and new raw materials provides new markets and
new investment opportunities for further expansion of capital.

Technical change requires theoretical treatment as an ongoing process within production. For the system of capitals as a whole it involves what Marx called the production of relative surplus value. It is also an aspect of competition among individual units of capital and as such is connected with the process of concentration and centralization of capital. So far as it involves development of new processes of production and new products that require new processes, it has to be made specific to the capital-goods-producing industries, or the industries of Department I. Technical change takes place unevenly, and so there is an important question as to the process by which diffusion of new techniques occurs across firms, industries, regions, and countries.

Production itself is a *labor* process. As such, it is inherently social in character and not purely technical. It is associated with divisions of property ownership and relations of hierarchy, control, subordination, and resistance. These relations define the fundamental *class* character of capitalist society. The analysis has to be situated in the context of a proper specification of those relations. In particular, that specification must be such as to give meaningful analytical content to the capital-labor relation as a basic structural condition with an objective existence in modern capitalist society. Recognition must also be given, at a more concrete level, to the changing forms of social differentiation and stratification that exist within the capital-labor relation as a whole, that are the consequence of historically changing technology, of changes in the concrete forms of property, and of the process of concentration of capital.

Analysis of the overall rate of accumulation and the process of technical change is necessarily connected with an understanding of the nature and operation of individual units of capital, or individual firms, as situated within a world of firms. This, in turn, requires correct specification of the conditions of competition and monopoly as structural and behavioral features of the capitalist economy, where those conditions are seen as undergoing changes in accordance with the process of concentration and centralization of capital. What is of importance in this connection is the emergence of the large corporation, operating usually on a global scale, to occupy a central position in the overall economic structure. This gives a distinctive character to modern capitalism and presents a problem of theoretical analysis that is specific to the conditions of this era. It calls for a new understanding of the firm, the interrelations among firms, and their relations with the state. In this context, expansion of the firm, innovation in both products and processes, capacity utilization, and the sales effort, all come to acquire new significance. Similarly, the structure and evolution of prices and of profit rates need to be given a determination specific to this context. The profit-retention or pay-out policies of the firm and the size of its mark-up or profit margin require theoretical treatment consistent with the position of the firm within the overall economic structure. For the individual firm, these relations govern its internal savings. Beyond this, the problem of savings for the firm becomes a matter of its access to finance, so that the structure and operation of the financial system have to be introduced. All of these conditions have to be situated within the growth process as a whole, which itself comes to acquire a form that is specific to those conditions.

The labor force has its own reproduction process and this requires analysis on its own terms. The reproduction process takes place in part outside the sphere of capitalist relations of production, for example in the family, or in a peasant sector, with the use of articles of consumption and labor services provided there. It follows that the value of labor power is not synonymous with the labor time that is embodied in the maintenance and reproduction of labor power. The implications of this difference for the accumulation process need to be examined. The significance of heterogeneity of labor power in terms of skills has to be considered in the context of the historical changes in methods of production and division of labor which give rise to such heterogeneity. Changes on the side of capital involving concentration and centralization of capital are mirrored on the side of labor in the form of concentration and structural divisions within the labor force. Together they constitute different manifestations of the same process and therefore have to be explained within that process viewed as a whole.

A systematic account is needed of the process of creation of the reserve army of labor on a world scale. Of crucial significance in this connection is the specific form of the process of accumulation and technical change involving the uneven development of different industries, sectors, and regions, as well as the erosion of noncapitalist relations of production. It is possible to provide, in this context, an explanation of the worldwide problem of unemployment, which is far removed from traditional Keynesian notions.

A fundamental question has to do with the role of the state. The answers are no doubt complex. But, in general terms, that role has to be seen as a developing one, which is conditioned by the requirements of reproduction of capital as a whole, by the contradictions associated therewith, and by the recurrent crises that arise in the course of the reproduction process. The role of the state also has to be made specific to the situation of the *national capitals* within a global setting of competition between different national capitals and under conditions of an increasing internationalization of capital.

Within the broad terms of the conception outlined here, the problem of underdevelopment acquires significance as a particular manifestation of the dual process of uneven and combined development taking place within capitalism. Uneven and combined development is the specific form that accumulation takes in the capitalist economy. That is to say, the capitalist economy in the course of its expansion integrates or combines different spheres of economic life into one, global, and interdependent system. At the same time, development proceeds unevenly within the different spheres of that system. This is generally so between different firms, industries, sectors, regions, and segments of the world economy. Underdevelopment is a particular manifestation of this process.

The character of this process requires elaboration as to its general form, its mechanisms, and its determining conditions. These have to do with shifting locational advantages associated with particular natural resources and raw materials, the pattern of development and diffusion of new techniques of production, differential effects of size in production and marketing of commodities, the operation of the market for finance, mechanisms of unequal exchange in the market for commodities, conglomeration effects resulting from technology, geography, and capitalist forms of organization, and the calculus of private profitability itself. In the particular instance of underdevelopment, the process also involves the mechanisms of imperialism and the relations between states. Beyond this, the roots of underdevelopment are to be found in the specific process of integration of previously noncapitalist social systems into capitalist relations, which thereby become stamped with a definite character involving a combination of seemingly disparate elements. There is a substantive question of exactly how the process of reproduction takes place in the context of those specific relations.

Of course, viewed in concrete historical terms, capitalist relations exist always in conjunction with noncapitalist relations as an organic whole— for instance, with feudal relations in eighteenth- and nineteenth-century Europe, with slavery in the Americas, and with peasant relations and various forms of simple commodity production everywhere. It is therefore a general requirement of the theoretical task as defined here that it seek to explain how the process of reproduction takes place within such historically specific social relations and how those relations themselves change in this process.

All of this should make it clear that perhaps the most basic requirement for the construction of theory is that it be rooted in an adequate understanding of history. Historical analysis is indispensable for the advance of theory, just as there can be no historical analysis without theory. In this sense the two are intimately interlinked.

Reference Matter

Appendix

Wages Paid Out of Capital or Revenue

In the analysis presented in Chapter 3, pp. 000–00, it is assumed for simplicity that wages are paid out of current revenue, so that the price system takes the form of

$$(A.1) \qquad P = a_0' w + A'(\delta + rI)P$$

However, for theoretical purposes, it may be regarded as a better representation of the institutional conditions of the capitalist economy to assume that wages are paid out of capital. This is the assumption usually employed by Marx. It may be taken as an abstract expression of a concrete social-historical condition. This condition is that the workers, because of their propertyless state, are incapable of providing on their own the means of their maintenance and reproduction and therefore must regularly turn up to offer their labor power in exchange with capital. In this respect, the relation between labor and capital involves a real, substantive condition that is established, so to speak, from the start of production. We consider here the implications of this assumption for the analysis of the price system.

In this case, the specification of the price system is

$$(A.2) \qquad P = a_0' w(1 + r) + A'(\delta + rI)P$$

Observe that (A.2) is equivalent to

$$P = [I - A'(\delta + rI)]^{-1} a_0' w(1 + r)$$

Expanding the matrix inverse gives

$$(A.3) \qquad P = \left(\sum_{t=0}^{\infty} [A'(\delta + rI)]^t \right) a_0' w(1 + r)$$

which has an interpretation similar to the corresponding relation from (A.1). In particular, prices are the sum of direct and indirect labor costs plus a mark-up due to the rate of profit. The mark-up is calculated here by a different weighting system such that prices are generally higher at the same rate of profit. They are higher by the proportional amount of profit calculated on the wage.

There exists also in this case a well-defined wage-profit curve, measured in terms of any numeraire, which is negatively sloped. For instance, with the price of a bundle of necessaries $b'P$ as numeraire, the wage-profit curve becomes

$$(A.4) \qquad \hat{w} = \frac{1}{b'\left(\sum_{t=0}^{\infty} [A'(\delta + rI)]^t \right) a_0'(1 + r)}$$

The intercepts of the curve are the same as in the case of the price system (A.1), but the real wage rate is lower at every intermediate level of the rate of profit, reflecting the fact that prices are higher. The difference in the wage is exactly equal to the amount of profit calculated on the wage. Thus, it is as if a proportional deduction were made from the wage in order to provide for profits on the amount of wages advanced.

We may note here that the worker, in any case, advances his labor power to the employer by hiring himself out to be employed for the duration of the production period. If wages are not similarly advanced by the employer, the costs of upkeep during the production period must be borne by the worker and if the worker does not have the means to bear these costs he must borrow from those who have. Therein lies the possibility of emergence of a group who obtain interest on loans to the workers. In that event, if the conditions governing the wage are undisturbed, wages have to be higher in order to enable the worker to pay interest on the loan. The amount of profits is lower by the amount of interest included in the wage. This gives a rationale for use of (A.1) if the wage is defined so as to include interest on the wage. But in that case, the magnitude of the rate of interest would have to be introduced as part of the problem. Otherwise, the distinction between payment for labor power and nonlabor income is lost. There is, of course, a distinction also between profit and interest. Profit accrues to capital owned in the form of the value sum tied up in commodities that are used for production. Interest accrues to capital owned in the form of money claims (loans). The question of what determines the rate of profit is accordingly quite separate from that of what determines the rate of interest. This distinction is suppressed in (A.2) by using the concept of rate of profit with reference to the whole of capitalists' income. But this procedure is justified in order to focus on the position of the class as a whole, thereby ignoring differences within the class.

Now, for the purpose of comparison, consider the relation between the conditions of exchange as specified in (A.1) and the sphere of production. Assume, as in Chapter 3, p. 85, that the wage is exactly equal to the purchase price of the bundle of necessaries, so that $w = b'P$. Then, substituting into (A.1) gives

(A.5)
$$P = [a_0'b' + A'(\delta + rI)]P$$

Under the usual assumptions, nonnegative solutions of this system exist for relative prices and the rate of profit. Associated with this solution is a strictly positive left eigenvector h^* such that

(A.6)
$$h^* = h^*[a_0'b' + A'(\delta + rI)]$$

Multiplying by the vector of labor values gives

(A.7)
$$h^*\Lambda = h^*a_0'b'\Lambda + h^*A'\delta\Lambda + rh^*A'\Lambda$$

Recall that $\Lambda = a_0' + A'\delta\Lambda$ and $\omega = b'\Lambda$. Therefore, by substituting into (A.7), we get

(A.8)
$$h^*(a_0' + A'\delta\Lambda) = h^*a_0'\omega + h^*A'\delta\Lambda + rh^*A'\Lambda$$

from which it follows that

(A.9)
$$r = \frac{h^*a_0'}{h^*A'\Lambda}(1 - \omega)$$

$$= \frac{1 - \omega}{k}, k = h^*A'\Lambda/h^*a_0'$$

Like the earlier result in equation (3.34), this result expresses the rate of profit in terms of production conditions in the economy as a whole, the value of labor power and the rate of exploitation. However, the particular form of the relation is different, reflecting the different conception of capital in this case as consisting only of purchase of means of production and excluding purchase of labor power.

Bibliography

Abramovitz, M., and P. A. David. 1973. "Reinterpreting economic growth: parables and realities," *American Economic Review, Papers and Proceedings* 63 (May): 428–39.

Allen, R. G. D. 1967. Macro-Economic Theory. New York: St. Martin's Press.

Althusser, L., and E. Balibar. 1970. Reading Capital. London: New Left Books.

Amin, S. 1976. Unequal Development. New York: Monthly Review Press.

Anderson, P. S. 1961. "The apparent decline in capital-output ratios," *Quarterly Journal of Economics* 75 (Nov.): 615–34.

Arrow, K. J., and F. H. Hahn. 1971. General Competitive Analysis. San Francisco: Holden-Day.

Asimakopulos, A. 1969. "A Robinsonian growth model in one-sector notation," *Australian Economic Papers* 8 (June): 41–58.

———. 1970. "A Robinsonian growth model in one-sector notation—an amendment," *Australian Economic Papers* 9 (Dec.): 171–76.

———. 1975. "A Kaleckian theory of income distribution," *Canadian Journal of Economics* 8 (Aug.): 313–33.

Baran, P., and P. Sweezy. 1966. Monopoly Capital. New York: Monthly Review Press.

Baumol, W. 1959. Economic Dynamics. New York: Macmillan.

———. 1974. "The transformation of values: what Marx 'really' meant (an interpretation)," *Journal of Economic Literature* 12 (March): 51–62.

Berle, A. A., Jr., and G. C. Means. 1932. The Modern Corporation and Private Property. New York: Macmillan.

Bhaduri, A. 1966. "The concept of the marginal productivity of capital and the Wicksell effect," *Oxford Economic Papers* 18 (Nov.): 284–88.

———. 1969. "On the significance of recent controversies on capital theory: a Marxian view," *Economic Journal* 79 (Sept.): 532–39.

Blaug, M. 1968. Economic Theory in Retrospect. Homewood, Ill.: Irwin.

Bliss, C. J. 1972. "Rates of return in a linear model." Discussion Paper No. 44, University of Essex, Department of Economics.

———. 1975. Capital Theory and the Distribution of Income. New York: American Elsevier.

Bohm-Bawerk, E. von. 1959. Capital and Interest. Vols. I, II, III. South Holland, Ill.: Libertarian Press.

Bortkiewicz, L. von. 1952. "Value and price in the Marxian system," *International Economic Papers* 2:5–60.

Braverman, H. 1974. Labor and Monopoly Capital. New York: Monthly Review Press.

Brown, M. 1969. "Substitution-composition effects, capital-intensity uniqueness and growth," *Economic Journal* 79 (June): 334–47.

Bruno, M. 1969. "Fundamental duality relations in the pure theory of capital and growth," *Review of Economic Studies* 36 (Jan.): 39–53.

Bruno, M., E. Burmeister, and E. Sheshinski. 1966. "The nature and implications of the reswitching of techniques," *Quarterly Journal of Economics* 80 (Nov.): 526–53.

Bukharin, N. 1972. Economic Theory of the Leisure Class. New York: Monthly Review Press.

Burch, P. H., Jr. 1972. The Managerial Revolution Reassessed. Lexington, Mass.: Lexington Books.

Burmeister, E. 1968. "On a theorem of Sraffa," *Economica* 35 (Feb.): 83–87.

Burmeister, E., and A. R. Dobell. 1970. Mathematical Theories of Economic Growth. New York: Macmillan.

Burmeister, E., and K. Kuga. 1970. "The factor-price frontier, duality and joint production," *Review of Economic Studies* 37 (Jan.): 11–19.

Burmeister, E., and P. Taubman. 1969. "Labour and non-labour income saving propensities," *Canadian Journal of Economics* 2 (Feb.): 78–89.

Burnham, J. 1941. The Managerial Revolution. New York: Day.

Buttrick, J. 1958. "A note on Professor Solow's growth model," *Quarterly Journal of Economics* 72 (Nov.): 633–36.

———. 1960. "A note on growth theory," *Economic Development and Cultural Change* 8 (Oct.): 75–82.

Cassel, G. 1932. The Theory of Social Economy. New York: Harcourt, Brace.

Champernowne, D. G. 1945. "A note on J. von Neumann's article on 'a model of economic equilibrium,'" *Review of Economic Studies* 13:10–18.

———. 1953. "The production function and the theory of capital: a comment," *Review of Economic Studies* 21:112–35.

———. 1971. "The stability of Kaldor's 1957 model," *Review of Economic Studies* 38 (Jan.): 47–62.

Chenery, H. B. 1960. "Patterns of industrial growth," *American Economic Review* 50 (Sept.): 624–54.

Clark, J. B. 1891. "Distribution as determined by a law of rent," *Quarterly Journal of Economics* 5 (April): 289–318.

Clark, J. M. 1931. "Distribution." Encyclopaedia of the Social Sciences. Reprinted in Readings in the Theory of Income Distribution. American Economic Association. Homewood, Ill.: Irwin.

Davidson, P. 1968. "Money, portfolio balance, capital accumulation and economic growth," *Econometrica* 36 (April): 291–321.

———. 1969. "A Keynesian view of the relationship between accumulation, money and the money wage-rate," *Economic Journal* 79 (June): 300–323.

Dobb, M. 1928. Wages. Cambridge: Cambridge University Press.

———. 1937. Political Economy and Capitalism. London: Routledge & Kegan Paul.

————. 1939. "A note on saving and investment in a socialist economy," *Economic Journal* 49 (Dec.): 713–28.

————. 1940. Political Economy and Capitalism. London: Routledge & Kegan Paul.

————. 1963. Studies in the Development of Capitalism. New York: International Publishers.

————. 1973. Theories of Value and Distribution since Adam Smith. Cambridge: Cambridge University Press.

Domar, E. D. 1946. "Capital expansion, rate of growth and employment," *Econometrica* 14 (April): 137–47.

————. 1957. Essays in the Theory of Economic Growth. New York: Oxford University Press.

————. 1961. "The capital-output ratio in the United States—its variation and stability." In F. A. Lutz and D. C. Hague, eds., The Theory of Capital. New York: St. Martin's Press.

Dorfman, R., P. A. Samuelson, and R. M. Solow. 1958. Linear Programming and Economic Analysis. New York: McGraw-Hill.

Drandakis, E. M. 1963. "Factor substitution in the two-sector growth model," *Review of Economic Studies* 30 (Oct.): 217–28.

Duesenberry, J. S. 1949. Income, Saving and the Theory of Consumer Behavior. Cambridge: Harvard University Press.

Eatwell, J. 1975. "Mr. Sraffa's standard commodity and the rate of exploitation," *Quarterly Journal of Economics* 89 (Nov.): 543–55.

Eichner, A. S. 1976. The Megacorp and Oligopoly: Micro Foundations of Macro Dynamics. New York: Cambridge University Press.

Eisner, R. 1958. "On growth models and the neo-Classical resurgence." *Economic Journal* 68 (Dec.): 707–21.

Emmanuel, A. 1972. Unequal Exchange. New York: Monthly Review Press.

Engels, F. 1939. Anti-Duhring (Herr Eugen Duhring's Revolution in Science). New York: International Publishers.

Evenitsky, A. 1963. "Marx's model of expanded reproduction," *Science and Society* 27 (Spring): 159–75.

Feiwel, G. R. 1975. The Intellectual Capital of Michal Kalecki. Knoxville: University of Tennessee Press.

Ferguson, C. E. 1969. The Neoclassical Theory of Production and Distribution. Cambridge: Cambridge University Press.

Foley, D. K., and M. Sidrauski. 1970. Monetary and Fiscal Policy in a Growing Economy. New York: Macmillan.

Galbraith, J. K. 1967. The New Industrial State. Boston: Houghton Mifflin.

Gale, D. 1960. The Theory of Linear Economic Models. New York: McGraw-Hill.

Gardiner, J., S. Himmelweit, and M. Mackintosh. 1975. "Women's domestic labour," *Bulletin of the Conference of Socialist Economists* (June).

Garegnani, P. 1960. Il Capitale Nelle Teorie Della Distribuzione. Milano: Giuffre.

————. 1966. "Switching of techniques," *Quarterly Journal of Economics* 80 (Nov.): 555–67.

————. 1970. "Heterogeneous capital, the production function and the theory of distribution," *Review of Economic Studies* 37 (July): 407–36.

Gordon, R. A., and L. R. Klein, eds. 1965. Readings in Business Cycles. Homewood, Ill.: Irwin.

Gram, H. 1976. "Two-sector models in the theory of capital and growth," *American Economic Review* 66 (Dec.): 891–903.

Haavelmo, T. 1954. A Study in the Theory of Economic Evolution. Amsterdam: North-Holland.

Hahn, F. H. 1965. "On two-sector growth models," *Review of Economic Studies* 32 (Oct.): 339–46.

————. 1966. "Equilibrium dynamics with heterogeneous capital goods," *Quarterly Journal of Economics* 80 (Nov.): 633–46.

————. 1968. "On warranted growth paths," *Review of Economic Studies* 35 (April): 175–84.

Harcourt, G. C. 1963. "A critique of Mr. Kaldor's model of income distribution and economic growth," *Australian Economic Papers* 2 (June): 20–36.

————. 1972. Some Cambridge Controversies in the Theory of Capital. Cambridge: Cambridge University Press.

Harris, D. J. 1967. "Inflation, income distribution, and capital accumulation in a two-sector model of growth," *Economic Journal* 77 (Dec.): 814–33.

————. 1972a. "Feasible growth with specificity of capital and surplus labor," *Western Economic Journal* 10 (March): 65–75.

————. 1972b. "Economic growth with limited import capacity," *Economic Development and Cultural Change* 20 (April): 524–28.

————. 1972c. "On Marx's scheme of reproduction and accumulation," *Journal of Political Economy* 80 (May/June): 505–22.

————. 1973. "Capital, distribution, and the aggregate production function," *American Economic Review* 63 (March): 100–113.

————. 1974. "The price policy of firms, the level of employment and distribution of income in the short run," *Australian Economic Papers* 13 (June): 144–51.

————. 1975. "The theory of economic growth: a critique and reformulation," *American Economic Review, Papers and Proceedings* 65 (May): 329–37.

Harrod, R. F. 1936. The Trade Cycle. London: Oxford University Press.

————. 1939. "An essay in dynamic theory," *Economic Journal* 49 (March): 14–33.

————. 1948. Towards a Dynamic Economics. London: Macmillan.

————. 1959. "Domar and dynamic economics," *Economic Journal* 69 (Sept.): 451–64.

————. 1960. "Second essay in dynamic theory," *Economic Journal* 70 (June): 277–93.

————. 1970. "Harrod after twenty-one years, a comment," *Economic Journal* 80 (Sept.): 737–41.

Harvey, P. 1976. "Marx's Theory of the Value and Price of Labor-Power." Ph.D. dissertation. New School for Social Research, New York.

Hicks, J. R. 1936. "Distribution and economic progress, a revised version," *Review of Economic Studies* 4: 1–12.

————. 1965. Capital and Growth. Oxford: Clarendon Press.

Hilferding, R. 1923. Das Finanzkapital. Wien: Wiener Volksbuchhandlung.

Hirshleifer, J. 1970. Investment, Interest, and Capital. Englewood Cliffs, N.J.: Prentice-Hall.

Inada, K. 1964. "On the stability of growth equilibria in two-sector models," *Review of Economic Studies* 31 (April): 127–42.

————. 1965. "On neoclassical models of economic growth," *Review of Economic Studies* 32 (April): 151–60.

————. 1966. "Investment in fixed capital and the stability of growth equilibrium," *Review of Economic Studies* 33 (Jan.): 19–30.

Jones, R. W. 1965. "The structure of simple general equilibrium models," *Journal of Political Economy* 73 (Dec.): 557–72.

Kahn, R. F. 1959. "Exercises in the analysis of growth," *Oxford Economic Papers* 11 (June): 143–56.

Kaldor, N. 1956. "Alternative theories of distribution," *Review of Economic Studies* 23 (2): 83–100.

————. 1957. "A model of economic growth," *Economic Journal* 67 (Dec.): 591–624.

————. 1959a. "Economic growth and the problem of inflation. Part I," *Economica* 26 (Aug.): 212–25.

————. 1959b. "Economic growth and the problem of inflation, Part II," *Economica* 26 (Nov.): 287–98.

————. 1960. Essays on Economic Stability and Growth. Glencoe, Ill.: Free Press.

————. 1961. "Capital accumulation and economic growth," In F. A. Lutz and D. C. Hague, eds., The Theory of Capital. New York: St. Martin's Press.

————. 1966. "Marginal productivity and the macro-economic theories of distribution," *Review of Economic Studies* 33 (Oct.): 309–19.

————. 1970. "Some fallacies in the interpretation of Kaldor," *Review of Economic Studies* 37 (Jan.): 1–7.

————. 1972. "The irrelevance of equilibrium economics," *Economic Journal* 82 (Dec.): 1237–55.

Kaldor, N., and J. A. Mirrlees. 1962. "A new model of economic growth," *Review of Economic Studies* 29 (June): 174–92.

Kalecki, M. 1937. "The principle of increasing risk," *Economica* 4 (Nov.): 440–47.

————. 1954. Theory of Economic Dynamics. London: Allen & Unwin.

————. 1971a. "Class struggle and the distribution of national income," *Kyklos* 24 (Fasc. 1): 1–9.

————. 1971b. Selected Essays on the Dynamics of the Capitalist Economy, 1933–1970. Cambridge: Cambridge University Press.

Keynes, J. M. 1936. The General Theory of Employment, Interest and Money. London: Macmillan.

Knox, A. D. 1952. "The acceleration principle and the theory of investment: a survey," *Economica* 19 (Aug.): 269–97.

Koopmans, T. 1957. Three Essays on the State of Economic Science. New York: McGraw-Hill.

————. 1965. "On the concept of optimal growth." In Salriucci et al., The Econometric Approach to Development Planning. Chicago: Rand McNally.

————. 1967a. "Objectives, constraints and outcomes in optimal growth models," *Econometrica* 35 (Jan.): 1–15.

————. 1967b. "Intertemporal distribution and 'optimal' aggregate economic growth." In W. J. Fellner et al., Ten Economic Studies in the Tradition of Irving Fisher. New York: Wiley.

Kregel, J. A. 1971. Rate of Profit, Distribution and Growth: Two Views. Chicago: Aldine.

————. 1973. The Reconstruction of Political Economy: An Introduction to Post-Keynesian Economics. New York: Wiley, Halsted Press.

Laing, N. F. 1969. "Two notes on Pasinetti's theorem," *Economic Record* 45 (Sept.): 373–85.

Lange, O. 1935. "Marxian economics and modern economic theory," *Review of Economic Studies* 2 (June): 198–99.

———. 1959. Introduction to Econometrics. New York: Pergamon.

———. 1969. Theory of Reproduction and Accumulation. New York: Pergamon.

Larner, R. J. 1970. Management Control and the Large Corporation. New York: Dunellen.

Leibenstein, H. 1957. Economic Backwardness and Economic Growth. New York: Wiley.

Leijonhufvud, A. 1968. On Keynesian Economics and the Economics of Keynes. A Study in Monetary Theory. New York: Oxford University Press.

Lekachman, R. 1964. Keynes' General Theory. Reports on Three Decades. New York: St. Martin's Press.

Lenin, V. I. 1939. Imperialism, the Highest Stage of Capitalism. New York: International Publishers.

———. 1964. "A note on the question of the market theory." In Collected Works. Vol. 4. Moscow: Progress Publishers.

Leon, P. 1967. Structural Change and Growth in Capitalism. Baltimore: Johns Hopkins Press.

Leontief, W. 1951. The Structure of the American Economy, 1919–1939. New York: Oxford University Press.

Levhari, D. 1965. "A nonsubstitution theorem and switching of techniques," *Quarterly Journal of Economics* 79 (Feb.): 98–105.

Levhari, D., and P. A. Samuelson. 1966. "The nonswitching theorem is false," *Quarterly Journal of Economics* 80 (Nov.): 518–19.

Levine, D. P. 1973. "Outline of a theory of technical change." Economics Department, Yale University.

———. 1975. "The theory of the growth of the capitalist economy," *Economic Development and Cultural Change* 23 (Oct.): 47–74.

———. 1977. Economic Studies: Contributions to the Critique of Economic Theory. London: Routledge & Kegan Paul.

Lewis, W. A. 1954. "Economic development with unlimited supplies of labour," *The Manchester School* 22 (May): 139–91.

Lutz, F. A., and D. C. Hague, eds. 1961. The Theory of Capital. New York: St. Martin's Press.

Luxemburg, R. 1951. The Accumulation of Capital. London: Routledge & Kegan Paul.

Malinvaud, E. 1961. "The analogy between a temporal and intertemporal theories of resource allocation," *Review of Economic Studies* 28 (June): 143–60.

Marris, R. 1964. The Economic Theory of "Managerial" Capitalism. London: Macmillan.

Marx, K. 1963, 1968, 1971. Theories of Surplus Value, Part 1 (1963), Part 2 (1968), Part 3 (1971). Moscow: Progress Publishers.

———. 1967. Capital. Vols. I, II, III. New York: International Publishers.

Marx, K., and F. Engels. N.d. Selected Correspondence. Moscow.

———. 1968. Selected Works. New York: International Publishers.

Mathur, G. 1965. Planning for Steady Growth. Oxford: Blackwell.

Matthews, R. C. O. 1960. "The rate of interest in growth models," *Oxford Economic Papers* 12 (Oct.): 249–68.

Mattick, P. 1969. Marx and Keynes. Boston: Porter Sargent.

McCallum, B. T. 1969. "The instability of Kaldorian models," *Oxford Economic Papers* 21 (March): 56–65.

Meade, J. E. 1961. A Neoclassical Theory of Economic Growth. London: Allen & Unwin.

———. 1963. "The rate of profit in a growing economy," *Economic Journal* 73 (Dec.): 665–74.

———. 1966. "The outcome of the Pasinetti process: a note," *Economic Journal* 76 (March): 161–65.

Meade, J. E., and F. H. Hahn. 1965. "The rate of profit in a growing economy," *Economic Journal* 75 (June): 445–48.

Medio, A. 1972. "Profits and surplus value: appearance and reality in capitalist production." In E. K. Hunt and J. G. Schwartz, eds., A Critique of Economic Theory. New York.

Meek, R. L. 1954. Marx and Engels on Malthus. New York: International Publishers.

———. 1967. Economics and Ideology and Other Essays. London: Chapman & Hall.

———. 1973. Studies in the Labor Theory of Value. 2d ed. London: Lawrence & Wishart.

Miliband, R. 1969. The State in Capitalist Society. London: Weidenfeld & Nicolson.

Morishima, M. 1956. "An analysis of the capitalist process of reproduction," *Metroeconomica* 8 (Dec.): 171–85.

———. 1964. Equilibrium Stability, and Growth. Oxford: Clarendon Press.

———. 1966. "Refutation of the nonswitching theorem," *Quarterly Journal of Economics* 80 (Nov.): 520–25.

———. 1969. Theory of Economic Growth. Oxford: Clarendon Press.

———. 1973. Marx's Economics, A Dual Theory of Value and Growth. Cambridge: Cambridge University Press.

———. 1974. "Marx in the light of modern economic theory," *Econometrica* 42 (July): 611–32.

Morishima, M., and G. Catephores. 1975. "Is there an 'historical transformation problem'?" *Economic Journal* 85 (June): 309–28.

Naqvi, K. 1960. "Schematic presentation of accumulation in Marx," *Indian Economic Review* 5 (Feb.): 13–22.

Nelson, R. R. 1956. "A theory of the low-level equilibrium trap in under-developed economies," *American Economic Review* 46 (Dec.): 894–908.

Neumann, J. von. 1945. "A model of general economic equilibrium," *Review of Economic Studies* 13: 1–9.

Newman, P. K. 1962. "Production of commodities by means of commodities," *Schweizerische Zeitschrift fur Volkswirtschaft und Statistik* 98 (1): 58–75.

Nichols, T. 1969. Ownership, Control, and Ideology. London: Allen & Unwin.

Niehans, J. 1963. "Economic growth and two endogenous factors," *Quarterly Journal of Economics* 77 (Aug.): 349–71.

Nuti, D. M. 1970. "Capitalism, socialism and steady growth," *Economic Journal* 80 (March): 32–54.

Pasinetti, L. 1962. "Rate of profit and income distribution in relation to the rate of economic growth," *Review of Economic Studies* 29 (Oct.): 267–79.

————. 1964. "A comment on Professor Meade's 'Rate of profit in a growing economy,'" *Economic Journal* 74 (June): 488–89.

————. 1966a. "The rate of profit in a growing economy: A reply," *Economic Journal* 76 (March): 158–60.

————. 1966b. "New results in an old framework," *Review of Economic Studies* 33 (Oct.): 303–6.

————. 1966c. "Changes in the rate of profit and switches of techniques," *Quarterly Journal of Economics* 80 (Nov.): 503–17.

————. 1969. "Switches of technique and the 'rate of return' in capital theory," *Economic Journal* 79 (Sept.): 508–31.

————. 1970. "Again on capital theory and Solow's 'rate of return,'" *Economic Journal* 80 (June): 428–31.

Phelps, E. S. 1961. "The golden rule of accumulation: a fable for growth-men," *American Economic Review* 51 (Sept.): 638–43.

————. 1966. Golden Rules of Economic Growth. New York: Norton.

Ramsey, F. P. 1928. "A mathematical theory of saving," *Economic Journal* 38 (Dec.): 543–59.

Riach, P. A. 1971. "Kalecki's 'degree of monopoly' reconsidered," *Australian Economic Papers* 10 (June): 50–60.

Ricardo, D. 1951–73. Works and Correspondence of David Ricardo. Edited by P. Sraffa (with M. H. Dobb). Cambridge: Cambridge University Press.

Ricardo, D. 1962. Principles. In P. Sraffa, ed. (with M. H. Dobb), Works and Correspondence of David Ricardo. Cambridge: Cambridge University Press.

Robinson, J. 1934. "Euler's theorem and the problem of distribution," *Economic Journal* 44 (Sept.): 398–14.

————. 1947. An Essay on Marxian Economics. London: Macmillan.

————. 1951a. "Introduction," in R. Luxemburg, The Accumulation of Capital. London: Routledge & Kegan Paul.

————. 1951b. Collected Economic Papers. Vol. I. Oxford: Blackwell.

————. 1952. The Rate of Interest and Other Essays. London: Macmillan.

————. 1956. The Accumulation of Capital. Homewood, Ill.: Irwin.

————. 1959. "Accumulation and the production function," *Economic Journal* 69 (Sept.): 433–42.

————. 1960. Collected Economic Papers. Vol. II. Oxford: Blackwell.

————. 1962a. Essays in the Theory of Economic Growth. London: Macmillan.

————. 1962b. "A neo-neoclassical theorem," *Review of Economic Studies* 29 (June): 219–26.

————. 1965. Collected Economic Papers. Vol. III. Oxford: Blackwell.

————. 1966. "Comment on Samuelson and Modigliani," *Review of Economic Studies* 33 (Oct.): 307–8.

————. 1969. "A further note," *Review of Economic Studies* 36 (April): 260–62.

————. 1970a. "Capital theory up to date," *Canadian Journal of Economics* 3 (May): 309–17.

————. 1970b. "Harrod after twenty-one years," *Economic Journal* 80 (Sept.): 731–37.

————. 1970c. "Harrod after twenty-one years, a reply," *Economic Journal* 80 (Sept.): 741.

————. 1971a. Economic Heresies. New York: Basic Books.

————. 1971b. "Continuity and the 'rate of return,'" *Economic Journal* 81 (March): 120–22.

————. 1973. "Ideology and analysis." In Sozialismus, Geschichte und Wirtschaft. Festschrift für Eduard Marz. Vienna: Europaverlag.

Robinson, J., and K. A. Naqvi. 1967. "The badly behaved production function," *Quarterly Journal of Economics* 81 (Nov.): 579–91.

Rothschild, K. W. 1959. "The limitations of economic growth models," *Kyklos* 12 (Fasc. 4): 567–86.

————. 1965. "Theme and variations—remarks on the Kaldorian distribution formula," *Kyklos* 18 (Fasc. 4): 652–69.

Rowthorn, R. 1974. "Neo-Classicism, neo-Ricardianism and Marxism," *New Left Review* (July/Aug.): 63–87.

Rubin, I. I. 1972. Essays on Marx's Theory of Value. Detroit: Black and Red.

Salter, W. E. G. 1966. Productivity and Technical Change. 2d ed. Cambridge: Cambridge University Press.

Samuelson, P. A. 1957. "Wages and interest: a modern dissection of Marxian economic models," *American Economic Review* 47 (Dec.): 885–912.

————. 1962. "Parable and realism in capital theory: the surrogate production function," *Review of Economic Studies* 29 (June): 193–206.

————. 1966. "A summing up," *Quarterly Journal of Economics* 80 (Nov.): 568–83.

————. 1973. Economics. 9th ed. New York: McGraw-Hill.

Samuelson, P. A., and F. Modigliani. 1966a. "The Pasinetti paradox in neoclassical and more general models," *Review of Economic Studies* 33 (Oct.): 269–301.

————. 1966b. "Reply to Pasinetti and Robinson," *Review of Economic Studies* 33 (Oct.): 321–30.

Sato, K. 1966. "The neoclassical theorem and distribution of income and wealth," *Review of Economic Studies* 33 (Oct.): 331–35.

Schefold, B. 1971. "Theorie der Kuppelproduktion." Ph.D. dissertation. University of Basel.

Schumpeter, J. 1934. The Theory of Economic Development. Cambridge: Harvard University Press.

————. 1954. History of Economic Analysis. New York: Oxford University Press.

Sen, A. K. 1963. "Neo-Classical and neo-Keynesian theories of distribution," *Economic Record* 39 (March): 53–64.

————. 1965. "The money rate of interest in the pure theory of growth." In F. H. Hahn and F. P. R. Brechling, eds., The Theory of Interest Rates. New York: St. Martin's Press.

Seton, F. 1957. "The 'transformation problem,'" *Review of Economic Studies* 24 (June): 149–60.

Shoul, B. 1957. "Karl Marx and Say's law," *Quarterly Journal of Economics* 71 (Nov.): 611–29.

Solow, R. M. 1956. "A contribution to the theory of economic growth," *Quarterly Journal of Economics* 70 (Feb.): 65–94.

————. 1957. "Technical change and the aggregate production function," *Review of Economics and Statistics* 39 (Aug.): 312–20.

————. 1958. "A skeptical note on the constancy of relative shares," *American Economic Review* 48 (Sept.): 618–31.

————. 1961. "A note on Uzawa's two-sector model of economic growth," *Review of Economic Studies* 29 (Oct.): 48–50.

————. 1963. Capital Theory and the Rate of Return. Amsterdam: North-Holland.

————. 1967. "The interest rate and transition between techniques." In C. H.

306   *Bibliography*

Feinstein, ed., Socialism, Capitalism and Economic Growth. Essays presented to Maurice Dobb. Cambridge: Cambridge University Press.
———. 1968. "Distribution in the long and short run." In J. Marchal and B. Ducros, eds., The Distribution of National Income. New York: St. Martin's Press.
———. 1970a. Growth Theory. New York: Oxford University Press.
———. 1970b. "On the rate of return: reply to Pasinetti," *Economic Journal* 80 (June): 423–28.
Spaventa, L. 1968. "Realism without parables in capital theory." In Recherches recentes sur la fonction de production. Centre de Recherches Economiques et Sociales, Université de Namur.
———. 1970. "Rate of profit, rate of growth and capital intensity in a simple production model," *Oxford Economic Papers* 22 (July): 129–47.
Sraffa, P. 1926. "The laws of returns under competitive conditions," *Economic Journal* 36 (Dec.): 535–50.
———. 1960. Production of Commodities by Means of Commodities. Cambridge: Cambridge University Press.
Steedman, I. 1975. "Positive profits with negative surplus value," *Economic Journal* 85 (March): 114–23.
Steindl, J. 1952. Maturity and Stagnation in American Capitalism. Oxford: Blackwell.
Stigler, G. J. 1941. Production and Distribution Theories. New York: Macmillan.
Stiglitz, J. E. 1967. "A two sector–two class model of economic growth," *Review of Economic Studies* 34 (April): 227–38.
Swan, T. W. 1956. "Economic growth and capital accumulation," *Economic Record* 32 (Nov.): 334–61.
Sweezy, P. M. 1937–38. "Expectations and the scope of economics," *Review of Economic Studies* 5:234–37.
———. 1953. The Present as History. New York: Monthly Review Press.
———. 1956. The Theory of Capitalist Development. New York: Monthly Review Press.
———. 1972. Modern Capitalism and other Essays. New York: Monthly Review Press.
———. 1973. "Some problems in the theory of capital accumulation." In Sozialismus, Geschichte und Wirtschaft. Festschrift für Eduard Marz. Vienna: Europaverlag.
Sylos-Labini, P. 1969. Oligopoly and Technical Progress. Cambridge: Harvard University Press.
Takayama, A. 1974. Mathematical Economics. Hinsdale, Ill.: Dryden Press.
Tobin, J. 1955. "A dynamic aggregative model," *Journal of Political Economy* 63 (April): 103–15.
———. 1965. "Money and economic growth," *Econometrica* 33 (Oct.): 671–84.
Tsuru, S. 1956. "On reproduction schemes." Appendix A in P. M. Sweezy, The Theory of Capitalist Development. New York: Monthly Review Press.
Urquhart, M. C. 1959. "Capital accumulation, technological change and economic growth," *Canadian Journal of Economics and Political Science* (Nov.): 411–30.
Uzawa, H. 1961. "On a two-sector model of economic growth," *Review of Economic Studies* 29 (Oct.): 40–47.
———. 1963. "On a two-sector model of economic growth, II." *Review of Economic Studies* 30 (June): 105–18.

Vaughan, R. N. 1971. "The Pasinetti paradox in neoclassical and more general models: a correction," *Review of Economic Studies* 38 (April): 271.

Walras, L. 1954. Elements of Pure Economics. Translated by W. Jaffe. Homewood, Ill.: Irwin.

Weintraub, S. 1959. A General Theory of the Price Level, Output, Income Distribution, and Economic Growth. Philadelphia: Chilton.

Wicksell, K. 1934. Lectures on Political Economy. Vol. I. New York: Macmillan.

Williamson, J. G., and A. C. Kelley, 1973. "Modelling economic development and general equilibrium histories," *American Economic Review, Papers and Proceedings* 63 (May): 450–58.

Williamson, O. E. 1970. Corporate Control and Business Behavior. Englewood Cliffs, N.J.: Prentice-Hall.

Wolfstetter, E. 1973. "Surplus labour, synchronised labour costs and Marx's labour theory of value," *Economic Journal* 83 (Sept.): 787–803.

Young, A. 1928. "Increasing returns and economic progress," *Economic Journal* 38 (Dec.): 527–42.

Index

Abstinence, 166, 186
Abstraction, 51
Acceleration principle, 31, 192, 268
Accounting ratio, 149, 151, 153
Aggregation problem, 20
Allocation of resources, 15–16, 21, 25, 247
Artisan economy, 20, 60
Austrian theory of capital, 19, 132
Average period of production, 132n

Basic commodity, 118
Book of blueprints, 123
Business cycle: and Harrod's dynamic equation, 30, 178; models of, 32–33; a cause of, 197; and degree of monopoly, 205; and crisis, 263

Capacity utilization: excess capacity, 28; at normal rate, 35, 206–7, 272
Capital: as a property relation, 7, 17, 19; as self-expanding value, 14; concentration of, 14, 287ff; marginal product of, 17, 132, 149n, 153n, 214–16, 231–34; as a factor of production, 17–18; and roundabout methods of production, 19, 132; deepening, 20, 187–88, 247; merchant capital, 66–68; as constant and variable, 87, 98, 256; circuit of, 89, 251–55; value of, 105, 113–15, 128; value related to profit rate, 132–39, 144–46, 148–54, 235–41; vintages of, 203n
Capital intensity, 132–39, 144–46, 148–54, 235–41
Capitalist economy: as specific mode of production, 10, 14, 20; abstract conditions of, 34–35, 68–74, 95–96
Choice of technique: in context of steady-state, 53–54; analysis of, 120–39; in neo-Keynesian analysis, 185; in neoclassical parable, 214–16
Classical economists: general theoretical system, 3–10; on technical change, 5n, 121; compared with Marx, 11–12, 21–24; compared with neoclassical, 19, 21–24; theory of wages, 73, 80–81, 116
Competition: meaning of, 34–35, 70, 203; and uniform rate of profit, 45–46; and choice of technique, 124–25
Composition effect, 113–15, 144, 152
Consumption: as objective of capitalist economy, 20f; as circular process, 21, 286; as criterion of social welfare, 43; related to accumulation, 91–93, 105–6, 167–72; by rentiers, 185; related to rate of profit, 241–43
Contradictions: inherent in accumulation process, 14, 284, 286, 289; internal, 39, 43, 283
Crisis: as inherent feature of capitalist economy, 14, 30, 43; of world economy in 1930's, 21, 26; Marxian theory of, 251; forms of, 269–76, 279

Demand: determination of, 67, 79; role in price determination, 78–79
Depreciation: and necessary costs, 7; as amortization, 36; specification of, 53–54, 98, 123, 147n; paid out of gross profits, 103–4